The Human Tradition in America

CHARLES W. CALHOUN
Series Editor
Department of History, East Carolina University

The nineteenth-century English author Thomas Carlyle once remarked that "history is the essence of innumerable biographies." In this conception of the past, Carlyle came close to modern notions that see the lives of all kinds of people, high and low, powerful and weak, known and unknown, as part of the mosaic of human history, each contributing in a large or small way to the unfolding of the human tradition. This idea forms the foundation for this series of books on the human tradition in America. Each volume is devoted to a particular period or topic in American history and each consists of minibiographies of persons whose lives shed light on that period or topic.

By bringing the study of history down to the level of the individual, these sketches reveal not only the diversity of the American people and the complexity of their interaction but also some of the commonalities of sentiment and experience that Americans have shared in the evolution of their culture. Our hope is that these explorations of the lives of "real people" will give readers a deeper understanding of the human tradition in America.

Volumes in the Human Tradition in America series:

Ian K. Steele and Nancy L. Rhoden, eds., *The Human Tradition in Colonial America* (1999). Cloth ISBN 0-8420-2697-5 Paper ISBN 0-8420-2700-9
Nancy L. Rhoden and Ian K. Steele, eds., *The Human Tradition in the American Revolution* (2000). Cloth ISBN 0-8420-2747-5 Paper ISBN 0-8420-2748-3
Ballard C. Campbell, ed., *The Human Tradition in the Gilded Age and Progressive Era* (2000). Cloth ISBN 0-8420-2734-3 Paper ISBN 0-8420-2735-1
Steven E. Woodworth, ed., *The Human Tradition in the Civil War and Reconstruction* (2000). Cloth ISBN 0-8420-2726-2 Paper ISBN 0-8420-2727-0
David L. Anderson, ed., *The Human Tradition in the Vietnam Era* (2000). Cloth ISBN 0-8420-2762-9   Paper ISBN 0-8420-2763-7
Kriste Lindenmeyer, ed., *Ordinary Women, Extraordinary Lives: Women in American History* (2000). Cloth ISBN 0-8420-2752-1 Paper ISBN 0-8420-2754-8

Michael A. Morrison, ed., *The Human Tradition in Antebellum America* (2000). Cloth ISBN 0-8420-2834-X   Paper ISBN 0-8420-2835-8

Malcolm Muir Jr., ed., *The Human Tradition in the World War II Era* (2001). Cloth ISBN 0-8420-2785-8   Paper ISBN 0-8420-2786-6

Ty Cashion and Jesús F. de la Teja, eds., *The Human Tradition in Texas* (2001). Cloth ISBN 0-8420-2905-2   Paper ISBN 0-8420-2906-0

Benson Tong and Regan A. Lutz, eds., *The Human Tradition in the American West* (2002). Cloth ISBN 0-8420-2860-9   Paper ISBN 0-8420-2861-7

Charles W. Calhoun, ed., *The Human Tradition in America from the Colonial Era through Reconstruction* (2002). Cloth ISBN 0-8420-5030-2   Paper ISBN 0-8420-5031-0

Donald W. Whisenhunt, ed., *The Human Tradition in America between the Wars, 1920–1945* (2002). Cloth ISBN 0-8420-5011-6   Paper ISBN 0-8420-5012-4

Roger Biles, ed., *The Human Tradition in Urban America* (2002). Cloth ISBN 0-8420-2992-3   Paper ISBN 0-8420-2993-1

Clark Davis and David Igler, eds., *The Human Tradition in California* (2002). Cloth ISBN 0-8420-5026-4   Paper ISBN 0-8420-5027-2

James C. Klotter, ed., *The Human Tradition in the Old South* (2003). Cloth ISBN 0-8420-2977-X   Paper ISBN 0-8420-2978-8

Nina Mjagkij, ed., *Portraits of African American Life since 1865* (2003). Cloth ISBN 0-8420-2966-4   Paper ISBN 0-8420-2967-2

Charles W. Calhoun, ed., *The Human Tradition in America: 1865 to the Present* (2003). Cloth ISBN 0-8420-5128-7   Paper ISBN 0-8420-5129-5

David L. Anderson, ed., *The Human Tradition in America since 1945* (2003). Cloth ISBN 0-8420-2942-7   Paper ISBN 0-8420-2943-5

Eric Arnesen, ed., *The Human Tradition in American Labor History* (2003). Cloth ISBN 0-8420-2986-9   Paper ISBN 0-8420-2987-7

PORTRAITS OF AFRICAN AMERICAN LIFE SINCE 1865

PORTRAITS OF AFRICAN AMERICAN LIFE SINCE 1865

No. 16
The Human Tradition in America

Edited by
Nina Mjagkij

A Scholarly Resources Inc. Imprint
Wilmington, Delaware

© 2003 by Scholarly Resources Inc.
All rights reserved
First published 2003
Printed and bound in the United States of America

Scholarly Resources Inc.
104 Greenhill Avenue
Wilmington, DE 19805-1897
www.scholarly.com

Library of Congress Cataloging-in-Publication Data

Portraits of African American life since 1865 / edited by Nina
    Mjagkij.
        p. cm. — (The human tradition in America ; no. 16)
    Includes bibliographical references and index.
    ISBN 0-8420-2966-4 (alk. paper) — ISBN 0-8420-2967-2 (pbk. :
alk. paper)
    1. African Americans—Biography 2. African Americans—History—19th century. 3. African Americans—History—20th century.
I. Mjagkij, Nina, 1961– II. Series.
E185.96 .P67 2003
920'.009296073—dc21   20022152539

♾ The paper used in this publication meets the minimum requirements
of the American National Standard for permanence of paper for printed
library materials, Z39.48, 1984.

About the Editor

NINA MJAGKIJ is professor of history and director of African American studies at Ball State University, Muncie, Indiana. She is the author of *Light in the Darkness: African Americans and the YMCA, 1852–1946* (1994), which received the Gustavus Myers Center Award. She coedited *Men and Women Adrift: The YMCA and the YWCA in the City* (1997) and edited *Organizing Black America: An Encyclopedia of African American Associations* (2001). She is also coeditor of Scholarly Resources' African American History Series.

Contents

Introduction

Nina Mjagkij

The lives of the fourteen African American men and women in this volume illustrate the broad spectrum of the black experience in the United States since 1865. These men and women were ordinary African Americans who lived in the South and the North as well as in the cities and the countryside. Some were born into slavery and had experienced poverty and the constant threat of the master's lash. Others grew up in freedom and economic comfort and had enjoyed a relatively carefree childhood. Among them were illiterate, self-taught, and poorly educated individuals as well as highly trained professionals and university graduates. They were farmers, teachers, businessmen, clubwomen, entertainers, art critics, politicians, labor organizers, civil rights activists, religious leaders, civil servants, and soldiers. Despite their different backgrounds, these men and women were united by a common goal: they sought to give meaning to freedom.

Although the Emancipation Proclamation had freed the slaves in the Confederacy in 1863, and the Thirteenth Amendment had abolished the institution of slavery in 1865, neither guaranteed the racial equality of the four million former slaves. To be sure, in the immediate aftermath of the Civil War, Congress did take several steps to ensure black political participation when it launched its Reconstruction plan. In 1866, Congress passed the Fourteenth Amendment, ratified in 1868, acknowledging the citizenship rights of African Americans. The Reconstruction Act of 1867 granted freedmen the right to vote, ordered the former states of the Confederacy to draft new state constitutions, and provided for the military occupation of the South. In addition, Congress passed the Fifteenth Amendment in 1869, ratified in 1870, removing racial restrictions on voting.

During the Reconstruction years the former slaves enjoyed unprecedented political freedom. Under the protection of the Union troops who occupied the South, freedmen elected black delegates to southern constitutional conventions where they helped draft progressive state constitutions. Many of these new state constitutions abolished property qualifications for voting and office holding, imprisonment for debt, and cruel punishments of criminals. Moreover, black politicians eagerly provided the former slaves with access to educational opportunities and helped create public school systems in many southern states. Access to education was one of the most important aspects of freedom, as Ronald E. Butchart demonstrates in his essay on the Highgate sisters.

Black political participation during Reconstruction raised the hopes of many African Americans that their years in bondage were finally over. However, such dreams of freedom and equality were soon shattered. In 1872 the federal government issued a General Amnesty, restoring the votes of white southerners. They elected politicians, the so-called Redeemers, who were intent on reinstating a racial order that ensured white supremacy. Soon thereafter white southerners started to reverse the gains that African Americans had made during Reconstruction. Following the removal of the last Union troops from the South in 1877, the Redeemers created a political, legal, economic, and social system that resulted in the virtual re-enslavement of African Americans.

During the Era of Jim Crow, as the period following 1877 came to be known, white southerners passed a series of laws that steadily deprived African Americans of the right to vote and eventually resulted in the complete racial segregation of the South. Black people who dared to challenge the system faced intimidation and violence. Lynchings soon reached a peak as white southerners tried to instill fear and terror in the hearts and minds of the black population. The federal government, never committed to racial equality and more interested in reaping the economic benefits of industrialization than addressing troubling questions about race, turned its back on the plight of African Americans. In 1896 the Supreme Court sanctioned racial discrimination in the infamous *Plessy v. Ferguson* case, which established the principle that separate-but-equal facilities did not violate the constitutional rights of African Americans. Segregation became the law of the land and, as historian Rayford W. Logan has noted, race relations reached a "nadir," an all-time low.

Abandoned by the federal government, unable to secure protection from state and local officials, and confined by oppressive economic conditions to ruinous tenant farming, the overwhelming majority of the black population nonetheless continued to live in the South. Lacking the financial resources to leave the region, they worked on white-owned land and paid for rent, tools, food, supplies, and equipment with a share of their crop, hoping that they would eventually pay off their debts and own the land. White landowners and merchants, however, routinely overcharged and defrauded black sharecroppers, keeping them in perpetual debt. Most African Americans thus remained trapped in a system of economic bondage in the rural South, limiting their ability to challenge their legal and political subjugation. Struggling to survive, they endured the climate of racial oppression while they worked to support their families and raised their children as best as they could.

African Americans resented their status as second-class citizens. Yet, the prospect for any immediate change was bleak, as long as African Americans lacked political and economic power. Believing that racial progress would be a slow and arduous process, characterized by small victories rather than radical change, many were willing to settle for gradual change.

After 1895 the main proponent of this gradual approach to racial advancement was Booker T. Washington, the leading black spokesman of the late nineteenth and early twentieth centuries. Washington urged African Americans not to challenge segregation and discrimination, in order to avoid antagonizing southern whites. Placing economic progress ahead of civil and political rights, he advised African Americans to pursue vocational training and acquire job skills that would allow them to gain economic independence. Once African Americans achieved economic self-sufficiency, he claimed, they would be in a better position to demand political and legal equality. Until they reached the ultimate goal of true equality, however, African Americans had no choice but to rely on themselves. A champion of racial solidarity and economic self-help, Washington urged African Americans to pool their financial resources and establish their own institutions and businesses in an effort to improve the black community's quality of life. Among Washington's supporters was Richard Henry Boyd, as Paul Harvey documents in his essay. Boyd rose from slavery to become one of the nation's leading black entrepreneurs by the turn of the twentieth century.

While some African Americans worked for gradual change, others insisted that blacks could only achieve racial equality through public protests and constant attacks on discrimination and segregation. Less patient than the gradualists, and most often associated with the scholar and activist W. E. B. Du Bois, they tried to force American society to live up to its promise of democracy and freedom for all. A vocal critic of gradualism, Du Bois attacked Washington and his followers for their willingness to accept the second-class citizenship status of African Americans while working for gradual change. African Americans could only achieve racial equality, Du Bois insisted, if they enjoyed civil and political rights. He also challenged Washington's advocacy of vocational training as the key to economic independence. Industrial education, Du Bois conceded, was appropriate for the working masses who needed skills to earn decent wages; but the race also needed highly educated and trained professionals, the so-called Talented Tenth, who would provide leadership in the struggle for civil rights. Yet, like those who pursued a gradual approach, these civil rights protestors had faith that racial equality was an attainable goal and that America was capable of becoming a just society in which blacks and whites could live in harmony.

While supporters of Washington and Du Bois pursued the same goal but disagreed about strategy, others questioned whether racial equality was possible or even desirable. Frustrated by the persistence of racism, they urged African Americans to take fate into their own hands and create a world that would meet their needs and in which they, and not whites, defined freedom. Scholars often characterize this philosophy, which advocated separation from white society, as black nationalism. Many of those embracing black nationalism supported cultural separation, fostering the creation of black-controlled institutions within American society. Others sought physical separation and urged the members of their race to move west and establish all-black farming communities or to emigrate to Africa.

Although the majority of the black population remained in the rural South in the late nineteenth century, some African Americans heeded the call of the nationalists and left the region. Trying to break the chains of economic dependency, political oppression, and heightened racial violence, several thousand of them uprooted their families and headed for the West. The Exodusters, as they came to be known, established all-black towns and agricultural settlements in Kansas and Oklahoma. Gary R. Entz traces the life of Benjamin "Pap" Singleton, the father of the Kansas Exodus, who urged African Americans to escape the racial humiliations and indignities they faced in the Jim Crow South and farm their own land in the West. Achieving economic self-sufficiency, however, was difficult for a people who, until very recently, had been unable to accumulate money or acquire property. The lack of financial resources ultimately led to the failure of many black agricultural settlements in the West. Increasingly frustrated with the deterioration of race relations, some blacks called on people of African descent to leave the United States and return to Africa. Few, however, made that daring move.

More frequently, African Americans left the southern plantations and headed for the cities of the South. Seeking to improve their lot, black migrants hoped to find a less racially oppressive climate as well as jobs in emerging industries. Their hopes were soon dashed. White city residents, alarmed by the influx of rural black migrants, often responded with restrictive municipal codes that made existing segregation and discrimination practices even more rigid. Several southern cities witnessed the eruption of race riots, while others greeted the arriving migrants with lynchings. African Americans also found that the southern cities offered them only limited employment opportunities. Competition with white workers and racist hiring practices forced most black migrants to perform poorly paid menial tasks as day laborers and domestics. Low income, the refusal of white landlords to rent or sell property to African Americans, and city ordinances that enforced residential segregation left the majority of the South's black urban population little choice but to live in the poorest neighborhoods.

Despite these conditions, a steady stream of rural blacks continued to move to the cities of the South during the late nineteenth and early twentieth centuries. There they encountered the members of a small educated and professional black elite, many of them with roots in the free black communities that had emerged prior to the Civil War. During slavery the South's free black urban populations had led precarious lives. Legally free, they nevertheless had lived in constant fear of slave catchers and faced exclusion and discrimination. Finding strength in numbers, free blacks had launched their own businesses, religious and educational institutions, social clubs, and mutual aid societies in an effort to sustain their communities. These black organizations provided spaces for social interaction, fostered education and leadership skills, promoted economic cooperation, raised funds for charitable work, and offered sickness, death, and burial benefits for their members. Moreover, as David M. Fahey's essay on fraternal society leader William Washington Browne illustrates, these organizations came to play an important role in the struggle for racial uplift.

The arrival of large numbers of rural migrants created a peculiar dilemma for black urban communities. While black businesses flourished and an emerging black middle class prospered as a result of the population growth, longtime black city residents also worried about the overcrowding of residential areas and the heavy burden the newcomers placed on urban resources. The resulting tensions between lower-class rural migrants and upper- and middle-class urban residents often divided black communities. Some black elites distanced themselves from the migrants and retreated into exclusive social clubs. They feared that the arrival of large numbers of rural blacks would contribute to a deterioration of race relations and undermine their precarious status in society. Thus, they discouraged the migrants from leaving the rural South. Other black urban residents, however, initiated programs and services in an effort to ease the newcomers' transition to city life.

Black middle- and upper-middle-class women in particular played a leading role in assisting rural migrants as well as other lower-class African Americans. They launched educational and vocational training programs; provided instruction in health, hygiene, and nutrition; offered child care; organized musical and literary groups; raised funds for hospitals and orphanages; and investigated housing and sanitation conditions. Fostering racial advancement through community uplift, the black women's club movement not only focused on civic reform but also propelled many of its members into political activism. Fighting racial as well as gender discrimination, many of the women joined the struggle for women's suffrage in the early twentieth century. Jacqueline M. Moore demonstrates how Anna Julia Cooper, a clubwoman and educator, challenged racism and sexism throughout her long life, which began in slavery and ended during the civil rights movement.

By the start of the twentieth century not much had changed for African Americans. They were free, but they remained second-class citizens. The color line had become firmly entrenched, and racism, segregation, and discrimination were facts of life throughout the United States. Behind the color line, African Americans had built a world of their own. They had established their own institutions, including businesses, churches, schools, hospitals, newspapers, social clubs, welfare agencies, fraternal orders, sororities, literary societies, and many other groups to serve the needs of the African American community.

As African Americans struggled to survive in the shadow of Jim Crow, new opportunities arose when World War I started in Europe in 1914. As a result of the war, defense production in the United States increased while the number of European immigrants, who had made up a significant portion of the American work force, dropped sharply. Driven by patriotism and the potential for making profits, northern industries recruited black workers from the rural South to fill the vacancies. Black southerners, encouraged by African American newspapers, particularly the *Chicago Defender*, began to make the move from field to factory in 1915. An estimated 400,000 African Americans, attracted by employment opportunities and hopes for a better future in the "Promised Land," moved to the industrial centers of the North during the war. The Great Migration, as the population movement from the rural South to the urban North came to be known, continued for the next twenty-five years.

When the United States entered World War I in 1917, labor shortages in the North became even more severe as millions of men left the production lines to serve in the army. Among them were 370,000 black soldiers, who served in segregated units, and more than 600 black commissioned officers. African Americans closed ranks and supported the nation's military effort overseas and on the home front, hoping that the war to "make the world safe for democracy" would also result in civil rights in the United States. However, when the war ended in 1918, heightened black expectations were met by violent white efforts to maintain the color line.

After the war numerous race riots, often sparked by white fears of labor competition, exploded in American cities and a revived Ku Klux Klan terrorized African Americans throughout the nation. Black participation in the war and the increase in racial violence in its aftermath generated different responses among African Americans. Disillusioned with the outcome of the war, some turned inward and sought refuge in the multitude of black storefront churches that promised racial justice and salvation in the afterlife. A. J. Scopino explores the life of Prophet Noble Drew Ali, the founder of the Moorish Science Temple of America, who attracted a large following, particularly among poor blacks living in cities.

Several million other members of the black urban working class joined Marcus Garvey's Universal Negro Improvement Association. The flamboyant, Jamaican-born Garvey appealed to the disaffected black masses largely because of his rhetoric. He expressed the postwar disillusionment of many black urban residents who lived in overcrowded ghettos and worked in low-paying, menial jobs. It was futile, Garvey claimed, to attempt to improve race relations in the United States because racism was so entrenched in American society that it was impossible for blacks and whites to live together in harmony. Instead, Garvey urged his followers to take fate into their own hands, recall their glorious past, and return to Africa. Members of the black educated elite who struggled to achieve racial equality in the United States frowned at Garvey's separatist message. Calling him a charlatan who was deceiving the urban poor, they helped government officials arrest and indict Garvey on charges of mail fraud. In 1925, Garvey was found guilty, and he spent the next two years in jail until he was deported in 1927.

While Garvey's "Back to Africa" movement had attracted millions of disenchanted African Americans, others were more determined than ever to fight for racial equality and civil rights in the aftermath of World War I. As W. E. B. Du Bois proclaimed in 1919, "We return from fighting. We return fighting." An important outlet for black protest efforts was the National Association for the Advancement of Colored People (NAACP), an interracial civil rights group that had been founded in 1910. During the postwar decade, the NAACP expanded its membership, recorded and publicized incidents of racial violence, started lobbying for antilynching legislation, and initiated lawsuits that challenged segregation and discrimination.

Some of the black activists, as Christine Lutz demonstrates in her essay on Addie Waites Hunton, extended the struggle for racial equality into the global arena and helped organize several Pan-African congresses in the decades following World War I. They urged African Americans to unite with nonwhite people throughout the world in the fight against racism and the struggle for human rights. African Americans could only enjoy freedom and equality, they argued, if racial oppression was eliminated wherever it existed.

Although Pan-Africanists, civil rights activists, and Garveyites pursued different strategies, they shared a common characteristic. They had been radicalized by the wartime experience and had grown impatient with the lack of racial progress in the United States. They were part of a new generation of African Americans, the so-called New Negro, who had come of age in the aftermath of slavery, rejected gradualism, and advocated protest and racial pride.

This new racial consciousness was also expressed by many black writers, painters, and sculptors of the 1920s, who celebrated African American life and culture as well as their African heritage. New York City's Harlem community, which had attracted large numbers of migrants during the war, was the center of this black literary and artistic movement that soon came to be known as the Harlem Renaissance. While the artists of the Harlem Renaissance appealed largely to the educated and financial elites, both black and white, jazz musicians and blues singers attracted black and white audiences from a broad economic spectrum. Tracing the life and career of Ma Rainey, one of the era's most successful black female performers, Spencer Davis examines how she helped popularize blues music. Silent movies, particularly the black-produced race films of the 1920s, also played an important role in the African American cultural renaissance. The race films not only provided black actors with employment opportunities but also allowed them to portray a broad range of characters. Hollywood films and theater productions usually cast black actors in limited roles that reflected and reinforced racist stereotypes. Journalist and drama critic Lester A. Walton, profiled by Susan Curtis, became a leading advocate of black actors, urging theater owners and, in later years, television executives to cast them in diverse roles both to secure jobs for them and to undermine racist perceptions of blacks.

The 1920s celebration of black life and culture ended abruptly when the stock market collapsed in 1929. In the aftermath of the crash, unemployment rates skyrocketed and African Americans, who had always been the last to be hired and the first to be fired, struggled for economic survival. As black workers lost their jobs and incomes, black businesses lost their patrons, forcing many entrepreneurs into bankruptcy. African Americans turned for help to the mutual aid societies and voluntary institutions that had sustained their community in the past. However, these community-based institutions were overwhelmed by the growing requests for assistance, particularly when revenues from membership dues and donations declined as a result of the Great Depression. Economic hardship was accompanied by the deterioration of race relations. As job competition between blacks and whites increased, lynchings and mob violence once again escalated.

While economic despair and a heightening of racial tensions characterized the black experience during the early years of the Great Depression, African Americans advanced the struggle for racial equality during the presidency of Franklin D. Roosevelt. Elected in 1932, Roosevelt initially did not do much to bolster the confidence of African Americans. As a Democrat he needed the support of white southerners and he was not about to alienate them by endorsing civil rights or anti-lynching legislation. Moreover, Roosevelt's New Deal programs, which provided assistance to the unemployed, subsidized farmers, and created jobs, were administered by local white officials who often discriminated against African Americans.

Although Franklin Roosevelt failed to introduce legislation to end racial discrimination and to ensure the color-blind administration of New Deal programs, he and First Lady Eleanor Roosevelt contributed to a change in the racial climate. Eleanor, an ardent advocate of racial justice and human rights, particularly reached out to African Americans. She frequently visited black institutions and organizations, befriended and sought the advice of black activists, and helped recruit a group of black civil servants into high-ranking federal government offices. Roosevelt's Black Cabinet, as the group of informal black advisers came to be known, used its rapport with Eleanor to ensure that African Americans would receive a fair share of New Deal funds. The high visibility of African Americans in the Roosevelt administration contributed to a shift of black voters from the Republican to the Democratic Party during the 1930s.

Members of the Black Cabinet had succeeded in improving black access to New Deal programs, but even they continued to work in segregated civil service offices. Moreover, despite the efforts of the Black Cabinet, the federal government refused to assume a leadership role in the struggle for racial equality. While most African Americans welcomed the New Deal programs and applauded what appeared to be an increase in black political power, some criticized the Black Cabinet's cautious behind-the-scenes approach as well as Roosevelt's lack of public support for civil rights.

While some African Americans used their connections in the Roosevelt administration to enhance black political involvement, others sought allies in the labor movement to improve the conditions of black workers. Significant numbers of African Americans had entered the industrial work force during World War I, but they soon discovered that whites, fearing job competition, excluded them from their unions. In response, African Americans established their own labor organizations, but they also continued to challenge white unions to end racial discrimination.

When the depression worsened the status of all workers, white labor leaders reconsidered their policy of exclusion. In 1935 the newly created Congress of Industrial Organizations (CIO) opened its membership to all workers. Eric Arnesen explores how Willard Townsend, the CIO's highest-ranking black official, fought to improve black working conditions and employment opportunities while challenging racism in the labor movement.

The economic crisis of the 1930s ended when World War II started in Europe in 1939. The war triggered an increase in defense production in the United States and the nation's economy began to improve. Defense plants, however, virtually excluded black workers. Determined to end the racist hiring practices, black labor leader A. Philip Randolph threatened to lead 100,000 African Americans to Washington, DC, in protest. He hoped that the March on Washington would embarrass Roosevelt, who had proclaimed that America was the "arsenal of democracy." The president, fearing that the Axis powers would exploit the protest for propaganda purposes, tried to convince Randolph to call off the march. Randolph, however, refused until Roosevelt signed Executive Order 8802 on June 25, 1941. The order prohibited discrimination in government employment and defense industries and established the Fair Employment Practice Committee (FEPC) to investigate charges of discrimination. Among the FEPC's investigators was Elmer W. Henderson. As Andrew E. Kersten illustrates, Henderson used his nearly fifty-year career as a civil servant to pressure the federal government to increase black employment opportunities and promote racial equality.

While the FEPC represented a major victory in the struggle for racial equality, African Americans had only limited success in challenging segregation and discrimination in the military. Throughout World War II the armed forces continued to segregate black troops, black blood supplies, and black United Service Organizations (USO) entertainers. Nevertheless, service opportunities for African Americans increased. By the end of the war, they were no longer barred from the U.S. Marine Corps, Coast Guard, and Army Air Corps; black women served in the Women's Army Corps; and Benjamin O. Davis Sr. became the first black man to be promoted to brigadier general. African American military service reached unprecedented numbers. Nearly one million black men and women served in the various branches of the armed forces, nearly half of them overseas.

Black military service and home-front support during World War II differed significantly from the previous war. In World War I, African Americans had closed ranks, hoping to be granted civil rights as a reward for their support of the nation's war effort. During World War II they planted the seeds for the modern civil rights movement when they launched the "Double V" campaign, insisting that a victory for democracy abroad had to be linked to a victory for racial democracy in the United States. African Americans were determined to continue the fight for racial equality during the postwar years.

Following World War II the nation embarked on a troubled peace when the United States started to compete with the Soviet Union for world leadership. The cold war not only increased international tensions between the two superpowers but also inspired a growing number of

African Americans to advance civil rights. If the United States was to lead the Free World, it had to live up to the democratic ideals it was propagating around the globe by putting an end to discrimination at home. The absence of civil rights in the United States, they argued, hampered the government's ability to attract democratic allies, particularly among developing nations.

In an effort to internationalize domestic racial problems, civil rights activists attended United Nations gatherings and submitted highly publicized petitions protesting racism in the United States in an attempt to mobilize world opinion. State Department officials became concerned about the damaging effects of domestic racism on foreign relations. Of particular embarrassment were incidents of segregation and discrimination involving nonwhite dignitaries visiting the United States. The international focus on America's domestic racial problems, State Department officials warned President Harry S. Truman, tarnished the image of American democracy abroad, undermined the government's foreign policy efforts, and posed a threat to national security.

Truman agreed and increasingly supported civil rights. In 1946 he appointed a committee to study the status of civil rights and to make recommendations to improve them. In the postwar years, Truman frequently addressed gatherings of the NAACP, visited black institutions, and introduced civil rights bills. In 1948, pressured in part by foreign policy considerations as well as by Randolph, who threatened to organize black mass resistance to military service, Truman issued Executive Order 9981 desegregating the U.S. Armed Forces.

African Americans found their greatest postwar ally in the struggle for civil rights in the Supreme Court. In 1954, after years of challenging Jim Crow in the courts, NAACP lawyers won their most important victory when the Supreme Court struck down the separate-but-equal ruling in *Brown v. Board of Education*. The *Brown* decision emboldened African Americans and moved the civil rights struggle from the courtrooms into the nation's streets.

The *Brown* ruling generated massive white resistance, but it also inspired a growing number of ordinary African Americans to challenge segregation and discrimination. In 1955 black residents of Montgomery, Alabama, launched a year-long bus boycott that propelled Rosa Parks and the Reverend Martin Luther King Jr. into the national limelight. Civil rights activist and labor leader Edgar Daniel Nixon attracted far less media attention, despite his crucial role in the boycott. John White documents how Nixon helped pave the way for the boycott, long before King's arrival in Montgomery. The success of the boycott illustrated the power of grassroots activism and nonviolent direct action and enhanced the determination of African Americans to end Jim Crowism once and for all. Following the boycott, black churches joined the civil rights struggle when King organized the Southern Christian Leadership Conference (SCLC) in January 1957.

As civil rights activities increased throughout the 1950s, President Dwight D. Eisenhower appeared to display little interest in advancing racial equality or implementing *Brown*. Without much fanfare, however, Eisenhower had appointed numerous African Americans to important federal posts. Roberta Church, a minority consultant in the Labor Department, was the highest-ranking black female appointee of the Eisenhower administration. As Beverly Greene Bond suggests, Church was more than a token of the Republican Party's commitment to racial progress. She used her position effectively and helped to increase the government's role in the fight against discrimination in hiring and promotion. Church and other members of Eisenhower's Black Cabinet worked behind the scenes and attracted little media attention, unlike the civil rights protesters who took to the streets.

In the fall of 1957 nine black students in Little Rock, Arkansas, enrolled in the city's white Central High School, sparking a highly publicized standoff between state and federal authorities. Eisenhower, like his predecessor, was aware of the international ramifications of domestic racism and became increasingly concerned about the worldwide media attention generated by Little Rock. In September 1957 he mobilized Arkansas National Guard units to protect the "Little Rock Nine." In the same month he signed the Civil Rights Act of 1957 into law, creating the U.S. Commission on Civil Rights and the Civil Rights Division of the Justice Department. While the legislation was the first civil rights act since 1875, some African Americans wondered if either agency would do more than gather information.

Meanwhile, the struggle for racial equality intensified. In 1960 black college students in Greensboro, North Carolina, initiated sit-ins at lunch counters that refused to serve African Americans. The movement spread rapidly to other southern cities with black colleges and universities and resulted in the creation of the Student Nonviolent Coordinating Committee (SNCC) later that year. White students in the North joined the protest. They helped launch SNCC chapters on northern campuses, raised funds, and picketed chain stores that practiced segregation in the South. In 1961 the freedom riders, an interracial group of activists, challenged segregation on interstate transportation and in bus depots and train stations in the South. Riding on two buses, the thirteen men and women were attacked by angry white mobs and one of the buses was firebombed. As newspaper and television shows depicted white southerners harassing and attacking sit-in participants and freedom riders, public concerns grew. Many white Americans, who had previously paid little attention to civil rights activities, became alarmed, particularly when they saw images of savagely beaten young white protesters.

The Kennedy administration did not ignore the escalation of violence and mounting public pressure, but its initial response was deliberately slow and evasive. Kennedy needed the support of Southern Democrats and decided to focus attention on the cold war, an issue that unified, rather than divided, his party. He could not, however, avoid racial unrest, particularly when it became tied to cold war propaganda. In 1963 after city officials in Birmingham, Alabama, used water hoses and police dogs against 6,000 peacefully protesting black children, international news coverage highlighted racism in America, making it a serious political liability. By the early 1960s thirty-three former colonies in Africa had become independent nations. Courted by American and Soviet diplomats, these African nations represented a potentially powerful bloc of votes in the United Nations. Meanwhile, many white Americans began to wonder why Kennedy, the defender of democracy abroad, did not take stronger action to defend it at home.

In addition to foreign policy considerations, concerns about the rise of black militancy were also partly responsible for Kennedy's decision to respond to the Birmingham crisis. Thus far civil rights activists had heeded King's call for nonviolent direct action. However, 1963 marked the 100th anniversary of the Emancipation Proclamation, reminding African Americans of the slow progress they had made toward racial equality. As African Americans grew increasingly impatient, politicians in Washington feared that King's leadership might be challenged by those who rejected nonviolence. Particularly, Malcolm X, the charismatic minister of the Nation of Islam, attracted a lot of media attention when he called for armed self-defense. Given the choice of dealing with the moderate King or the militant Malcolm X, Kennedy promised to introduce comprehensive civil rights legislation in June 1963, one month after the Birmingham crisis. In August 1963, nearly 250,000 black and white protesters joined the March on Washington, celebrating the civil rights victory, demonstrating their continued commitment to the struggle for racial equality, and reminding the president of his promise. Kennedy, however, was assassinated in November 1963, before his civil rights bill became law.

When Vice President Lyndon B. Johnson succeeded Kennedy, many African Americans feared that the new president from Texas would not support civil rights legislation. Yet, despite his southern roots, Johnson became a much more forceful advocate of racial equality than Kennedy. He appointed numerous African Americans to high government posts, including Thurgood Marshall, the first black Supreme Court justice, and Robert Weaver, who, as Secretary of the Department of Housing and Urban Development, became the first black cabinet member. Johnson also secured congressional support for Kennedy's civil rights bill. In 1964, Congress adopted the Civil Rights Act, which prohibited racial discrimination and segregation in public accommodations, education, and employment and extended to the federal government the power to enforce its provisions.

The struggle for racial equality, however, was not over as long as white southerners continued to exclude African American voters from the polls. In 1964 civil rights activists launched a massive attack on the denial of black voting rights in the South when they initiated the Mississippi Freedom Summer Project. Black and white volunteers, many of them college students from the North, went to Mississippi to register black voters and to set up freedom schools in rural areas. They were met by violent white opposition. The most widely publicized incident was the disappearance and subsequent murder of three of the volunteers: Michael Schwerner, Andrew Goodman, and James Chaney. Undeterred by the violence, student volunteers continued their efforts.

In addition to increasing the number of registered black voters in the South, civil rights groups urged the president to submit a Voting Rights Act to Congress. In an effort to expose black disfranchisement, Martin Luther King announced plans for a protest march from Selma to Montgomery, Alabama, in 1965. Violent opposition to the march captured the attention of the media and the nation. In response, Congress passed the Voting Rights Act of 1965, which allowed federal government officials to register voters and enforce the Fifteenth Amendment.

Despite legal victories the movement began to lose momentum after 1965. The Selma protest had heightened tensions among the various civil rights organizations and activists. SNCC organizers were outraged when King obeyed court injunctions against the march. Arguing that he had conceded too much to the federal government, they challenged his leadership. Indeed, divisions within the civil rights movement had existed from the start. As the movement expanded, competition for members, funds, and media attention increased among different groups. Moreover, there was little agreement on strategy. Some civil rights groups advocated using the legal and political system to advance their cause, while others organized grassroots protests. Age and gender also contributed to numerous disagreements. Many women complained about sexism, and a growing number of young black activists questioned the usefulness of nonviolence as well as the involvement of whites.

In the aftermath of Selma the movement disintegrated. Many white volunteers, hoping that the Civil Rights and Voting Rights Acts would ensure racial equality, went home. Other whites were driven out of the movement by a growing number of young black activists who rejected integration as a goal and nonviolence as a strategy. Proclaiming "Black Power," they embraced black nationalism, advocated separation from white society, and insisted on racially exclusive organizations. The Black Panther Party, founded in 1966, reflected this new militancy. Armed with rifles, Panthers asserted their right to self-defense: "We want power to determine the destiny of our Black Community." In the same year, the SNCC excluded whites from membership.

Other civil rights groups and activists shunned the militant rhetoric and continued to rely on nonviolent direct action in their pursuit of racial and social justice. King, alarmed by a wave of riots that erupted in cities of the North and West, focused the SCLC's attention on the plight of the urban poor. Demanding better jobs, schools, and housing, King announced plans for a Poor People's Campaign. He called on Americans of all races to gather in Washington, DC, in late April 1968. The protesters were to remain in the nation's capital until they secured federal legislation that guaranteed government support of full employment and the construction of low-income housing. Preparations for the campaign were nearing completion when King was assassinated in Memphis on April 4. King's death further weakened the black freedom struggle.

By the late 1960s many white Americans had lost interest in the civil rights movement. The escalation of the war in Vietnam and antiwar protests in the United States captured the nation's attention and pushed the black freedom struggle out of the headlines. While America's involvement in Vietnam polarized the nation, African Americans were particularly critical of U.S. troop deployments in Southeast Asia. They charged that the draft was racially biased because black men were less likely to qualify for college deferments than whites. Disproportionately high casualty rates among black combat troops and the 1967 conviction of heavyweight boxing champion Muhammad Ali on charges of draft evasion further enraged African Americans.

While the majority of the more than 300,000 black soldiers in Vietnam were reluctant young draftees, others had chosen a career in the military. James E. Westheider shows that the number of black professional soldiers increased steadily following the desegregation of the armed forces in 1948. A career in the military was attractive to many African Americans, because it allowed them to advance economically, without having to face the racist hiring and promotion practices prevalent in civilian employment. Sgt. Allen Thomas Jr., who served three tours of duty in Vietnam, witnessed the tensions between draftees and professional soldiers as well as black and white troops. Moreover, he observed the men's growing disillusionment with American involvement in the war and the resulting decline in troop morale.

Many Americans who did not serve in Vietnam shared the soldiers' sense of despair. Television coverage of the carnage in Vietnam as well as the urban riots and the civil rights and antiwar protests at home reinforced a growing sense of insecurity, particularly among white Americans. They wondered if the nation was coming apart. African Americans, who had always lived apart from, yet inside, American society, wondered if the nation could ever come together. As W. E. B. Du Bois had observed in 1903, racism had created a "double-consciousness" among African Americans, a sense of "two-ness," being both American and black. Most whites had paid little attention to the two racial worlds that existed in the midst of American society until the turmoil of the 1960s. In 1968 a highly publicized report on the causes of the urban violence concluded: "Our Nation is moving toward two societies, one black, one white—separate and unequal." As the biographies in this volume illustrate, African Americans knew only too well that those two societies already existed.

Although there was no longer a unified civil rights movement by 1968, the foundation that it had laid provided a basis for further progress. At the start of the twenty-first century, African Americans occupy important and highly visible posts in the federal government, including the cabinet, the armed forces, and the Supreme Court. The number of black elected officials in Congress as well as in state and local politics has increased dramatically. Overall, economic conditions of African

Americans have improved considerably. Median incomes of black house-holds have risen substantially and black poverty rates have dropped. The black middle class has experienced a particularly impressive growth as an unprecedented number of African American professionals have entered white-collar employment. A much larger percentage of black students finish high school and many of them continue their education at the college level.

Despite these advances, African Americans continue to earn less than equally qualified whites. They are more likely to live in poverty or on welfare, often lack access to adequate health care, and have higher infant mortality, teen pregnancy, and unemployment rates than whites. The percentage of black students completing high school or college, while improving, is still significantly lower than that of whites. African Americans are also more likely to become victims of crime than the white population. High crime rates in black neighborhoods, African American residents claim, are exacerbated by a slow response of white law enforcement officials as well as police harassment and brutality. Although incidents of lynchings and other forms of mob violence have declined dramatically, racially motivated intimidation and violence continue.

Improvements in the social, political, and economic status of the black population indicate that African Americans have made great strides toward equality since 1865. Yet the persistence of racial disparities also points to the struggle that still lies ahead. While population figures are important indicators of changing conditions, statistics cannot convey the human experience. Indeed, figures, charts, and tables depersonalize human beings and reduce them to faceless numbers and percentages.

The biographies in this volume provide a very personal window on the African American past. They illustrate the experiences of ordinary men and women who faced extraordinary challenges because they were black. All of them encountered racism, yet their responses to racial oppression varied, reflecting the diversity of the African American experience. Although they lived in the shadow of well-known individuals such as Booker T. Washington, Martin Luther King Jr., or Malcolm X, they are no less significant for an understanding of the African American past. Perhaps they are more important because they were ordinary people.

1

Edmonia G. and Caroline V. Highgate

Black Teachers, Freed Slaves, and the Betrayal of Black Hearts

Ronald E. Butchart

Even before the end of the Civil War many northerners headed to the South to aid the freedpeople in making the transition from slavery to freedom. Both blacks and whites, many of whom had been active in the abolitionist movement, hoped to relieve the suffering of the nearly four million former slaves. With the support of missionary societies established by northern churches as well as secular humanitarian groups, these men and women provided much-needed welfare services. They furnished medical assistance, distributed clothing and food, and organized churches and schools. In the closing months of the war, Congress came to the aid of the northern reformers and the private charities that had funded their work. On March 3, 1865, Congress created the Bureau of Refugees, Freedmen, and Abandoned Lands, better known as the Freedmen's Bureau. The agency was charged with assisting southern white refugees, providing for the welfare of the freedpeople, and managing abandoned and confiscated southern property.

The former slaves welcomed the efforts of the Freedmen's Bureau and the numerous northern freedmen's aid societies, particularly their educational work. Allocating over $5 million to freedmen's education, the Freedmen's Bureau transported teachers and educational supplies to the South, provided government buildings for schooling, and was instrumental in launching many southern black colleges. The former slaves, young and old, flocked to the schools. As slaves they had been denied an education; now they thirsted for it. Learning how to read and write, they asserted their freedom and broke the shackles of slavery.

Among those who went to the South to aid freedmen's education were Edmonia G. and Caroline V. Highgate. Born and raised in Syracuse, New York, the well-educated Highgate sisters left the relative comforts of their home and headed for the war-torn South. As members of the free black community in the North they had lived privileged lives, yet they were no strangers to discrimination, segregation, and racism. As Ronald E. Butchart demonstrates, the lives of the Highgate sisters symbolized the widespread black thirst for knowledge as well as the determination of African Americans

1

to achieve equality. Both women dedicated their lives to careers as teachers in the new black schools of the South, where they taught the less fortunate members of their race. Teaching, however, meant more than providing the former slaves with useful skills; it also served as a means for racial uplift. Both women's careers were cut short when they fell in love with white men. Edmonia died of a failed abortion; and Caroline, deserted by her husband, struggled to provide for her six children.

Throughout their history, African Americans have demonstrated a thirst for knowledge and education equaled by few groups with similar resources. Surviving slavery demanded solidarity, wit, critical insight, and a culture of intelligent resistance. Thriving despite the relentless, dehumanizing practices and restraints of racial slavery and postslavery racist culture nurtured a hunger among African Americans for asserting and demonstrating the racial superiority of people of African descent. A central strategy for surviving and thriving was learning, in order to break the codes of white power. The well-honed study of the habits and tempers of white people; clandestine literacy; reconstructed theologies, which consigned white Christians to eternal damnation while exalting black spirituality; a rich and subtle oral tradition, which communicated resistance and solidarity under the unsuspecting eyes of slave owners; the use of information about the white power structure in order to turn it into cultural capital—these and other traditions of study and education distinguished African American culture. Further, traditions of respect for knowledge spawned high regard in the black community for those who taught.

With such educational traditions, America's former slaves greeted freedom differently than any other people coming out of bondage. As black scholar and activist W. E. B. Du Bois observed, most emancipated people "regard ignorance as natural and necessary, or even exalt their own traditional wisdom and discipline" over formal education. Others accept that knowledge is the prerogative of social superiors. "American Negroes never acted thus," Du Bois continued. "The very feeling of inferiority which slavery forced upon them fathered an intense desire to rise out of their condition by means of education."[1]

The result was an unparalleled social phenomenon: a demand for schools, teachers, books, and literacy from the moment of emancipation, a demand that the nation could not begin to meet. From the opening skirmishes of the Civil War in 1861 to the end of Reconstruction in 1877, northern groups, black and white, joined with literate southern African Americans to open schools and support teachers for the freedpeople. Between 1865 and 1870 the federal government contributed halfheartedly to that effort through the limited resources of the Freedmen's Bureau.

For a time during and after the Civil War, young and old went to school. When the lash of economic necessity and the prod of labor contracts drove African American adults back to the fields, they sacrificed their children's labor potential to keep them in school more often and for longer periods than southern poor whites did. African American efforts to obtain formal education faced severe limits when, in angry and ugly retaliation, white political leaders and white organized violence reduced access to public schools in the years following Reconstruction as part of the white Redemption of the South. Yet even after the partial dismantling of the public education system that the former slaves had helped to create during Reconstruction, African Americans sought such schooling as they could get from the state and from northern philanthropists. They sustained their teachers and built and supported institutions of higher education.

The lives and experiences of the Highgate sisters, who were literate and well-educated black women and teachers, epitomized the nineteenth-century African American experience in at least three ways. First, their own learning symbolized a widespread black thirst for knowledge. Second, like thousands of other black women and men in the tumultuous years of the Civil War and Reconstruction, they dedicated their lives to careers as teachers in the new black schools of the South, exemplifying the desire of black teachers to foster racial uplift through formal education. Finally, their intimate lives, tragically, stand as symbols of the universal experience of nineteenth-century African Americans: the hearts of both women were betrayed by white men, symbolic of the social, economic, and political betrayal black men and women experienced constantly at the hands of white men and women.

Edmonia Goodelle Highgate and Caroline Victoria Highgate were the first and fourth children of Charles and Hannah Francis Highgate. Hannah Highgate was born in Virginia, though whether she was born free or slave is not known. The sisters were born and raised in the black community in Syracuse, New York. Edmonia, five years her sister's senior, was born in 1844. Her father, a barber and native of Pennsylvania, died when she was seventeen and Caroline was twelve. Charles left his widow with six children, the youngest six years of age. Charles Highgate was not a wealthy man, even by the standards of a small, northern black community. Yet he attended to the education of his children rather than putting them to work. Edmonia was among the small group of young people in the first class to graduate from Syracuse High School and apparently the only African American in her class. She graduated with honors in 1861. In her high-school studies she emphasized the "normal course," the era's name for teacher education. Nonetheless, it is clear from her subsequent career that her schooling provided her with a broad education, including French. Her knowledge of that language enabled her to hold her own in conversational French during an audience with a European actress eight years later and to assist her French-speaking Creole students in Louisiana. Writing in 1867 of her experience as a bilingual educator, she remarked, "My little knowledge of French is put in constant use in order to instruct them in our language."[2]

Upon graduation, Edmonia received a teaching certificate from the Syracuse Board of Education. She learned soon enough, however, that her certificate could not buy her a position in the city of her birth, because of her race. Thus, in 1861, as the Civil War divided the nation, Edmonia Highgate took a teaching position in a black school in Montrose, Pennsylvania, just across the state line from Binghamton, New York, about sixty miles from her home. After one term she accepted a position as principal of a larger black school in Binghamton. The educational needs of millions of African Americans in the South soon changed the path of her career.

By 1863 the war had ground down to a bloody stalemate, and Edmonia, like all northern African Americans, was acutely aware that slaves by the thousands had made their way to freedom behind Union lines and were clamoring for schools and teachers. Early in the war many voluntary northern aid societies had sprung up, and existing missionary societies had shifted their attention to assist the former slaves, then called "contraband of war." The aid societies reprinted in their many monthly journals the letters of scores of northern teachers who spoke of the suffering and destitution in the freedmen's camps. They wrote also of the churches, barns, and sheds that had been transformed into makeshift schools, where frequently more than one hundred students of all ages learned their letters from a single teacher. By 1864, Edmonia knew she had to be part of this challenging and exciting effort to educate the millions of former slaves. In January she wrote to the American Missionary Association asking for a position among that organization's teachers. "I have felt an intense interest in the education of my freed brethren [in the] South," she explained, "and have been actuated to enter into this work simply by a desire to be a pioneer in trying to raise them up to the stature of manhood and womanhood in 'Christ Jesus.' "[3] One month later she left her position in Binghamton and spent four weeks raising funds for the National Freedmen's Relief Association of New York, then left for Norfolk, Virginia. In Norfolk she taught with three other black women, two of them graduates of Oberlin College. She earned less than half of the salary she had received in New York and worked much harder under extraordinary conditions.

Edmonia worked herself to exhaustion in her first months in Norfolk. In the autumn she returned to Syracuse to recuperate. During her stay the city hosted a convention of African American men, one of a series of such conventions, dating back two decades. By invitation, Edmonia addressed the convention, which was attended by the nation's leading black abolitionists, ministers, and thinkers. She was one of very few black women to speak, testimony both to her charisma and learning and to the respect those men had for the freedmen's teachers.

In early 1865, Edmonia returned south to organize a school in Darlington on Maryland's Eastern Shore. By summer, she had moved her mother and her youngest sister, Willella, to Maryland to assume control of her school. Once assured that her mother and sister were capable of carrying the school forward, Edmonia left for New Orleans. Though no longer an employee of the American Missionary Association nor of any other freedmen's aid society, she dedicated herself to organizing schools for the former slaves. "We have a flourishing school in the Creole district, called after our eloquent champion, Frederick Douglass," she wrote in early 1866, adding, "your *amie de plume* [faithful correspondent] is principal, assisted by an able corps of educated colored teachers."[4] Her sister, Caroline V. Highgate, who had also pursued the "normal course" shortly after Edmonia left Syracuse in 1861, joined her in New Orleans, assuming the principalship of another freedmen's school, the General Baird School.

Edmonia also assisted in organizing the Louisiana Educational Relief Association that spring. It was a primarily black organization intended to raise money to support schooling for indigent black children and to hasten "the equalization of political and social recognition of manhood irrespective of color." Never one to mince words with white northerners who fancied themselves friends of the freedmen, she appealed for aid in the *Christian Recorder*, the weekly newspaper of the African Methodist Episcopal (AME) Church:

> I only wish that our northern radical spoken friends, who are now at their fashionable summer resorts, while we teachers are laboring on a salary, only

what our certificate calls for and less by a third what our expenses are, would feel it their duty to enclose some substantial evidence of their interest in this work, in a cheerful letter to us. We dare not send away twenty or thirty children from our schools, because they cannot pay their tuition fee. . . . Yet we expend our strength teaching them, and have not wherewith to supply ourselves with more than one meal a day, or money for a car-ride, but must foot two or three miles of weary distance beneath a tropical sun. Think of these things, theorists, and withhold your aid if you can.[5]

In addition to financial problems, racial violence also hampered Edmonia's work. On July 30, 1866, white policemen in New Orleans fired shots at a peaceful assembly of black and white Republicans, killing dozens and injuring over one hundred. That incident touched off two days of rioting by white southerners, venting their wrath on northerners in general and African Americans in particular. The Highgate sisters nursed the wounded in hospitals while continuing their schools, but by autumn they felt it best to leave the city. Caroline returned to the North and took charge of a black school in Woodbury, New Jersey. Edmonia moved to Lafayette Parish, well to the west of New Orleans, where she taught day, night, and Sabbath schools. Her new location, however, did not protect her from white violence. "There has been much opposition to the school," she wrote in December 1866. "Twice I have been shot at in my room. My night scholars have been shot, but none killed. . . . The rebels here threatened to burn down the school and house in which I board."[6] Edmonia's absence from New Orleans lasted only a few months. By March 1867 she had returned and opened another school where she taught 125 indigent students supported by the Louisiana Educational Relief Association.

Upon her return to New Orleans, Edmonia found that the riot of the previous year had chastened most of the city's black teachers and principals. When a committee from the Orleans Parish School Board interviewed all of the black school principals in August and September 1867 to ascertain their and, presumably, the black community's attitudes regarding racially integrated schools, all but Edmonia spoke circumspectly, careful not to offend the segregationist leanings of the board. Edmonia, on the other hand, spoke as forthrightly to southern white men as she had to her northern white supporters. She offered no apologies for her position "that there should be no distinction made in the schools" between white and black students. She did concede that, given the temper of the time, "mixing the races now may create difficulties and injure the cause of education for the time being," but in the long run, equality of access was essential. Her interviewers remarked to the board, "Miss Highgate is a very intelligent, and apparently highly educated lady."[7]

Meanwhile, Caroline, who had left New Orleans in the aftermath of the riot to assume a teaching position in the North, returned to the South. In the autumn of 1867 she resigned from her post in New Jersey, despite pleas from students and members of the black community, and established a school in Jackson, Mississippi. She taught there without any financial assistance from northern organizations except for one year, 1868–1869, when the Pennsylvania Freedmen's Relief Association paid a portion of her salary.

In January 1868, shortly after Caroline's arrival in Jackson, Edmonia also moved to Mississippi, where she opened a school in Enterprise, eighty miles east of her sister's school. The reasons for Edmonia's departure from New Orleans are not clear. When New Orleans established its own public schools in the late 1860s, built on the structure put in place by Edmonia and others in the city's black community, Edmonia either sought a new field of labor or perhaps she was frozen out of the new system, both too outspoken and too northern for the white city fathers.

After Edmonia moved to Mississippi, she and Caroline arranged for their mother and youngest sister, Willella, to join them to establish a school in Canton, twenty miles north of Jackson. By 1869 their two surviving brothers, James and William, had joined the rest of the family as teachers in Mississippi. The oldest brother, two years younger than Edmonia, had died of wounds suffered at the Battle of Petersburg.

After establishing her family as educators to the freedmen of Mississippi, Edmonia spent part of 1870 in the north raising money for her school. In February she spoke before the Massachusetts Anti-Slavery Society, observing ominously that the work of abolitionists was "not yet half done; and if it is not now thoroughly done, it will have to be done over again."[8] In a single decade, Edmonia had gone from an honor graduate of a fledgling New York high school to a pioneer teacher in the dark heart of a former slave kingdom whose body was broken but whose spirit was alive and virulent.

Edmonia's learning was always evident: she spoke effectively before churches, conventions, and the last meeting of the Massachusetts branch of the American Abolition Society. She also became a frequent contributor to the *Christian Recorder*, and her letters appeared in the *American Freedman* and the *American Missionary*. By 1870 she had attracted the attention of Theodore Tilton, editor of the *Independent*, a widely read weekly newspaper with a national distribution. At one point,

Edmonia even turned her hand to fiction. While teaching at Darlington, Maryland, she wrote a didactic novella, "Congojoco," serialized in three parts by the *Christian Recorder* under the pen name "E. Godelle H.," either an intentional misspelling of her middle name, Goodelle, or a printer's error. She later published most of her correspondence with the *Christian Recorder* under the name "E. Goodelle Highgate." Because "Congojoco" was a metaphor for her own intentions, consciously or not, the story is worth a moment's digression. "Congojoco"—the title is never explained—was a short, religious romance in which the heroine spurns various suitors, one of whom dies of a broken heart. Edmonia describes her heroine who has just turned away her final suitor:

> Ursula Nicolas had as gentle and womanly a nature as ever slumbered in any bosom. At last it was aroused, and she determined to make some amends for the guilt that lay at the door of her heart. Clad in the quiet Quaker drab, she visited the haunts of vice and wretchedness and spoke life-words to those who had gone away from virtue and happiness; she admonished them to cast themselves into the lily white of redeeming love; encouraged fallen sisters to go to the Saviour, who had, while on earth, manifested a special sympathy for them. She had her reward in the joy of getting out of self; of getting away from the sepulchre within and of loosing that old clinging feeling of weariness.[9]

In the last installment of the novella, Ursula Nicolas works as a nurse in a military hospital in Virginia, when a former suitor, gravely wounded, falls under her care. She nurses him back to health; when he fails again to win her, he asks her why she has saved him. She replies, "To develop within you the latent powers of your soul; to awaken you to a sense and duty of true manhood, that you may, hereafter, properly use and apply the rare intellectual gifts with which you are endowed." Months later, "walking through a luxuriant grove of trees, in the interior of South Carolina, she discovered a cluster of graves." Among them she found the grave of her late suitor. " 'Thank God, he came to the hospital before he died,' she said, with an upturned glance."[10]

A vibrant young woman in her twenties when she wrote "Congojoco," Edmonia constructed Ursula as her alter ego. Ursula was a strong-willed woman who by sheer willpower stared down romantic and sexual longings to devote her life to a higher calling in mission work to the downtrodden. Edmonia's novella was a metaphor for how she envisioned her own life: elevated above passion, embracing resolutely the twin goals of the spiritual and political elevation of the freedpeople, awakening them "to a sense and duty of true manhood" so that they might "properly use and apply [their] rare intellectual gifts." Five years later, as

Edmonia was preparing to take a position as one of the first faculty members of the new Tougaloo College in Mississippi, her ability to separate romantic passion and spiritual ministry met a challenge she was not prepared for, with fatal results.

Meanwhile, romance and love disrupted Caroline's life in Mississippi. In the autumn of her third year of teaching in Jackson, a dashing young former Union Army officer visited her school. Col. Albert T. Morgan, a white native of Wisconsin, had leased a plantation in Mississippi after the war and gained a seat in the state senate. As he and a colleague approached the school, they heard the children singing, and above their voices he heard Caroline's pure tones, a sound that captivated him. He met Caroline, then just twenty years old, described by others as a young woman of simple grace and a spontaneous smile. Morgan himself recalled that Caroline was one of the most popular teachers in Jackson. She had "not only won the love of all the freed people" but had also "won the profound respect of even 'the enemy,' who treat her with great deference, notwithstanding her calling." Morgan continued: "She is as tireless in her work as she is skillful. Think of it, she not only manages that large day school—sometimes numbering a hundred— but she attends to her religious duties, superintends . . . the Sabbath-school, runs a temperance society, and has put in execution various other plans for the social elevation of the freedpeople." When asked how she withstood the strain, Morgan replied that it was "the cause in which she is engaged—the cause."[11] Caroline Highgate and Albert T. Morgan fell in love, but Mississippi laws prohibited interracial marriage in 1870. Morgan prevailed upon his fellow legislators to rescind the laws, and the two were married in Jackson on August 3, 1870.

The newlyweds departed immediately for the North for their honeymoon. They arranged to meet Edmonia and other friends in McGrawville, New York, forty miles south of Syracuse. The town had, up to a decade earlier, been the home of New York Central College, an abolitionist school that from its inception had been interracial and co-educational. Although the town proved ultimately not to be supportive of interracial education, it was a place sacred to nineteenth-century dreams of an interracial America.

In that setting, watching the happy interracial couple, twenty-six-year-old Edmonia, too, fell in love with a white man, John Henry Vosburg, who was some years her senior. She was preparing to return to Mississippi to work in the normal school at Tougaloo College, and had written some weeks earlier, "I have no other expectation and much prefer to devote the remainder of my years to that branch of the work," teacher training.[12] But unlike the heroine in her novella, Edmonia chose not to turn her suitor away. Two months later she died as a result of a failed abortion. Her train tickets to Tougaloo were found in her trunk. Her paramour, Vosburg, had betrayed her, abandoning her to the abortionist's blade to return to the wife he had never revealed to her.

Though less tragic than Edmonia's fate, Caroline's life was also marred by the betrayal of a white man. Caroline and Albert T. Morgan had six children. Morgan, unsuccessful at nearly everything he attempted, moved his family from Mississippi to the District of Columbia and then to Kansas. He left for Colorado in search of work, but never returned or sent for his wife and children. Caroline successfully raised her children, training her four daughters, "beautiful and talented young women," in music. They supported themselves as a professional quartet with their mother acting as manager and chaperone. One daughter, Caroline Victoria, said later of her mother that she "became a mental healer, Christian Science practitioner and dramatic reader . . . . Those are her professions but she is wonderfully equipped in all phases of literature, art, and religion, and she long ago decided that more children were not to be desired and that people, even married couples, should refrain from the closest intimacy." Caroline died in 1926 in London, where she was living with one of her daughters. Explaining Morgan's betrayal of the family, his son, Albert Jr., remarked, "my father never made a success and he became so disheartened that he was really ashamed to come home."[13] Morgan died in 1922.

Although there may be no uniform experience that describes the human tradition in African American history, common elements mark particular periods in that history. The Highgate sisters symbolize several of those elements. Though from a humble family, they were broadly educated. At only sixteen or seventeen years of age, they became teachers and strove to extend their privileges to others of their race. They advocated racial uplift through education, a perspective on schooling that is almost uniquely African American, and one that challenges dominant notions of education for individual advancement and personal gain. They personify traditions of learning and teaching despite poverty and disadvantage. The Highgates are symbolic, too, of the many northern black teachers who flooded into the South even before the end of the Civil War "to do something for my people who have been less fortunate than myself," as their mother, Hannah Francis Highgate, wrote in 1865.[14] Their white counterparts have long been celebrated or, by traditional southern historians, vilified. Yet it was black teachers who served in disproportionate numbers in the schools for the freedpeople, who taught longer, and who worked in more dangerous and less prestigious places than white teachers. Like Edmonia and Caroline Highgate, black teachers were much more likely than their white counterparts to go fearlessly into the urban and rural South to establish schools independently of the northern aid societies, confident that "the keen relish which [the freedmen] have for knowledge" would sustain them.[15]

The work of black teachers such as the Highgate sisters provided the foundation for state systems of public education, something that did not exist for either race in the slave South. The work of black teachers sustained the southern black demand for schooling in the face of white racist fears of educated black women and men. In the final analysis, as James D. Anderson has observed, southern African Americans, despite their disfranchisement, poverty, and enforced social marginality, contributed more to the creation of universal schooling in the South than any other group.[16] Edmonia and Caroline typify the teachers who carried messages of hope and resistance through knowledge.

Ironically, however, Edmonia and Caroline Highgate also symbolize, at a personal and intimate level, the experiences of African Americans at a social and political level. Their hearts were betrayed by white men, as many white men have betrayed the hearts, minds, bodies, and futures of the black race in America. For Edmonia, the betrayal was brutal and fatal. Caroline, on the other hand, survived betrayal, and symbolized in her remaining years yet another tradition in the black community—the resilience and inventiveness, bolstered by education, that allowed her and her children to thrive.

Notes

1. W. E. B. Du Bois, *Black Reconstruction in America, 1860–1880* (1935; reprint, Cleveland, OH: World Publishing Co., 1964), 637–38.

2. Edmonia G. Highgate to M. E. Strieby, December 17, 1866, American Missionary Association Archives, Amistad Research Center, Tulane University, hereafter cited as AMA.

3. Edmonia G. Highgate to S. S. Jocelyn, January 30, 1864, AMA.

4. *Christian Recorder* 6 (March 17, 1866), 41. The *Christian Recorder*, a weekly newspaper written primarily for the nation's African Americans, was the official publication of the African Methodist Episcopal (AME) Church.

5. *Christian Recorder* 6 (July 7, 1866), 105.

6. Edmonia G. Highgate to M. E. Strieby, December 17, 1866, AMA. See also her note in *Christian Recorder* 6 (November 3, 1866), 173.

7. "Report of Committee on Colored Schools," September 16, 1867, in Orleans Parish School Board, Minutes, August 29, 1865–June 2, 1869, No. 7, 209–10. Orleans Parish School Board Meetings and Related Committees, Special Collections, New Orleans University.

8. Quoted in Dorothy Sterling, ed., *We Are Your Sisters: Black Women in the Nineteenth Century* (New York: W. W. Norton, 1984), 301.

9. *Christian Recorder* 5 (May 20, 1865), 78.

10. *Christian Recorder* 5 (May 27, 1865), 82.

11. A. T. Morgan, *Yazoo; or, On the Picket Line of Freedom in the South: A Personal Narrative* (1884; reprint, New York: Russell and Russell, 1968), 345–46.

12. E. G. Highgate to E. P. Smith, June 23, 1870, AMA.

13. Richard Nelson Current, *Those Terrible Carpetbaggers* (New York: Oxford University Press, 1988), 411–12.

14. H. F. Highgate to George Whipple, April 23, 1864, AMA.

15. Edmonia G. Highgate, in "Monthly Report of Darlington School for the Month of March, 1865," AMA.

16. James D. Anderson, *The Education of Blacks in the South, 1860–1935* (Chapel Hill: University of North Carolina Press, 1988), 4–32.

Suggested Readings

There have been no biographies of the Highgate family. The family information included here comes from analyses of manuscripts and census records, city directories, newspaper accounts, correspondence, and other primary sources.

The traditions that the Highgate sisters exemplify, however, have been explored by several historians. Regarding education for survival, see particularly Thomas L. Webber, *Deep Like the Rivers: Education in the Slave Quarter Community, 1831–1865* (New York: W. W. Norton, 1978). Lawrence W. Levine, *Black Culture and Black Consciousness: Afro-American Folk Thought from Slavery to Freedom* (New York: Oxford University Press, 1977), studies the uses of knowledge in black culture. Leon F. Litwack, *Been in the Storm So Long: The Aftermath of Slavery* (New York: Alfred A. Knopf, 1979), tells the dramatic story of African Americans coming out of bondage.

Henry L. Swint, *Northern Teacher in the South, 1862–1870* (Nashville: Vanderbilt University Press, 1941), the traditional source on freedmen's education, has been superseded by a rich literature in the last two decades, beginning with Ronald E. Butchart, *Northern Schools, Southern Blacks, and Reconstruction: Freedmen's Education, 1862–1875* (Westport, CT: Greenwood Press, 1980); Jacqueline Jones, *Soldiers of Light and Love: Northern Teachers and Georgia Blacks, 1865–1873* (Chapel Hill: University of North Carolina Press, 1980); and Robert C. Morris, *Reading, 'Riting, and Reconstruction: The Education of Freedmen in the South, 1861–1870* (Chicago: University of Chicago Press, 1981). On African American teachers in the freedmen's education movement, see Butchart, "Perspectives on Gender, Race, Calling, Commitment in Nineteenth-century America: A Collective Biography of the Teachers of the Freedpeople, 1862–1875," *Vitae Scholastica* 13 (Spring 1994): 15–32. James D. Anderson, *The Education of Blacks in the South, 1860–1935* (Chapel Hill: University of North Carolina Press, 1988), provides the best overview of formal black schooling between the Civil War and the Great Depression, and establishes the central role of African Americans in the struggle for universal education in the South.

2

Benjamin "Pap" Singleton
Father of the Kansas Exodus

Gary R. Entz

In 1879 the news that thousands of impoverished former slaves were abandoning their southern homes in search of a better life in Kansas stunned many white Americans. Following the Civil War most African Americans had remained in the South, working as sharecroppers or tenant farmers on white-owned plantations. Cultivating small family plots, they paid for housing, tools, and supplies with a share of their crop. Many whites believed that sharecropping allowed the freedpeople to provide food and shelter for their families, if they worked hard and accepted a subservient position in society. They could not comprehend why so many African Americans turned their backs on the South for what, at best, would be a harsh life on the western prairie.

For black southerners, however, the mass migration to Kansas was anything but surprising. They were free in name, but emancipation had not resulted in economic or political freedom. White landlords had used the sharecropping system to keep black tenant farmers in perpetual debt and bound to the land. Moreover, the Hayes administration's acceptance of the conservative Democrats' takeover of Louisiana and South Carolina, the last two Republican states in the South, led many former slaves to believe that the federal government had no interest in enforcing black freedom and equality but was willing to acquiesce in southern white efforts to create a strict racial caste system that closely resembled slavery. As white southerners deprived African Americans of the right to vote, migration to the West became an attractive alternative to economic bondage and political oppression in the South. Thus, for black southerners, the westward migration not only represented a search for economic opportunity but also a means for asserting their autonomy, protecting their citizenship rights, and articulating their opposition to white supremacy.

Few people understood this better than a former slave named Benjamin "Pap" Singleton. Gary R. Entz documents the important role that Singleton played in the black migration to Kansas. Beginning in 1875, Singleton urged black southerners to migrate to the West, and two years later he led the first group of black settlers to Kansas. With only limited financial resources, however, most of the black agricultural settlements in the West failed. Embittered by this failure, Singleton concluded that African Americans could only achieve economic independence and political autonomy if they separated completely from the United States. Thus, instead of continuing to encourage black southerners to migrate to the West, Singleton embraced Pan-Africanism and began to urge them to return to Africa, however, without much success.

Benjamin Singleton was born into slavery in 1809 near Nashville in Davidson County, Tennessee. Details of his early life in bondage are elusive. Trained as a carpenter and cabinetmaker, Singleton apparently had a history of defying slavery. He claimed that he had made nearly a dozen attempts to escape his bondage before he finally made good on his bid for freedom in 1846. At the age of thirty-seven, Singleton escaped through Indiana to Detroit, Michigan. He never credited any individual or group with assisting his escape and in subsequent years recalled, "when the nostrils of the blood hounds were trailing at my heels" there was "no eye to pity or hand to deliver."[1] He made his way to Canada but returned to the United States within a year.

In Detroit, Singleton lived the hardscrabble life of a scavenger, constantly fearing his capture by fugitive slave catchers. The passage of the Fugitive Slave Law of 1850, which made it easier for slave catchers to apprehend fugitives as well as free blacks, further threatened Detroit's African American community. Singleton, like all fugitives, had to maintain a nondescript existence for his own safety. In later years, however, he claimed that he had labored as a member of the Underground Railroad, aiding fellow fugitives during the final leg of their journey across the border to Canada. Singleton undoubtedly contributed whatever aid he could and continued in this capacity until 1861, when the outbreak of the Civil War ended the fugitives' need to seek refuge in Canada. "There was a time," he later said, "when we could not see the clouds of heaven for the smoke of angry men until after it was settled, and the slaves could stare freedom in the face, and cry with a loud voice, 'We are free at last!' "[2] Singleton took advantage of the Union occupation of Nashville to return home, rebuild his life, and search for family and friends. Singleton apparently had children before he escaped to Canada. But since he remained illiterate and left no personal papers, little is known about his family.

Nashville occupied a unique position among southern cities. In February 1862, Confederate forces abandoned the city, and its citizens surrendered to the Union army with minimal resistance. As a result, Nashville avoided the widescale destruction other southern urban areas experienced, and its subsequent status as headquarters for Union troops kept money flowing into the region. Tennessee's state capital took on

Courtesy of the Kansas State Historical Society, Topeka

the characteristics of a frontier boomtown, attracting large numbers of black and white residents from the North and the South. Many freedpeople, particularly from the upper South, migrated to Nashville in search of economic opportunities.[3]

As the number of former slaves who flocked to the Union camps and shantytowns on the outskirts of Nashville grew, white legislators and city residents became alarmed and started to exclude African Americans from social and political life. In 1870, Tennessee enacted laws prohibiting interracial marriages, and it became the first southern state to adopt a poll tax, requiring prospective voters to pay for the privilege of voting. As a result, the majority of African Americans, who had limited financial resources, were virtually excluded from voting. In 1873, Tennessee segregated its school system, and two years later the state assembly gutted the federal Civil Rights Act of 1875, which sought to end racial discrimination in the selection of juries and in public accommodations. At the same time, Tennessee enacted contract labor and vagrancy laws, coercing African Americans to work for white planters and allowing for the incarceration of those who had no means of support. In the 1870s, Nashville became a focal point for antiblack sentiments, resulting in lynchings, black church burnings, and other manifestations of mob violence.[4]

Nashville's black residents recognized this ominous trend even before the state legislature passed the first of its exclusionary laws. In September 1869 a group of African Americans gathered in Nashville under the leadership of Randall Brown to discuss the possibility of relocating to the West. Brown, a former slave and Republican politician whom conservative Democrats had recently ousted from the city council, however, was more interested in reorganizing his own political base than in leading an emigration movement. While the meeting did not generate a black mass migration to the West, those who attended discussed the matter thoroughly. They understood that drastic changes were necessary to end black economic dependence on whites, which virtually ensured that African Americans remained second-class citizens in the South.[5]

Although there is no evidence that Benjamin Singleton ever collaborated with Brown, several of Singleton's associates had attended the 1869 convention. Singleton, aware of the deterioration of black economic, social, legal, and political conditions in the South, shared the meeting delegates' grim outlook for African Americans in the region.[6] Unlike Brown, however, Singleton eschewed politics. Distrustful of politicians, Singleton had nothing but contempt for those who used the black community to gain elective office and line their pockets. He had little patience with what he saw as the endless posturing of black leaders who talked without acting. In 1869, Singleton joined forces with Columbus M. Johnson and several other former slaves and began looking for ways to free African Americans from economic dependency by providing them with their own land.

The group, however, lacked the funds to purchase land and distribute it among the freedmen. Thus, the initial goal was to encourage blacks to seek out small farms that they could bargain for at favorable terms. Singleton and his associates had little immediate success and encountered stiff resistance from white landowners who either refused to sell land to former slaves or demanded an inflated price far above the fair market value of the property.[7] Johnson may have raised these issues when he served as a delegate to the 1872 Republican National Convention in Philadelphia and again at the party's 1876 convention in Cincinnati. A conservative resurgence, however, undermined the efforts of those in the Republican Party who sought to aid the former slaves and frustrated African American hopes for any federal assistance.[8]

Despite such discouragements, Singleton and his colleagues continued their efforts to find land for the freedmen in Tennessee, until the depression that followed the panic of 1873 ended Nashville's postwar economic boom. The depression had a severe impact on the city's African American population, as limited employment opportunities heightened the job competition between black and white workers.[9] Singleton realized that the economic crisis created potentially dangerous conditions for black residents. Singleton, who had worked as a coffin maker, had witnessed firsthand the horrifying results of lynchings. Given the racially explosive climate as well as the limited legal and political protection that the state provided for its black residents, Singleton feared that African Americans could no longer guarantee the safety of their families. It was at this point that he began to argue aggressively for black separatism. In September 1874 he and eight others organized the Edgefield Real Estate Association to assist former slaves living in the Nashville area in the acquisition of land.[10]

White opposition, however, remained a major obstacle to black land ownership in the South. Thus, Singleton and his partners began to explore the possibility of relocating African Americans to Kansas or other parts of the West. In May 1875 they became the leading participants in a black state convention that discussed the systematic resettlement of

African Americans. Convention delegates agreed that black economic, political, legal, and social conditions had deteriorated, but they were initially split over the necessity of leaving Tennessee. It was not until the delegates considered the recent lynchings of David Jones, Joseph Reed, and schoolteacher Julia Hayden that those who advocated migration to the West finally forged a majority. Proclaiming that "prejudice is stronger than law," the convention concluded that the state was unable and unwilling to protect African Americans. Thus, the delegates declared, "as we desire . . . peace and prosperity, we deem it best for the negro to seek a place, where he can enjoy the privileges of mankind, where justice is too blind to discriminate on account of color."[11]

To implement their plan the delegates established a Board of Emigration Commissioners in Nashville and appointed recruiting agents for each county in Tennessee.[12] Local agents conducted emigration meetings and appointed subagents for each ward and civil district in the state. This communications network enabled Singleton's associates to spread their separatist message and generate statewide interest in black migration to the West. Furthermore, the commissioners directed Henry A. Napier to take a three-man scouting party to explore the Kansas plains in search of suitable land. The Napier team spent the summer of 1875 near Great Bend, Kansas. Returning to Nashville in August, Napier reported that he was pleased with the quality of the land. His report concluded, however, that given the limited resources of African Americans, black settlers would encounter more financial and environmental obstacles in Kansas than they could overcome. He calculated that each settler would need more than $1,000 to survive and warned that "it is not advisable for anyone to go to Kansas with a less amount than the above named sum at his command, with any hope of bettering his temporal condition."[13] Without sufficient funds to feed and clothe the migrants, Napier considered it folly to exchange one form of suffering for another. Not all of the commissioners agreed with Napier's blunt assessment. Another commissioner argued that $200 would be sufficient for the frugal settler who opted for a government homestead.[14]

Individual migration, however, was not what Singleton had in mind. He believed that black migrants could overcome the financial obstacles through mutual aid, cooperation, and, most important, racial solidarity. Singleton used the emigration commissioners' network of agents to encourage potential recruits to attend his real estate association's twice-weekly meetings in Edgefield and at the Second Baptist Church in Nashville. He also encouraged local ministers to spread word of his plans for a cooperative migration among their congregations.[15]

It took him a year, but by August 1876, Singleton had recruited between fifty and 100 African Americans who were willing to relocate to Kansas. Although his association had collected enough money to pay for most of the migrants' transportation expenses, the settlers had virtually no money to purchase land or support themselves after their arrival. Hence, Singleton sought an external source of aid. He asked Kansas governor Thomas A. Osborn if the state government would be willing to assist the colonists with land, work, or any type of relief that would help them get a start in the West. He assured Osborn that his followers were industrious workers and within a few years of getting settled would gladly repay any aid received. This was no idle request on Singleton's part, and he wanted the governor to understand the sense of urgency blacks felt about leaving Tennessee. "We are Bound to leve [*sic*] the State just as soon as we can get a way," he declared, "for Starvation is Staring us in the face."[16]

Osborn's staff never responded to the letter, but Singleton remained undeterred. In the late fall of 1876 he made a personal trip to Kansas to see if he could make other arrangements. Accompanied by Columbus Johnson, he visited Cherokee County in the southeastern part of the state. In December 1876 he may have reached a verbal understanding with agents of the Missouri River, Fort Scott and Gulf Railroad to reserve two thousand acres of ground north of the town of Baxter Springs.[17] Singleton returned to Nashville with the good news and during the summer of 1877 accompanied seventy-three settlers to Cherokee County. Reflecting his belief in black separatism, Singleton emphasized the importance of race unity to those leaving Nashville. Yet he also realized that because of the migrants' limited funds, temporary wage labor was an economic necessity. Thus, he encouraged his followers to "make their sustenance and their first gains by working for wages on the new farms of the more forehanded white settlers."[18]

The settlers who migrated to Cherokee County did so with every intention, as a local journalist observed, "of laying out a town, [and having] a post-office, newspaper and all the parapharnalia [*sic*] of an enterprising town."[19] Their dream was complete economic independence, but with the simultaneous development of lead mines in the nearby towns of Galena and Empire City the colony site rapidly increased in value. The black settlers had not made any down payments on the land before the mining boom, and when they arrived the railroad's land agents felt obliged to charge them seven dollars per acre with a 7 percent interest rate payable over ten years. The price was reasonable for the area but significantly more than Singleton's followers could afford. There were few employment opportunities for black unskilled laborers in the mines and towns, and without this source of income, on which the association had counted, the entire project collapsed. By 1878, African Americans in Cherokee County were appealing to the governor for aid to prevent starvation, and Singleton withdrew his support of the colony.[20]

Singleton was upset at having to abandon the Cherokee County colony but remained convinced that a separate economic existence was the only way for African Americans to succeed. Since land prices had defeated his first effort, Singleton turned his attention toward obtaining government homesteads. In 1878 the only government land still open to settlers in the eastern part of Kansas was along the Neosho River valley in Morris and parts of Lyon counties. This area had been part of the Kansa Indian Reservation, and the federal government had been selling the Kansa trust lands piecemeal since the removal of the tribe in 1873. Squatters and the railroads had long since claimed the best ground, but some marginal lands, selling for $1.25 and $2.00 per acre, near the village of Dunlap were still available. This area was where Singleton made his second effort, and between April 1878 and March 1879 his association directed almost two hundred settlers to the region. Most managed to make the initial down payment on a small claim in four distinct settlements in Dunlap and its vicinity, although they had nothing left for homes and had to live in dugouts or brush shelters. Nevertheless, their fortitude impressed the local postmaster, who commented, "they have got along better than the same class of whites would."[21] Within a year the settlers were building small houses from local stone, and it appeared as if Singleton's dream of a black separatist haven might come true. That is, until the Exodusters arrived.

Literally thousands of rural black southerners started arriving in Kansas when the Great Exodus began in the spring of 1879. Many whites, who had no understanding of the anxieties that stirred black people to leave the South, were initially surprised by the mass migration. They claimed that land sharks and other "unscrupulous men," who for their own profit shamelessly "deluded" impoverished African American people with false promises of free land in the West, were responsible for the Exodus. Only men with financial means, whites insisted, could overcome the hardships of prairie life, and they urged poor blacks to remain

Ho for Kansas!

Brethren, Friends, & Fellow Citizens:

I feel thankful to inform you that the

REAL ESTATE

AND

Homestead Association,

Will Leave Here the

15th of April, 1878,

In pursuit of Homes in the Southwestern
Lands of America, at Transportation
Rates, cheaper than ever
was known before.

For full information inquire of

Benj. Singleton, better known as old Pap,

NO. 5 NORTH FRONT STREET.

Beware of Speculators and Adventurers, as it is a dangerous thing
to fall in their hands.

Nashville, Tenn., March 18, 1878.

Courtesy of the Kansas State Historical Society, Topeka

in the South. Assumptions of this sort angered Singleton, who countered, "it's because they are poor . . . that they want to get away, and ought to get away. If they had plenty, they wouldn't want to come. It's to better their condition that they are thinking of. That's what white men go to new countries for, isn't it? And do you tell them to stay back because they are poor?"[22] Members of Singleton's association in Topeka, including Columbus Johnson, immediately began organizing efforts to look after the welfare of the new settlers.[23]

Meanwhile, Singleton stopped conducting organized migrations from Tennessee so that he could remain in Kansas and act as an advocate for the largely voiceless Exodusters. In June 1879 he incorporated the Singleton Colony of Dunlap and accepted appointment as the "agent to procure aid for the destitute of the Colony." He had been calling himself the "Father of the Kansas emigration from Tennessee" since 1877 but now adopted the title "Father of the Kansas Exodus" to encourage racial unity and cooperation between blacks already settled in Kansas and those just arriving from other parts of the South.[24] Singleton rejoiced that African Americans were "now waked up to a sense of their duty," which was, as he saw it, to separate from the South and join together as a nation in the West. "The morning light has appeared to them," he proclaimed, "and they have got that light and are now traveling by it to the glory and promised land." Singleton's associates provided aid to the Exodusters while directing selected groups of new arrivals to the Dunlap colony. Singleton's resources, however, were limited and he hoped that African Americans throughout the nation would support the settlers. He urged black associations and churches to "come forward and contribute towards the relief of their brethren who are fleeing in their poverty."[25]

By spring many white Kansans had become worried about growing racial tensions in Topeka. Concerned individuals, under the leadership of Governor John P. St. John, realized that some form of assistance was necessary and organized the interracial Kansas Freedmen's Relief Association (KFRA). The KFRA helped relocate African American migrants to several colonies in Kansas, and a little more than 100 of them went to Dunlap in 1879. Unfortunately the influx was more than the struggling colony could bear. Although the original colonists had agreed to encourage migration and assist the newcomers, by the end of the year they were overwhelmed and had to appeal to the KFRA for help in meeting their fifteen-dollar annual land payments.[26] The KFRA provided some food, clothing, and shelter to those individuals it helped relocate, but to survive on their own the settlers needed land, money, and tools. The needed assistance came, but at the cost of the colony's independence.

In 1879 the Presbyterian Synod of North America appointed the Reverend John M. Snodgrass as missionary to blacks in Dunlap and to coordinate church relief efforts in the area. Snodgrass, in addition to helping with direct relief efforts, petitioned his church to sponsor construction of a literary and business school. In 1881, Snodgrass's labors resulted in the opening of the Freedmen's Academy of Dunlap, a primary school that also offered adult degrees in teaching, business, and vocal music as well as sewing classes for young women. Working with the Freedmen's Aid Association of Dunlap, the academy solicited land donations to distribute among the settlers in five- and ten-acre allotments. In 1882, Andrew Atchison, the academy's principal, declared the colony and school a success, although he admitted that farm crops remained "disheartening."[27] As a result of the Presbyterian Church's relief efforts, the Dunlap colony had become entirely dependent on donations from white philanthropists. When whites began to withdraw their support toward the end of the decade, the academy folded and the colony entered its final decline. Singleton's involvement with the Dunlap colony ended once the Presbyterian Church assumed relief efforts. Columbus Johnson and a few of his longtime associates remained in Dunlap to run the church-sponsored Freedmen's Aid Association, but Singleton could not subordinate himself to a white organization.[28]

Although Singleton ceased his formal association with the Dunlap colony, his advocacy on behalf of the Exodusters had earned him a measure of national prominence. In 1880, when the U.S. Senate convened an investigating committee to determine the causes of the Exodus, he received a subpoena to testify. The Senate investigation was sparked largely by concerns that the continued westward migration of African Americans threatened to deprive southern white landowners of their cheap agricultural workforce. With the exception of Republican William Windom of Minnesota, members of the investigating committee were hostile to the black migration. Singleton, determined to make a case for those still suffering in the South, refused to be intimidated by their hostility.[29] He admonished the senators to consider the plight of the majority of black southerners who were living in grinding poverty and without equal protection under the law. "I am a man," he insisted, "that will live in a country where I am going to cope with the white man, where the white man will lift himself to the level of justice; but when the white man will think that equal rights under the law to the colored man is a violation of his . . . dignity, I am going to leave." Singleton concluded that as long as the federal government shirked its responsibility of protecting African Americans, black separation was the only answer. Thus, he proclaimed that he would continue to encourage black people to migrate out of the South "if there ain't an alteration and signs of change."[30]

Traveling back to Kansas, Singleton continued to criticize the committee, particularly its Democratic chairman, Senator Daniel Voorhees. He attacked Voorhees in a speech, charging that the senator had manipulated the witness list to ensure that the committee would hear primarily from men "who were interested in keeping the colored people South." Singleton, who in the past had rejected politics as a viable means of fostering racial advancement, now encouraged his audience to vote against the Democratic ticket. Northern Democrats, decried Singleton, "say they are not like these Southern Democrats—they are as bad or worse—they are helping them, who boast of a solid South to carry out their purpose."[31]

Following his Washington testimony, Singleton realized that owning a parcel of land in the West was not enough to guarantee either black economic independence or racial equality. Rather than concentrating his efforts on encouraging blacks to leave the South, Singleton now started to focus his energy on uniting all African Americans into one national organization. Individual members of the race, he argued, had limited power to fight racial discrimination, but collectively they would have the strength "to be a great and prosperous people."[32] Singleton urged black ministers to help him disseminate his plans among their congregations while opening their churches as meeting halls "in the interest of consolidating my race."[33] Singleton envisioned an organization that would combine the financial resources of all African Americans to build black-owned factories, businesses, and trade schools. His efforts soon bore fruit.

On March 4, 1881, during an open-air rally in Topeka, Singleton launched a new organization designed to unite all African Americans in the struggle against racial discrimination. Those attending the rally acknowledged Singleton's charge that "as a race we have been since our enfranchisement, merely drifting along each pursuing his or her separate or private interests." This state of affairs had to end, and those attending proclaimed it was the "duty of every intelligent colored man to step forward and unite himself with his brethren in an earnest and unceasing effort to evolve a satisfactory solution" to the problem of racial discrimination in America. Addressing the rally, Singleton declared, "we the colored people form an organization to be known as the Colored United Links" (CUL).[34]

The CUL never gained the nationwide following Singleton envisioned. In Kansas, however, the organization became powerful enough to attract the attention of the Greenback-Labor Party. Both groups agreed to a joint convention in Topeka in August 1881. Singleton, who had shunned party politics in the past, hoped that the CUL's collaboration with the Greenback-Labor Party would secure social and political protection for blacks in an increasingly hostile and competitive job market. The prospect of a fusion between the Links and the Greenbackers so frightened local white Republicans that they embarked on a campaign to destroy the CUL. Singleton criticized such Republican tactics, even though most African Americans believed that they owed their freedom to the party of Lincoln. Disappointed about the lack of support the Republican Party had extended to the former slaves, Singleton proclaimed that he felt no obligation to the Republicans: "I . . . say good bye to the party and sing a funeral dirge." For Singleton racial unity was more important than party loyalties, and he explained, "we are not on politics but on a sure platform, [so] step on board and do not fall asleep. No difference in the fare, one fare for all."[35]

While James B. Weaver of the Greenback-Labor Party highlighted the Topeka convention festivities, Alonzo D. DeFrantz, a longtime associate of Singleton, articulated the CUL's position. "We recollect," declared DeFrantz, "that the Constitution is a depository of every precious right of its citizens." He reminded the audience that blacks were entitled to the full privileges of citizenship, "and as we feel and know that our race has been deprived of those rights . . . we ask the sympathy of the Nation to enforce such laws as will secure our rights in common with other citizens." DeFrantz emphasized the CUL's continuing concern for African Americans in the South and stressed, "we want the freedom of speech, in the protection of life, liberty, and prosperity in the Southern States in the free exercise of the ballot inasmuch as the Constitution provides." In addition to these fundamental rights, he insisted that black people should have access to an "impartial trial by the juries of the country, and not the mob law that has taken possession of it." This message was the one the CUL wanted politicians of all parties to hear, and DeFrantz punctuated it with a final appeal to white northerners: "Dear people of the North, will you hear us cry for freedom, and suffer us to die! We don't believe that you will."[36]

Despite the apparent success of the August 1881 convention, the CUL never achieved the unity of effort for which Singleton had hoped. He felt that "the Spirit of the Lord" had instructed him "to call his people together to unite them from their divided condition," but his expectations never included a specific program beyond the vague promises of success through racial cooperation. Without any concrete agenda the CUL's membership dispersed after the August convention. The realization that the CUL was faltering struck Singleton particularly hard. "I have been slighted," he bemoaned, "all my work prevaileth nothing. I seek no more honor from man. I have got all the honor I want and what I have got would not pay my burial expenses." At seventy-two years of age, Singleton was exhausted, but not quite ready to withdraw from public life.[37]

Singleton spent the next year contemplating the collapse of the CUL and by 1883 came to the conclusion that African Americans needed a "fresh start where the color line is not too rigid." Disillusioned with the entrenchment of segregation and the deterioration of race relations in the South, Singleton advised blacks to "never cast another vote in the south for it is just getting you all murdered up and slaughtered in a brutal manner." He was equally troubled by continued white efforts to prevent African Americans from achieving economic independence. "When we were delivered from slavery," he observed, "we were delivered with nothing and have been trying to rise up and be respected." Yet white southerners, he complained, "still try to hold us down but we can't stand to be treated in this manner." Singleton concluded that racial advancement was only possible if African Americans separated completely from the United States. His call captured the attention of Joseph Ware, a white businessman in St. Louis, who convinced Singleton that he should solicit the British government to open the Mediterranean island of Cyprus to black separatists.[38]

Singleton moved to St. Louis to work with Ware and John Williamson, an African American minister, on the formation of a "Chief League" for emigration to Cyprus. The project attracted little support, however, and fell apart in 1884 when Ware's business failed. The entire Cyprus debacle left Singleton embittered, and before returning to Topeka he unleashed a harsh epistle to the black community in St. Louis. His efforts to unite the race, he charged, had been undermined by members of the educated black urban elite, "some of the imported slippery chaps from Washington, Oberlin, [and] Chicago." Interested in safeguarding their own status in society, they had conspired and sent provocateurs in the form of "intriguing reverends, deputy doorkeepers, military darkeys or teachers; to go around the corrals, and see that not an appearance of a hole exists, through which the captives within can escape, or even see through."[39]

Although the Cyprus project never progressed beyond the planning stage, it gave Singleton a global perspective and pushed his separatism toward Pan-Africanism. He moved to Kansas City and in June 1885 organized his final venture, the United Transatlantic Society (UTS). The goals of the UTS were to colonize people of African descent in Africa and to "better the condition of the African race politically, socially and financially throughout the world." Like all of Singleton's projects, the UTS counted on African Americans to unite and donate their "assistance in labor of brain and finance to accomplish this great and grand purpose." The UTS served primarily as an outlet for the black collective rage that had been growing since the end of the Civil War. Black people had struggled in poverty for twenty years and, having received little assistance since emancipation, owed no allegiance to the United States. The officers of the UTS pointed out that whites' willingness to hire European immigrants, rather than African Americans, illustrated that racial discrimination would always prevent blacks from attaining full equality. Singleton wholly condoned this line of reasoning and blamed immigrants for forcing African Americans to consider leaving the land of their birth. "We cannot feed, clothe, and school our children on starvation wages," lamented Singleton, "and when we have attained an education, of what use is it to them here? None whatever."[40]

Although the UTS held several conventions through 1887, and never compromised its declaration "that nothing short of a separate national existence will ever meet the wants and necessities of our people," it lacked the funds to send African Americans across the Atlantic. The organization collapsed in the summer of 1887, and Singleton returned to Topeka in October of that year to address a meeting of young civil rights activists who had united under the banner of the Afro-American League. This speech marked one of his last public appearances, and he closed his career with a formidable warning of dark days to come. Singleton told his youthful audience, "as the volcano bursts, with a louder explosion, when the combustible matter is confined within its bosom, so will a nation's revenge find vent the more their wrongs are repressed." He returned to Kansas City in ill health and made no further public appeals until 1889, when he raised his voice for the final time. Singleton had been observing the efforts of Edward P. McCabe and others who had been encouraging Congress to set aside part of the Oklahoma Territory for an all-black state. Singleton issued a brief statement of support and asked the railroads to give discounts to African Americans migrating to the region.[41] Following this appeal, he slipped into obscurity. Singleton died in St. Louis in 1892 at the age of eighty-three.

Historians have called Benjamin Singleton the Moses of the black Exodus, but this is a misnomer. He was first and foremost a nationalist who urged African Americans to seek a separate and dignified existence on the western plains of Kansas. His separatism failed, but he left an activist legacy in the West that placed him ideologically alongside Marcus Garvey and other advocates of a "race first" philosophy.

Notes

1. *Kansas City Gate City Press*, clipping, n.d., in Benjamin Singleton, Scrapbook, 53, Kansas State Historical Society, Topeka, Kansas (hereafter cited as Singleton, Scrapbook).

2. Ibid.

3. Howard N. Rabinowitz, *Race Relations in the Urban South, 1865–1890* (New York: Oxford University Press, 1978), 15.

4. Yollette Trigg Jones, "The Black Community, Politics, and Race Relations in the 'Iris City': Nashville, Tennessee, 1870–1954" (Ph.D. diss., Duke University, 1985), 58–59; and Rabinowitz, *Race Relations*, 52–53.

5. *Nashville Daily Press and Times*, September 21–28, 1869; *Nashville Union and American*, September 28, October 10, 1869; Rabinowitz, *Race Relations*, 250; Alrutheus Ambush Taylor, *The Negro in Tennessee, 1865–1880* (Washington, DC: The Associated Publishers, Inc., 1941), 108–10; May Alice Harris Ridley, "The Black Community of Nashville and Davidson County, 1860–1870" (Ph.D. diss., University of Pittsburgh, 1982), 83–84.

6. "The Negro Hegira," *Chicago Tribune*, March 27, 1879.

7. U.S. Senate, *Report and Testimony of the Select Committee of the United States Senate to Investigate the Causes of the Removal of the Negroes from the Southern States to the Northern States*, 46th Cong., 2d sess., 1880, S. R. 693, serial 1899 (Washington, DC: Government Printing Office, 1880), 389; *St. Louis Globe-Democrat*, April 21, 1879.

8. *Chicago Tribune*, March 27, 1879.

9. Rabinowitz, *Race Relations*, 24–25.

10. Charles N. Gibbs, Secretary of the State of Tennessee, Letter of Incorporation, Singleton Miscellaneous Collection, Kansas State Historical Society; U.S. Senate, *Report and Testimony of the Select Committee*, 387.

11. *Nashville Union and American*, May 20, 1875.

12. Ibid., May 21, 1875.

13. Ibid., May 25, 29, August 15, 1875.

14. Ibid., August 15, 1875.

15. "See What Colored Citizens Are Doing for Their Elevation," promotional handbill, Singleton, Scrapbook, 32.

16. Benjamin Singleton and W. A. Sizemore to Thomas A. Osborn, August 7, 1876, Correspondence, Thomas A. Osborn Administration, Records of the Governor's Office, Library and Archives Division, Kansas State Historical Society.

17. *Great Bend Inland Tribune*, December 23, 1876.

18. *Chicago Tribune*, March 27, 1879; and "Call for an Investigating Meeting," clipping, May 30, 1877, Singleton, Scrapbook, 50.

19. *Columbus Republican Courier* (Kansas), August 9, 1877.

20. Gary R. Entz, "Image and Reality on the Kansas Prairie: 'Pap' Singleton's Cherokee County Colony," *Kansas History* 19 (Summer 1996): 132–35.

21. Promotional handbills, Singleton, Scrapbook, 40, 52; Joseph V. Hickey, " 'Pap' Singleton's Dunlap Colony: Relief Agencies and the Failure of a Black Settlement in Eastern Kansas," *Great Plains Quarterly* 11 (Winter 1991): 24–26; London Harness, interview by Douglas Thompson and Arthur Finnell, February 6, 1974, Flint Hills Oral History Project, Emporia State University Archives, Emporia, Kansas; and *New York Daily Tribune*, May 20, 1879.

22. *St. Louis Globe-Democrat*, April 21, 1879.

23. "Kansas Colored State Emigration Board," *Topeka Colored Citizen*, May 24, 1879; "The Right Thing," *Topeka Commonwealth*, April 23, 1879; and "Kansas Colored State Emigration Bureau," *Topeka Commonwealth*, May 1, 1879.

24. "Certificate of Incorporation," June 1879; petition, Dunlap, Kansas, August 9, 1879, Singleton, Miscellaneous Collection, Kansas State Historical Society; and "To the Colored People of the United States," clipping, October 4, 1879, Singleton, Scrapbook, 28.

25. "A Prophecy," *Topeka Commonwealth*, July 31, 1879; and *Topeka Colored Citizen*, October 11, 1879.

26. Minutes of a meeting between the African American citizens of Dunlap, August 9, 1879, Singleton, Miscellaneous Collection; *Morris County Times*, December 19, 1879; and Hickey, " 'Pap' Singleton's Dunlap Colony," 29.

27. *Kansas Colored Literary & Business Academy* (Council Grove: Republican Print, 1881), in "Kansas Education Society" folder, Kansas State Historical Society; *Topeka Daily Capital*, October 19, 1882; and "Quarterly Report of the Freedmen's Aid Association of Dunlap, Kansas," 1882, Papers of the Freedmen's Aid Association of Dunlap, Kansas, Freedmen's Academy of Dunlap, Kansas State Historical Society.

28. *Topeka Daily Capital*, October 19, 1882.

29. *Topeka Herald of Kansas*, March 12, April 9, 1880; and clipping, n.d., Singleton, Scrapbook, 32.

30. U.S. Senate, *Report and Testimony of the Select Committee*, 381, 390.

31. Untitled notes from a Singleton speech, n.d., Singleton, Miscellaneous Collection.

32. "Declaration by Colored Citizens," clipping, n.d., Singleton, Scrapbook, 11.

33. Benjamin Singleton to Elder Merritt, February 12, 1881, Singleton, Miscellaneous Collection.

34. "Topeka, March 4th, 1881," "A Colored Conference," and "Convention of Colored Men," clippings, Singleton Scrapbook, 15, 8.

35. "The Convention of Links," *Topeka Commonwealth*, June 4, 1881; "The Colored Links," clipping, Colored United Links Convention Poster, Singleton, Scrapbook, 6, 20; and "A Few Words from Pap Singleton," *Topeka Daily Kansas State Journal*, July 22, 1881.

36. "Colored United Links," *Topeka Commonwealth*, August 2, 1881.

37. "From 'Pap Singleton,' " clipping; and "Pap Singleton Sees the Sign," *Topeka Daily Kansas State Journal*, September 1881, Singleton, Scrapbook, 39.

38. "To the Freed Slaves of the South," *North Topeka Times*, September 28, 1883; and "Negro Colonization," *Topeka Commonwealth*, October 21, 1883.

39. " 'Pap' Singleton. The Great Exoduster Arrives in the City—Off for Cyprus"; "A New Exodus"; and "Good Advice. Old 'Pap' Singleton Writes an Epistle to the Negroes of St. Louis," *St. Louis Post-Dispatch*, clippings, n.d., Singleton, Scrapbook, 32, 36, 54.

40. Handbill, "The United Trans-Atlantic Society," n.d.; and "Constitution of the United Transatlantic Society," Singleton, Scrapbook, 56, 61.

41. Clipping, n.d., Singleton, Scrapbook, 64, 56, 40; *North Topeka Benevolent Banner*, October 8, 1887; and *St. John Weekly News* (Kansas), October 11, 1889.

Suggested Readings

Benjamin Singleton was illiterate and left no writings. He did, however, maintain a scrapbook collection of newspaper articles about his activities. The Singleton Scrapbook is housed at the Kansas State Historical Society in Topeka and is available on microfilm. For Singleton's Senate testimony, see U.S. Senate, *Report and Testimony of the Select Committee of the United States Senate to Investigate the Causes of the Removal of the Negroes from the Southern States to the Northern States*, 3 vols., 46th Cong., 2d sess., S. Rep. 693 (Washington, DC: Government Printing Office, 1880). There is little information about Singleton's early life, but David M. Katzman, *Before the Ghetto: Black Detroit in the Nineteenth Century* (Urbana: University of Illinois Press, 1973), provides a good overview of Detroit's black community during the time of Singleton's residence. For race relations in 1870s Nashville and Singleton's activities in the black community, see Alrutheus Ambush Taylor, *The Negro in Tennessee, 1865–1880* (Washington, DC: The Associated Publishers, Inc., 1941); Howard N. Rabinowitz, *Race Relations in the Urban South, 1865–1890* (New York: Oxford University Press, 1978); and Bobby L. Lovett, *The African-American History of Nashville, Tennessee, 1780–1930* (Fayetteville: University of Arkansas Press, 1999). Singleton's involvement with the Exodusters in Kansas is covered in Nell Irvin Painter, *Exodusters: Black Migration to Kansas after Reconstruction* (Lawrence: University Press of Kansas, 1986), and Robert G. Athearn, *In Search of Canaan: Black Migration to Kansas, 1879–80* (Lawrence: The Regents Press of Kansas, 1978). For a well-written overview designed for younger readers, see Jim Haskins, *The Geography of Hope: Black Exodus from the South after Reconstruction* (Brookfield, CT: Twenty-First Century Books, 1999). Topeka's black community has been explored in Thomas C. Cox's *Blacks in Topeka, Kansas, 1865–1915: A Social History* (Baton Rouge: Louisiana State University Press, 1982). For studies of the two Singleton colonies, see Gary R. Entz, "Image and Reality on the Kansas Prairie: 'Pap' Singleton's Cherokee County Colony," *Kansas History* 19 (Summer 1996): 124–39; Joseph V. Hickey, " 'Pap' Singleton's Dunlap Colony: Relief Agencies and the Failure of a Black Settlement in Eastern Kansas," *Great Plains Quarterly* 11 (Winter 1991): 23–36; and Philip R. Beard, "The Kansas Colored Literary and Business Academy," *Kansas History* 24 (Autumn 2001): 200–217. Dated but still useful articles include Walter L. Fleming, " 'Pap' Singleton: The Moses of the Colored Exodus," *American Journal of Sociology* 15 (July 1909): 61–82; and Roy Garvin, "Benjamin, or 'Pap,' Singleton and his Followers," *Journal of Negro History* 33 (January 1948): 7–23.

3

William Washington Browne
Fraternal Society Leader

David M. Fahey

In the late nineteenth century many African Americans joined a growing number of fraternal societies, particularly in the urban South. African Americans had been active in fraternal organizations since 1775, when black men in Boston, in response to their exclusion from membership in the city's white Freemasons, had launched the Prince Hall Masons. In the following decades African American men in other cities eagerly embraced the opportunity for male fellowship and established numerous lodges in many northern states. Attracting a largely urban middle-class following, other black fraternal societies as well as women's auxiliaries emerged prior to the Civil War. In 1843, African Americans in New York City obtained a charter for the Grand United Order of Odd Fellows, which soon became the largest black fraternal organization.

Fraternal societies were popular among nineteenth-century African Americans because they provided their members with important services. They created spaces for social interaction, offered sickness and burial benefits, assisted members in financial distress, and encouraged economic cooperation and entrepreneurship. In addition to fostering fellowship and mutual aid among their members, black fraternal societies also came to play an important role in the struggle for racial advancement.

William Washington Browne, a former slave, was among the first African Americans who realized the potential of fraternal societies as tools for racial uplift. In 1880, Browne took charge of the True Reformers lodge in Richmond, Virginia. The True Reformers, a fraternal society for black men and women, had been founded in the early 1870s by the Good Templars, a white temperance organization. Browne, a zealous temperance advocate, initially rejected segregated fraternal societies. By the end of Reconstruction in 1877, however, he accepted them as unavoidable. Eventually, when he became head of Virginia's Grand Fountain, he came to prefer separate black fraternal societies because they guaranteed black leadership and promoted racial solidarity as well as black economic empowerment.

As David M. Fahey demonstrates, Browne had little interest in pageantry, rituals, and regalia. Instead, he hoped that fraternal societies would provide African Americans with the means to advance financially, both as individuals and as a race. Browne used the organizational structure of the True Reformers to pool the resources of its members and help black people become owners of homes, farms, and businesses. Placing economic progress ahead of civil and political rights, Browne transformed the fledgling Richmond lodge into a black business empire. He initiated a life insurance society with which he funded a savings bank, a 150-room hotel, a real estate agency, an old folks home, retail stores, and a newspaper, creating employment opportunities for many African Americans. By the 1890s, the True Reformers had erected a $24,000 building that housed their general offices and meeting rooms.

William Washington Browne was born a slave on the plantation of Benjamin Pryor in Habersham County in northeastern Georgia on October 20, 1849. Unlike many other black leaders of the late nineteenth century, he was entirely of African descent, a fact that his supporters pointed to proudly. He was the seventh child of Joseph and Mariah Browne, both born in Virginia and both field slaves. As a young child he was called Ben Browne.

Ben Browne was not destined to follow his parents into the fields. Acknowledged from early childhood as unusually bright, he was chosen to be the servant and companion of his master's son, who was about the same age. He did not easily accept the status of inferiority expected in this relationship and once was severely beaten for having dared to fight with the white boy. When Browne was about eight years old his master died, and the widow remarried and sold the plantation, including Ben's parents. She took Ben with her when she joined her new husband in Rome, Georgia.

Browne followed a variety of livelihoods as a slave. First, his new master hired him out to a storekeeper, but the arrangement ended when Browne complained that the storekeeper was mistreating and cheating black customers. Browne then was hired out as an office boy to a prominent lawyer, an outspoken atheist. The lawyer's death after a prolonged and painful illness made an impression on his young servant, who thereafter never went to sleep without first praying. It was about this time that Ben persuaded his owner to let him be known by a new name, William Washington Browne, which eliminated the disliked "Ben" and honored the "father" of the United States.

Although his master tolerated this request, he was displeased with the boy's independent spirit and, as a result, took him to Memphis to be sold to the highest bidder. Wanting only to return to the plantation where his parents still lived, Browne at first refused to cry out the customary "buy me, master, buy me," but the whip forced him into humiliating submission at the slave pen. He was purchased by a horse

From D. Webster Davis, *The Life and Public Services of Rev. Wm. Washington Browne, Founder of the Grand Fountain, U[nited].O[rder]. of True Reformers and Organizer of the First Distinctive Negro Bank in America* (Philadelphia: Mrs. Mary A. Browne-Smith, 1910).

trader to be trained as a jockey on a race circuit that included parts of Tennessee and Mississippi. Once again, William's lack of docility angered his new owner.

Insolent slaves, such as Browne, became particularly dangerous after the outbreak of the Civil War in 1861. Thus, Browne's owner sent the twelve-year-old to a plantation in Mississippi, with orders that he be watched closely and not be allowed to talk with other slaves. Nevertheless, Browne joined two slaves in escaping to Memphis, fifty miles away, which was occupied by Union troops. For a time he found employment as a servant to an officer but soon discovered that fugitive slaves were not safe at the camp. The Union commander returned several runaways to their owners. In defiance of the commander's policy, the soldiers helped light-skinned fugitive slaves pass as whites, but they told Browne that "you are so black, you will have to look out for yourself."[1] For a brief period, Browne worked in town for a Jewish pawnbroker before sailing north as a stowaway on a Mississippi River vessel.

At Cairo, Illinois, Browne found employment at $10 per month as a family servant and bartender with a saloon keeper. The scenes that he witnessed at the saloon turned Browne into a lifelong teetotaler and temperance reformer. When one brawl ended in murder, Browne's testimony helped convict the murderer. Shortly afterward, Browne decided to leave Cairo, a decision prompted by nightmares about the murder, fear of vengeance at the hands of the murderer's friends, and, above all, after a white Kentuckian crossed the Ohio to claim his runaway slave, worry that even in Illinois a fugitive was not safe from being returned to his owner.

Browne continued to hurry through a variety of occupations. He joined the crew of the Union gunboat *New National* as bootblack and general servant. He soon was promoted, from dishwasher to cook to cabin boy, and volunteered to assist a gun crew. After the fall of Vicksburg on July 4, 1863, Browne left the navy and for the first time in his life became a fieldhand, harvesting wheat in Illinois. Having learned that black people were allowed to attend school in Wisconsin, he went to Prairie-du-Chien, in the southwestern corner of the state, where he combined work with school. Although this first stint of formal education amounted to less than a year, Browne regarded it as "the changing point in his life." Next he enlisted in the army as a substitute for a wealthy farmer. Browne served in the Eighteenth United States Infantry regiment until 1866. According to his biographer, D. Webster Davis, he had been promoted to the rank of sergeant major, which seems unlikely for a teenager.[2]

After his military discharge, Browne returned to Wisconsin. He had given $600 of his fee for serving as a substitute to a former employer to hold in trust. The man, however, refused to turn over the money or the horse that Browne had received in lieu of wages. Despite this betrayal, Browne agreed to work for him again while planning his revenge. When his employer purchased a house, which he intended to move on the public highway with the aid of rollers, a capstan, and rope, Browne arranged accidents with the rope that left the house stranded on the highway at night. He then took out an attachment against the building to get back his money. The attachment made it illegal to move the house, and Browne's employer was subject to a large daily fine for obstructing the highway. He quickly decided to settle with Browne on Browne's terms. Afterward, Browne took his final farm job in Wisconsin, this one lasting for three years. Because of his skill with horses he was paid handsome wages, $25 per month. During these three years he attended school on a part-time basis.

In September 1869, Browne returned to Georgia. At the age of twenty he was a changed man, with at least the rudiments of literacy and numeracy, a bit of money, and experience in a variety of work. When he wrote his former master about his mother, he learned that she was still alive. Homesick, Browne left the North for good. He found more than his mother in Georgia. He also found a new livelihood as a teacher, and he found religion. According to his biographer, Browne had "a restless, forceful, aggressive disposition" and in the North had "engaged in many questionable acts and unholy feelings."[3] It was in Georgia, under the influence of a black preacher named Hunt, that Browne underwent a conversion and became a committed Christian. He briefly studied for the ministry in Atlanta at the African Methodist Episcopal Church school, which later became Gammon Theological Seminary.

In 1871, Browne moved to Alabama where he continued to teach school. There he met Mary A. (Molly) Graham, whom he married in 1873. The couple had no children, although later they adopted a boy and a girl. Browne's marriage was solemnized by a white minister, although assisted by a pastor of the Colored Methodist Episcopal Church. Both white and black people attended Browne's wedding. A few years after his marriage, Browne was ordained a minister in the Colored Methodist Episcopal Church.

While living in Alabama in the early 1870s, Browne was less accepting of racial separation and exclusion of blacks from political power than he later became. The white minister and the white wedding guests could not have been imagined following the end of Reconstruction in 1877 when Browne boasted that he "never mingled with white men," that "you do not see me among them except on business."[4] In his early years in Alabama he also was bold in confronting white supremacists. He declared "that a bullet from a Winchester" might convince whites not to threaten blacks. He took part in a convention at Atlanta directed against the Ku Klux Klan. The convention appointed him to tour the southern states as a lecturer and organizer. When he spoke before a mixed-race audience in Lowndes County, Alabama, he "laid two heavy navy pistols on the stand in front of him," a defiant answer to the threats against his life. Shortly after his marriage, Browne served as special U.S. marshal to supervise the elections in Piedmont, Alabama. After an altercation at the voting place, a white man threatened to shoot him. When his bride heard of the danger he was in, she hurried to her husband with "two pistols under her apron."[5]

During this same time period, Browne, who had abstained from alcohol since his bartending days in Cairo, Illinois, also joined in a temperance agitation that began with a meeting of blacks and whites in Montgomery, Alabama. A special motive for black temperance reformers such as Browne was to end the disfranchisement of black men linked to intoxication. Many black men, convicted for public drunkenness or crimes they committed after consuming alcohol, had lost the right to vote.[6] Moreover, since the majority of southern blacks were poor, they could not afford to waste money on alcoholic beverages. "All that the masses of our Race own," Brown observed, "is [a grave of] three by six feet of earth."[7] In response to these conditions, Browne organized temperance clubs and juvenile Bands of Hope.

Browne decided that none of his work would endure without a formal organization to unite the local temperance clubs. In 1874 he spoke at a meeting of the white Grand Lodge of Alabama, affiliated with a fraternal temperance organization called the Good Templars, to plead for the creation of black Good Templar lodges. Fearful that his proposal would antagonize whites, other black temperance leaders repudiated Browne's initiative, and one of them even called him a fool.[8]

Although whites in Alabama and other southern states refused to charter black lodges, they were willing to sponsor a temperance organization for black men and women called the True Reformers, which had been created by white Good Templars in Kentucky. In the beginning the True Reformers were under white control. Good Templars created all the True Reformer literature, rituals, and regalia. When blacks organized enough local lodges, called fountains, they were allowed to form statewide organizations, called Grand Fountains. At this point the whites gladly withdrew. They never were comfortable about their association with black temperance reformers.

Browne became a stalwart of the True Reformers and dedicated the final twenty-two years of his relatively brief life to them. In March 1874 he became a full-time organizer for the True Reformers in Alabama. A Grand Fountain was organized in the state in 1875, and Browne was elected to the office of grand worthy secretary to keep the books and accounts. In practice he was more important than the official head of the organization, the grand worthy master—a curious title for a society of former slaves.

On February 7, 1876, Browne, only twenty-seven years old, was elected grand worthy master of the Alabama Grand Fountain. After the withdrawal of the white Good Templars from control, there was never a national or regional True Reformer organization, only independent statewide chapters, but a newspaper that Browne published, *True Reformer*, circulated throughout many of the southern states. It was this newspaper that enabled the True Reformers in Virginia to know about Browne's work.

The instability of the True Reformers in Alabama frustrated Browne. For instance, between March 1876 and February 1877, the organization nominally grew from twenty-seven subordinate fountains with 2,000 members to forty-five fountains with 5,000 members. In practice many of the fountains ceased to exist soon after they were formed. Even those elected to Grand Fountain offices often lacked commitment. Browne complained that of twelve officers, only three remained active a year after their election.

Browne hoped to retain members of the Grand Fountain by creating a life insurance program. He later claimed that he had collected $50,000 from people who wanted to participate and had obtained promises from others for another $100,000. His success aroused the envy of rival black leaders. They first tried to take over the convention in charge of implementing the insurance program and, having failed, spitefully persuaded the Alabama legislature to deny Browne a charter for an insurance society. In disgust, Browne decided to move on. In late 1880 he left Alabama and appears to have had no further connection with the True Reformers there.

Browne relocated to Virginia, the birthplace of his parents. Several years earlier, black temperance reformers in the Old Dominion had invited Browne to join them. A new invitation came in December 1880. Both invitations resulted from a continuing crisis that the True Reformers of Virginia experienced when rival white Good Templar factions maneuvered for African American support.

The Good Templar international fraternal temperance society had split in 1876 over the question of black membership in the former slave states. A breakaway faction, supported by most Good Templars in England and Scotland, insisted on the right of blacks to receive lodge charters from the existing statewide white Grand Lodges. When this "British" faction tried to recruit members in the American South, it had no success with whites but some with blacks. This practice led to the creation of new all-black Grand Lodges. Whites in the former slave states had refused to charter black lodges, but even before 1876 there were a few in North Carolina, organized by a Good Templar from Connecticut. These black North Carolinians in turn had helped organize blacks in neighboring Virginia.

At first the southern white Good Templars had sponsored the True Reformers as an alternative to chartering black Good Templar lodges. After the schism of 1876, some southern white Good Templars offered a new compromise to assuage the conscience of northern whites: the creation of parallel white and black Grand Lodges. Blacks could become Good Templars but not in the same state organization as whites. Several dual Grand Lodges were established in Dixie. Both the "British" and "American" Good Templar factions raided the True Reformers in search of black recruits. For instance, the Grand Fountain of Virginia, United Order of True Reformers lost most of its membership after the "British" faction of the Good Templars sent its most celebrated black organizer, Dr. William Wells Brown, to the state.[9] The True Reformer remnant struggled to survive as a distinct organization.

Their difficulties led to the invitation to Brown to come to Virginia. Browne arrived in Richmond shortly after Christmas 1880, met with the state's True Reformer leadership on January 3, 1881, and was elected grand worthy master on January 11. The Virginia True Reformers were decimated, dispirited, and divided. By June 1881, Browne had only fourteen subordinate fountains, with perhaps 100 or 150 members contributing sickness and funeral dues, and assets of no more than $150. The quality of the members was dismal: "we had the very worst of our Race; not a decent man . . . wanted to bother with us."[10] In addition to these problems, the old guard changed its mind about Browne within months of installing him as the head of the Grand Fountain. They tried to oust him and even sought to get him arrested for refusing to surrender official records.

Few in the Virginia membership had confidence in Browne's ambitious scheme, devised in Alabama, of reconstituting the True Reformers as an insurance society. Although Browne was a teetotaler, he did not think total abstinence from alcoholic drink to be a viable basis for membership. Moreover, he had little interest in the ritual aspect of fraternalism and regarded lavish expenditures on regalia and fancy funerals as a waste of money. And he thought that in the 1880s it was money that African American men and women needed more than anything else. He wanted the True Reformers to provide life insurance benefits that were substantial enough to help survivors of a deceased member and did more than simply pay for burial expenses. At a time when decent jobs were scarce for black people, Browne also hoped that his society would be capable of offering employment to black men and women in True Reformer-owned businesses. Browne's vision contrasted sharply with what was then the reality: black fraternal and mutual benefit societies that assessed local members to pay for a respectable funeral, and white-run commercial insurance companies that overcharged blacks and almost never employed them as agents.

Browne's all-consuming devotion to True Reformerism often entailed financial sacrifice as well as the risk of public ridicule. He lost his position as a pastor in the Colored Methodist Episcopal Church when the Richmond bishop objected to the time he spent on True Reformer work. Brown switched his affiliation to the African Methodist Episcopal Church but never served as a pastor. The salary that the True Reformers paid him in his first years in Virginia was small and often in arrears. In the early 1880s it was sewing by Browne's wife that provided most of the couple's meager income.

Tireless in his efforts to recruit new members for the Grand Fountain, Browne focused initially on Richmond and the surrounding countryside. In 1880 about 44 percent of the population of the state capital was African American. The nearly 28,000 blacks in Richmond worked in the tobacco industry, as domestic servants, or in service trades. Most were very poor. Browne traveled on foot throughout the Richmond district, sometimes with nothing to eat but wild fruit. He spoke at shoe shops and barber shops, in homes and from the pulpits of small country churches. In these early days he was ridiculed as "True Reformer" Browne, an obsessed fanatic, who wore in all seasons a long black clerical coat "slick" with wear and age. "Wherever this coat was seen, men knew that there was W.W. Browne with a plan of a Negro Insurance Society. No one believed that the plan was worth anything, and no respectable man cared to be seen in Browne's company, for fear that he would be thought crazy, too, as many said Browne was."[11]

Browne made an indispensable early recruit when he persuaded William Patrick Burrell to join him in January 1881. Browne sought out this fifteen-year-old schoolboy so that he would have a literate helper to keep True Reformer records. Burrell served the True Reformers for about thirty years, first as Browne's private secretary and later as grand worthy secretary.

After several difficult years, Browne defeated his old-guard enemies, implemented an increasingly sophisticated insurance scheme, and created a children's auxiliary. In 1884 his enemies, who had organized what they called the Supreme Fountain, sued the Grand Fountain; the circuit court of Richmond ruled that Browne's was the authentic True Reformer society. In the same year, Browne supplemented ordinary True Reformer life insurance with the Class Department, which offered members an additional policy that paid up to $500, later up to $1,000, in case of death. In 1885 the True Reformers began to charge different rates depending on the members' ages, and shortly afterward insisted on answers to a medical questionnaire and sometimes a physical examination before agreeing to issue insurance. In the same year the membership reached a milestone, 1,000 True Reformers in Virginia. In addition, women True Reformers organized the Rosebuds for children under age fourteen.

In the late 1880s and the 1890s the True Reformers became the dominant black fraternal society in Richmond and throughout Virginia. During these years, whites sometimes lent a helping hand to black leaders who told their followers to focus on economic improvement rather than seeking political equality. Faced with the formidable reality of white racism, Browne restrained his confrontational personality and followed what he regarded as the only practical strategy: "Hush up that mouth of yours until a Negro can die on his own land and go to heaven from his own house."[12]

Aided by black migration from the Old Dominion, Browne's Grand Fountain also established itself outside Virginia, particularly in northern cities. In the mid-1880s a worsening political climate favored Browne's ideology of economic self-help. Richmond's interracial Knights of Labor collapsed, and the Readjusters, a white faction that was relatively moderate on race relations, lost power at the state level. Later, during the economic crisis of the 1890s, most of the rival black fraternal societies in Virginia were crippled by large losses in membership as members could not pay their dues.

With the help of insurance premiums, the Grand Fountain created a savings bank. In March 1888 the Virginia legislature chartered a True Reformers' savings bank to serve as a depository for insurance-generated funds. It was the first black-owned and -operated bank in America. The bank, however, did not open for business until 1889. In the intervening time, African Americans in the nation's capital had opened the Capitol Savings Bank of Washington, DC, claiming that it was the first black financial institution.

Originally the True Reformers' savings bank was located in Browne's home, but in 1891 it moved to a new three-story building. True Reformers' Hall, which had cost $24,000, also provided offices, storerooms, meeting rooms, and a concert auditorium. During the dedication ceremony, which included a parade and a visit by the mayor, Browne praised his supporters, claiming that he could easily find "ten thousand [black] men who have drunk the cost of this building, seven times this year, at five cents a drink."[13] He also reminded his audience to deposit at least one dollar in the savings bank on what he called "Money-Stone Day," a kind of financial cornerstone-laying.

At this stage the Grand Fountain had 15,000 members and was growing rapidly. Soon the society operated a 150-room hotel, published a newspaper, and operated Westham Farm. By 1896 the Grand Fountain had 250 employees, helping to fulfill Browne's dream of providing jobs for black people. Browne had other plans. He began to raise money for an old-age home for black men and women, not restricted to True Reformer members. A few years later, W. E. B. Du Bois, one of the nation's most prominent black civil rights activists, called the True Reformers "probably the most remarkable Negro organization in the country."[14]

In the last years of Browne's life he alienated old friends. Part of the problem was that he wanted money from the True Reformers to repay him for his "plans" for an insurance order. He quarreled with John Mitchell Jr., the editor of Richmond's principal black newspaper, the weekly *Planet*, with several of Richmond's leading Baptist preachers, and with other former supporters when he persuaded the Grand Fountain to promise him the enormous sum of $50,000 for the purchase of his "plans." Many people believed that the True Reformers already paid him enough: $1,800 annually, plus traveling expenses. The society gave Browne and his wife $29,500 before insurance regulators intervened to prevent further payments for the "plans."

Another major controversy erupted over race relations. Robert T. Teamoh, a black legislator from Massachusetts, came to Virginia in March 1895 as part of a tour by northern legislators of the southern states. The local organizers invited *Planet* editor Mitchell to join the Richmond part of the tour as Teamoh's escort. After visits to local tobacco factories, whites and blacks left to eat lunch separately. The governor had agreed to meet the northerners in the afternoon. To the surprise of whites, Teamoh and Mitchell turned up, which angered white opinion in Richmond. The *Dispatch* newspaper hinted at retaliation against blacks in general. Browne responded with a public letter criticizing Mitchell and Teamoh for worsening race relations and asking whites not to blame other black people. Browne said that "legal equality and cordial relation—to the extent of building up the negro race—are the desires of respectable and sensible negroes; and they are as much opposed to social equality between whites and blacks as are the whites themselves."[15] In Richmond and throughout the country, African Americans denounced Browne as an Uncle Tom.

The destructive battle between Browne and Mitchell took on new forms. Browne turned the *Reformer* newspaper into a weekly and tried to make it a rival of the *Planet* and also took financial control of a second newspaper, the *Virginia Baptist*, although he himself was a Methodist minister. In the 1896 municipal elections, Browne battled Mitchell for control of the predominantly black Jackson ward. In the end neither black slate took office, as the Democrats who supervised the elections awarded the seats to white candidates. This effectively disfranchised the ward's black majority.

In the last year of his life an increasingly autocratic Browne turned on his inner circle. Burrell, who had been at his side since the early 1880s, was publicly humiliated when he dared to suggest that there was a shortage in the old folks'-home account. The editor of the *Reformer*, a former minister to Liberia, was fired when he published an editorial too friendly toward Mitchell. Browne's judgment and temper may have been affected by the cancer that soon took his life. He arranged in 1897 to get a year of sick leave at full pay. In choosing an interim chief officer he passed over his senior lieutenants, the True Reformers' secretary, and the bank cashier. He then wandered vainly from physician to physician in search of a cure before he died in Washington, DC, on December 21, 1897, a few weeks after his forty-eighth birthday.

For more than a decade the Richmond-based True Reformers continued to prosper. The membership grew and spread far beyond Virginia, while the Grand Fountain opened new retail businesses in Richmond. In 1907, according to a senior officer, the society counted over 70,000 members; since its founding, it had paid out over $2,000,000 in insurance benefits. The True Reformers proudly published an official history in 1909, and Browne's widow arranged for the publication of her husband's biography in 1910. In the latter year the savings bank collapsed, and the True Reformers quickly shrank to the status of a second- or third-rank fraternal society. During the Great Depression of the 1930s it disappeared altogether. As the Grand Fountain faded away, so did the public's memory of Browne.

Whatever his failings, embarrassingly evident in his last years, Browne was one of the giants of late nineteenth-century African American life. Rising from the depths of slavery, Browne built a black business empire, and his dream of black economic empowerment inspired many of his followers. Within a few years after Browne's death, numerous African Americans who had worked with the Richmond True Reformers launched their own life insurance companies and banks, including John Merrick, who founded the North Carolina Mutual Life Insurance Company, which became one of the largest black-owned businesses in the early twentieth century. Maggie Lena Walker, who had been a paid staff member of the True Reformers, assumed leadership of another fraternal society, the Independent Order of St. Luke. Implementing Browne's vision, she established the St. Luke Penny Savings Bank, which by the mid-1920s had deposits of nearly $500,000 and provided numerous black families with mortgages to purchase their own homes. Thus, Browne's pioneering vision continued to have an impact on African Americans throughout the nation long after his death.

Notes

1. W. P. Burrell and D. E. Johnson Sr., *Twenty-Five Years History of the Grand Fountain of the United Order of True Reformers, 1881–1905* (Richmond, VA: Grand Fountain, United Order of True Reformers, 1909; reprinted, Westport, CT: Negro Universities Press, 1970), 12.

2. D. Webster Davis, *The Life and Public Services of Rev. Wm. Washington Browne, Founder of the Grand Fountain, U[nited]. O[rder]. of True Reformers and Organizer of the First Distinctive Negro Bank in America* (Philadelphia: Mary A. Browne-Smith, 1910),

63–250, as reprinted in David M. Fahey, ed., *The Black Lodge in White America: "True Reformer" Browne and His Economic Strategy* (Dayton, OH: Wright State University Press, 1994), 93.

3. Davis, *Life and Public Services*, reprinted in Fahey, *Black Lodge*, 102–3.

4. Browne, speech, April 1895, quoted in Burrell and Johnson, *Twenty-Five Years*, 30.

5. Davis, *Life and Public Services*, reprinted in Fahey, *Black Lodge*, 106–7.

6. Ibid., 109.

7. Browne, speech, February 1877, quoted in Burrell and Johnson, *Twenty-Five Years*, 26.

8. Browne, speech, April 1895, quoted in Burrell and Johnson, *Twenty-Five Years*, 20.

9. David M. Fahey, *Temperance and Racism: John Bull, Johnny Reb, and the Good Templars* (Lexington: University Press of Kentucky, 1996).

10. W. P. Burrell, report to Grand Fountain, 1890, in Burrell and Johnson, *Twenty-Five Years*, 114.

11. Ibid., 112–13.

12. (Richmond) *Planet*, May 23, 1891, quoted in Fahey, *Black Lodge*, 4.

13. Davis, *Life and Public Services*, reprinted in Fahey, *Black Lodge*, 210.

14. W. E. B. Du Bois, ed., *Economic Co-Operation among Negro Americans* (Atlanta: Atlanta University Press, 1907), 101.

15. Reprinted in (Richmond) *Planet*, March 30, 1895.

Suggested Readings

The standard work is David M. Fahey, ed., *The Black Lodge in White America: "True Reformer" Browne and His Economic Strategy* (Dayton, OH: Wright State University Press, 1994), which provides a substantial introductory essay and includes the text of D. Webster Davis's *The Life and Public Services of Rev. Wm. Washington Browne, Founder of the Grand Fountain, U[nited]. O[rder]. of True Reformers and Organizer of the First Distinctive Negro Bank in America* (Philadelphia: Mary A. Browne-Smith, 1910), written at the request of Browne's widow, as well as the True Reformer pamphlet *1607–1907, From Slavery to Bankers, Grand Fountain, UOTR* (Richmond: Grand Fountain, United Order of True Reformers, 1907). The other principal source for the history of the True Reformers in Virginia is W. P. Burrell and D. E. Johnson Sr., *Twenty-Five Years of the Grand Fountain of the United Order of True Reformers, 1881–1905* (Richmond,VA: Grand Fountain, United Order of True Reformers, 1909; reprinted, Westport, CT: Negro Universities Press, 1970), which can be supplemented by the (Richmond) *Planet*. Burrell also wrote "The True Reformers," *Colored American Magazine* (April 1904): 267–69, 285–88, and (May 1904): 340–46. There is a thoughtful, well-documented article by James D. Watkinson, "William Washington Browne and the True Reformers of Richmond, Virginia," *Virginia Magazine of History and Biography* 97, no. 3 (May 1989): 375–98, based on his master's thesis at the University of Virginia. For an analysis of black involvement in the temperance movement, see David M.

Fahey, *Temperance and Racism: John Bull, Johnny Reb, and the Good Templars* (Lexington: University Press of Kentucky, 1996). Also of interest are James D. Watkinson, "William Washington Browne," 324–26, and John T. Kneebone, "William Patrick Burrell," 420–22, in *Dictionary of Virginia Biography*, ed. Sara B. Bearss et al. (Richmond: Library of Virginia, 2001), and David M. Fahey, "W. W. Browne," in *American National Biography*, 24 vols., ed. John A. Garraty (New York: Oxford University Press, 1999), 3:764–65.

4

Richard Henry Boyd
Black Business and
Religion in the Jim Crow South

Paul Harvey

Richard Henry Boyd was a stalwart of America's small, embattled black urban middle class during the rise of Jim Crow, the system of segregation that defined race relations in America in the years following the Civil War. As segregation excluded African Americans from equal participation in American society and relegated them to second-class citizenship, Boyd became an advocate of black-controlled institutions. In particular, he fostered religious independence from white denominations and economic self-sufficiency through black-owned businesses.

Boyd was a leading force in the creation of the black separatist National Baptist Convention in 1895. The Baptist Church had attracted a large following among African Americans since its emergence during the religious revival of the 1730s and 1740s known as the Great Awakening. The Baptist faith appealed to African Americans because it proclaimed spiritual equality and promised salvation to all, regardless of race. During the eighteenth and early nineteenth centuries, black and white Baptists often worshipped together and addressed each other as brothers and sisters, and black ministers preached to white congregations. While Baptists embraced religious egalitarianism, they advocated neither racial equality nor abolition of slavery. It was not until the early nineteenth century that the issue of slavery increasingly started to divide Baptists. In 1845, Southern Baptists split from the denomination, insisting that the Bible sanctioned slavery. In the aftermath of the schism, Baptist masters continued to proselytize among their slaves, emphasizing Scripture passages that exhorted them to be obedient servants. Not surprisingly, African American Baptists pushed for independent, black-controlled churches after gaining their freedom.

Boyd's support for black denominational autonomy allowed him to combine his religious and business interests. In 1896 he established the National Baptist Publishing Board, which distributed Sunday school literature to black churches. By the time of his death in 1922, he had turned the small, Nashville-based company into the largest black-owned publishing house in the nation. Boyd's other business ventures included the One-Cent Savings Bank and Trust Company, founded in 1904; the *Nashville Globe*, which he launched in 1906; and the National Negro Doll Company, created in 1911.

Boyd's business career exemplified the racial advancement strategy of Booker T. Washington, the nation's leading black spokesman. In 1895, Washington, in his famous Atlanta Exposition address, had advised African Americans to stay in the South and sacrifice political rights and social equality in exchange for a chance to pursue economic self-sufficiency with the assistance of sympathetic whites. Unlike Washington, however, Boyd also challenged racial segregation publicly. In 1905, for example, he helped organize a black boycott of Nashville streetcars. Moreover, he used his newspaper, the *Globe*, to voice black opposition to segregation. Paul Harvey demonstrates that Boyd, like other members of the black urban middle class, maintained a careful balancing act between acknowledging segregation and testing its limits.

On March 5, 1843, Indiana Dixon, a slave woman from Mississippi, who had been sold away from her parents at age seven, bore her first son. She named the boy Dick Gray, in memory of her long-lost father. After the Civil War, Dick Gray would rename himself Richard Henry Boyd. In the late 1850s, Martha Gray, the owner of Indiana and her children, died, and her possessions, including her slaves, were sold to pay off creditors. Benonia Gray, a relative of Martha's, purchased Dick for $1,200 and settled in Texas. Indiana also moved to Texas, but with a different family, thus parting from Dick.

In Texas, Dick Gray grew into a strong young man with close ties to his white owners. When the Civil War started in 1861, Dick accompanied Master Gray and his three sons to the Confederate army. He worked, as did many other slave men, as a body servant to his masters and as a day laborer in the army. In 1863, at the battle of Chattanooga, Master Gray and his two eldest sons were killed in battle, and the youngest son was injured. Dick tended to his injured young master, took him back to Texas, and worked on the Gray plantation until the conclusion of the war. It is not surprising that later in life Boyd demanded pensions for black men who had served in the Confederate army. Moreover, he cooperated successfully with whites in business enterprises, drawing on his experience as a trusted laborer and body servant during his time as a slave.

Following the Civil War and the end of slavery, Dick Gray worked on a ranch and in a mill in southeastern Texas. In the meantime, he taught himself to read and tried to locate his mother, who was living in Grimes County, Texas. In 1867 the two reunited and subsequently remained close until Indiana's death in Nashville in 1915. In 1867, Dick

Gray changed his name to Richard Henry Boyd.[1] Two years later he was converted and joined a Baptist church in Montgomery County, Texas. He also began attending Bishop College in Marshall, Texas, an institution founded by the American Baptist Home Mission Society to train young freedmen for preaching and teaching. It is ironic that it was a conflict with the society in the 1890s that set Boyd on a career that would result in the establishment of the largest black-owned publishing enterprise in the country.

While in Marshall, he met a young woman named Harriett Albertine Moore, a former slave, and the two married in 1869. She remained his lifelong partner and supporter. The marriage produced nine children. Five of them survived their parents: Mattie B. Johnson, Annie L. Hall, Lula B. Landers, Henry Allen Boyd, and Theophilus Bartholomew Boyd. Henry Allen was his father's true business partner, carrying on the family's enterprises until his own death in 1959. The other four children died when they were very young.

In the early 1870s the financial demands of providing for his family compelled Richard Boyd to leave Bishop College before receiving his degree. While sup-

Courtesy of the Southern Baptist Historical Library and Archives, Nashville, Tennessee

porting his family as a minister and day laborer, he began organizing Baptist associations and churches throughout Texas, impressing white and black citizens alike with his vigor and administrative skills. In 1876, for example, Boyd was selected as the representative of black Baptists to the country's centennial celebration in Philadelphia. As a leader of Texas Baptists, he established churches at Waverly, Old Danville, Navasota, Crockett, Palestine, and San Antonio. In 1891 he capped his career in Texas by becoming pastor of a prestigious black Baptist congregation in San Antonio.

In the 1890s, as a well-known pastor and Baptist leader, Boyd became involved in a controversy that threatened to divide black Baptists. Some African Americans advocated separation from the white-controlled American Baptist Home Mission Society, while others supported continued affiliation with the white Baptists. Proponents of separation criticized the society for its failure to involve African Americans in its governance, particularly the distribution and control of funds. They insisted that only an independent black-controlled organization could serve the needs of black Baptists.

African American ministers had first made attempts to launch a separate group in 1866 in Cincinnati, when they established the Consolidated American Baptist Missionary Convention to provide a central forum for black Baptist churches. This group ceased to function about 1873, primarily because of a lack of funds after white northern Baptists redirected some of their monies to other projects. (Until 1873, white northern Baptist groups contributed to separate black denominational organizations. That year they began to fund white northern-directed missionary groups such as the American Baptist Home Mission Society.) Black Baptists opposed to separate enterprises argued that black denominational independence was not feasible economically, as the difficult experience of the Consolidated American Baptist Missionary Convention had shown. They claimed that the work of impoverished black congregations depended on the financial support of white Baptists.

In Texas and many other states, however, the separatists eventually won. In 1893 a group of black Baptists, led by Boyd and Sutton E. Griggs, who soon became a well-known minister and novelist in Nashville, founded a separate black Baptist state convention in Texas, called the Missionary Baptist General Convention of Texas. Boyd and Griggs charged that the American Baptist Home Mission Society failed to encourage black economic and social progress by neglecting to involve African Americans in its governance. In particular, Boyd and his Texas colleagues objected to the plans of the society to consolidate and reorganize schools for the freedpeople, which would have resulted in the closing of some schools, including Guadalupe College in Seguin, Texas, which had been established by African Americans. The society also blocked the creation of additional black-controlled institutions by insisting that churches direct their money, energies, and young students to institutions controlled by the society. In doing so, Boyd and others charged, the white northern Baptists hindered the development of "manhood" among the race, which they defined as the ability to sustain independent institutions. In the midst of one such controversy in Texas in 1893, Boyd expressed his frustrations this way: "We believe in letting all our Baptist schools live. . . . [Whites] simply say, let your field grow up in weeds and work my land for fifty years. Let your wife and children do without the home for fifty years, and work for me; but they forget when the fifty years are out the Negro is just where he was when he started. Not one whit higher, cornered and unprotected."[2] Despite their criticism of the American Baptist Home Mission Society, Boyd and Griggs justified their move with language that even black Baptists opposed to separation could appreciate. "The Holy Spirit come to us and forbid the Negro taking a second place," they explained.[3]

After establishing a separate state convention in Texas, Boyd and his allies sought to create a national organization for the numerous black Baptist congregations that had emerged in the aftermath of the Civil War. A major obstacle, however, was the administrative structure of the Baptist church, which provided for the complete autonomy of local congregations. Each church set its own policy, hired and fired its own ministers, and collected and distributed money according to the desires of the congregation. Such congregational independence historically had made it a challenge to create larger Baptist organizations. Black denominational independence, however, often faltered at local levels, where poorly paid ministers, preaching to poverty-stricken congregants, relied on white financial support to help fund the work of their small churches. Realizing that black religious autonomy depended on financial independence, Richard Henry Boyd searched for a viable strategy to utilize all available resources, including those of whites from both North and South, in building a black-controlled national organization. Some black Baptists, especially those who had benefited from the educational institutions operated by the American Baptist Home Mission Society, were reluctant to alienate their white northern allies who provided substantial and crucial support. White northerners, for their part, worried about the "race feeling" developing among black Baptists such as Boyd and others, who were becoming what some were beginning to call "race men."

The efforts of black Baptist separatists, including Boyd, resulted in the formation of the National Baptist Convention, which first met in Atlanta, Georgia, in 1895. The new denomination took on a structure like that of its white Baptist counterparts: it was a central organization whose purpose was to encourage various kinds of religious endeavors, such as publishing religious material, conducting missionary work, and establishing new churches and educational institutions. Black Baptist congregations that supported the new National Baptist Convention were declaring themselves in favor of creating separate black-controlled organizations, apart from the dominant northern missionary societies and publishing houses.

By 1906 the Baptist faith was more firmly entrenched than ever among African Americans. Baptists represented 60 percent of black churchgoers, or about 2,250,000 communicants, most of them belonging to churches affiliated with the National Baptist Convention. By 1916 the organization claimed nearly 3,000,000 communicants, more than the Southern Baptist Convention, the largest white denomination in the South, which had some 2,700,000 members. In fact, the black denomination had become the third largest religious organization in the country, outranked only by the Catholic Church and the Methodist Episcopal Church.[4]

From its inception, the National Baptist Convention debated the wisdom of setting up an independent black-controlled publishing house to provide its members with black-produced religious literature. Supporters of the proposal argued that such an agency would serve as an important means to counter the growing tide of white supremacist rhetoric, create employment for African Americans, promote literacy among the black population, and provide a forum for black scholars and theologians who could not find publishing opportunities elsewhere. As one supporter pointed out, "all races have a literature."[5]

The proposal, however, met with much opposition from black Baptists. Opponents stressed the historic attachment of black Baptists to the white-controlled American Baptist Publication Society. Since the Civil War, the Philadelphia-based society had placed inexpensively produced pamphlets, tracts, Bibles, and Sunday-school literature in the hands of black congregations, often distributing them free of charge. Moreover, the society had hired black agents to sell its publications, and it had been instrumental in aiding literacy efforts among freedpeople in the years following the Civil War by creating and funding schools at all levels, distributing teaching material, and employing hundreds of teachers throughout the South. African American opponents of an independent black publishing house were concentrated in the southeastern states, especially Virginia and North Carolina, where cooperation with the American Baptist Publication Society was historically the strongest. Indeed, as Lewis G. Jordan, a black Baptist historian, observed, "nearly all who fought the idea were employees of the Northern Societies, which were then furnishing literature for the Sunday schools of our churches, and these workers felt that such steps would be construed as enmity against our white brethren and friends who had given so much, and endured so much for us."[6] Opponents defeated the proposal, claiming that if the business venture failed, it would prove to whites the inability of African Americans to conduct their own affairs. Moreover, given the poverty of black churches, many felt that it was unrealistic to expect them to support a separate publishing enterprise.

Boyd, however, continued to push hard for the creation of a black-controlled publishing house. His efforts were aided by a controversy that resulted in the growing estrangement of many southern black Baptists from their northern white coreligionists. In 1890 the American Baptist Publication Society had offered to print a series of articles by black Baptist authors. When the white-controlled publishing house withdrew the offer, because of objections from white southern Baptists, black religious leaders were offended. The corresponding secretary of the society, A. J. Rowland, tried to appease African Americans by offering the black authors an alternative outlet for their writings. The damage, however, was done.

Capitalizing on this affront to black Baptists, Boyd used his considerable oratorical skills to impress his fellow Baptists with visions of an independent black-controlled publishing house. The success of such a business venture, Boyd knew, was contingent on the patronage of the black urban middle class, which had the financial means to purchase black-produced books and pamphlets. Thus, Boyd set out to persuade black congregations in cities with a sizeable African American middle class to support the creation of a black Baptist publishing house. Within a year following the formation of the National Baptist Convention, Boyd succeeded in gaining the support of many of the most prominent black urban ministers, such as Emmanuel K. Love, pastor of Savannah's historically influential First African Baptist Church, whose congregation had more than 1,000 members. Love pledged to provide seed money for the enterprise and support it by buying its publications. Pastors of other sizeable congregations, such as Sutton Griggs in Nashville, Lewis G. Jordan in Kentucky, and Elias Camp Morris in Helena, Arkansas, also backed the enterprise.

In 1896 the National Baptist Convention established a publishing board, placed it under the auspices of its Home Mission Board, and named Boyd secretary-treasurer of both boards. Boyd secured a charter for the publishing agency, placing it under the control of a self-perpetuating board of nine African American men. In this way, the publishing house was in effect an independent business enterprise, as Boyd saw it, and not an "auxiliary" to the National Baptist Convention. The publishing board could thus serve denominational needs but operate as a separate and distinct business, not as a subsidiary of the denomination. The denomination, for example, could not legally demand power of appointment to the agency's board of directors, since the board could set its own rules and appoint its own members.

Boyd located the enterprise in Nashville, Tennessee. Dubbed the Athens of the South, the city served Boyd's purposes ideally. Davidson County, Tennessee, which was dominated by the capital city of Nashville, had a population of approximately 43,000 African Americans, including a substantial urban working class as well as a community of professionals associated with the numerous colleges and churches in the city. Nashville was home to several black educational institutions, including Fisk University, the Baptist Roger Williams University, and Methodist-run Central Tennessee College. Several influential black ministers resided in the city, such as Sutton Griggs of East First Baptist Church and Nelson Merry of Nashville's downtown black Baptist congregation. Thus, Boyd could draw on a pool of educated and competent talent. Nashville was also a Baptist stronghold, with dozens of congregations, most of which were affiliated with the National Baptist Convention. The railroads passing through the city made it an ideal location to reach the majority of African Americans who lived in the South.

Moreover, Nashville was the home of the publishing house of the white Southern Baptist Convention, established in 1891 and headed by a layman named James Marion Frost. The Southern Baptist Convention itself had emerged in 1845 as part of the antagonism over slavery between northerners and southerners that had affected nearly every denomination prior to the Civil War. The white Southern Baptists in their early years had attempted to publish their own material, without success, and thus remained after the Civil War still dependent on the American Baptist Publication Society for religious literature to use in their churches. In 1891, however, Frost successfully convinced leaders of the Southern Baptist Convention to support the creation of a publishing house owned and controlled by the denomination. Frost's efforts were spectacularly successful, and his agency, the Sunday School Board of the Southern Baptist Convention, grew quickly into a major force in religious publishing. From this vantage point, then, Frost was well equipped to aid Boyd's efforts to establish an independent black-controlled publishing house.

Upon arriving in Nashville in 1895, Boyd secured the aid of Frost, including funds, technical advice, printing presses, and literature. Frost saw his support of Boyd as part of the racial paternalism to which God had called southern whites. Frost also recognized that he and Boyd shared the same business competitor, the American Baptist Publication Society, which had continued its efforts to extend its market share in the South. Frost and other white leaders of the Southern Baptist Convention supported racially segregated enterprises, believing that this practice would aid African Americans in assuming their proper place in the southern social order. Thus, Frost had both theological and business reasons for his remarkable alliance with and assistance of Boyd. Initially, some of Boyd's black Baptist associates apparently feared that the white Sunday School Board would subsume the black publishing agency. Frost, however, aided black Baptist endeavors without seeking to influence the content of Boyd's publications. The Southern Baptist Convention expressed itself "gratified" that black Baptists were producing publications "which do credit to their religious enterprise, intelligence, and their literary taste."[7]

These white Southerners supported the National Baptist Publishing Board because Boyd's Sunday-school publications focused exclusively on religious indoctrination and did not challenge segregation. Indeed, by supporting the black publishing house, they were assisting in creating the right kind of segregated order, one contributing to the "uplift" of both races, separately. Boyd, for his part, had considerable experience in working for and with southern whites, and was well able to speak the accommodationist rhetoric that this type of communication entailed. Boyd felt too that in the era of segregation, black southerners were best advised to nurture cooperative relationships with southern whites, and to use those alliances to help build their own black business ventures.

For Boyd and for the white southern Baptists, continued reliance on northern Baptist publications was detrimental to denominational self-development. White northern Baptists in the American Baptist Home Mission Society and its corresponding publishing arm, the American Baptist Publication Society, saw themselves as the true benefactors of their black brethren in the South. White northern Baptists had, of course, been instrumental in establishing numerous schools, colleges (including Bishop College, where Boyd was educated), churches, and other black institutions. White northern Baptists supported a large number of missionaries in the South, both white and black, who had conducted ministries of salvation and education among the freedpeople. Boyd recognized this honorable history, but saw the late nineteenth century as a time when African Americans had to make their own history, with white assistance but not white control.

He viewed the support of white southern Baptists in precisely the same way. They were to provide funds, advice, and assistance without heavy-handed control. As Boyd saw the matter, white northern Baptists had opposed his endeavor, even enlisting black allies of the northern American Baptist Publication Society in the process. Meanwhile, white southern Baptists eagerly helped the fledgling black Baptist publishing enterprise, understanding that this would aid in "racial self-development." Boyd hoped the northern white Baptists would learn the proper lesson from this kind of black religious and business independence: "The National Baptist Convention has a right to own and control its own business enterprises, to maintain, on a larger scale, distinctive educational institutions, and in the exercise of this priestly prerogative, no band of white brethren anywhere should undertake to embarrass or molest them. With the recognition of these rights and corresponding brotherly treatment, our white brethren will find in the constituency of the National Baptist Convention *ardent friends* and *loyal supporters*."[8]

Moreover, Boyd believed that the publishing house could serve as an important instrument of black cultural expression. White religious literature, he pointed out, often reinforced racist stereotypes. White northern Baptist publications, for example, depicted angelic figures as whites, and demons who guarded the gates to Hell as blacks. Such portrayals, Boyd insisted, would lead black children to assume "that the latter belong to an inferior creation." Only a black publishing house, Boyd concluded, could provide positive images of African Americans that challenged the racist stereotypes of the nation's denominational publishers.[9]

In January 1897, a year after the National Baptist Convention launched the Publishing Board, Boyd released the first series of Sunday-school lessons, using printing plates donated to him by Frost and the white Sunday School Board. Boyd sold his publications to black Baptist churches throughout the country and soon established a sizeable market. Frost assisted Boyd by providing some printed literature from the white Sunday School Board's growing stable of authors. By 1900, Boyd had hired his own authors and had begun producing his own material. By 1910 the Board's presses produced more than 11,000,000 pieces of literature each year and employed more than 150 black workers. In 1915 the Board reported that $158,298 had passed through the publishing house the previous year, with a cumulative total of over $2,500,000 of business during Boyd's incumbency since 1896. Boyd plowed back into the enterprise the agency's growing yearly gross income. With some of the proceeds he spun off a related enterprise, the National Baptist Church Supply Company, which soon furnished pews, benches, hymnals, pulpits, choir robes, and children's dolls to black churches. Perhaps more important, the Publishing Board held together the diffuse and loosely organized National Baptist Convention, largely because the publishing house was the only denominational agency that could sustain itself financially.

Located in downtown Nashville on the main thoroughfare of Second Avenue North, the city's central business district, the headquarters of the Publishing Board was purchased by Boyd for $10,000 in 1898. A savvy businessman, Boyd took advantage of fire sales conducted by bankrupt companies, including one of his former creditors, to bargain for inexpensive printing equipment, an electric motor, and other items for the new building. Boyd intended for his publishing house to print its own literature, rather than simply distribute material printed by privately contracted presses, as was the case with most denominational publishing houses, white and black. In some cases, Boyd hired white intermediaries to conduct the business transactions, knowing that some whites would not sell or lease land, equipment, or buildings to blacks.

While many black Baptists applauded Boyd's successful management of the Publishing Board, his position of financial power also generated jealousy among some leaders of the National Baptist Convention. Challenging Boyd's control of the publishing house, they charged that he had diverted funds for personal gain. In 1908, after Boyd had paid $7,600 toward the purchase price of the new building, the convention ordered him to pay the remaining $2,400. By 1912, however, the Publishing Board's debt had increased to $5,000, which Boyd insisted was due to investments in the enterprise and not to his mismanagement of funds. Boyd's family had taken out personal mortgages on property that, National Baptist Convention officials believed, belonged to them. Boyd also had taken out mortgages and borrowed money against the Publishing Board's property and used the funds to help finance several of his other ventures, including the National Negro Doll Company, the One-Cent Savings Bank, and the National Baptist Church Supply Company.

Boyd defended his and his family's actions by pointing out that these mortgages had been used to fund the Publishing Board's growing business interests, which served black Baptists as a whole. Boyd saw all of this as advancing the interests of the denomination, even while he believed his board was outside of denominational ownership, since it had been incorporated, financed, and organized separately from the National Baptist Convention in 1898, whereas the convention itself was not incorporated until 1916. Boyd also reminded convention leaders that in the board's early days, much of the financing came from Boyd's own mortgaging, leasing, bargain hunting, and personal sacrifices. Indeed, initially, he had lived in a small room behind the publishing house and had devoted literally every waking hour to the fledgling endeavor, overseeing the entire operation from distributing the literature to sweeping the floors. Boyd had invested some of his own money in the enterprise as well, giving him further claim to the venture. During that time, most of Boyd's family had remained in Texas until, in the early 1900s, he was solvent enough to move them to Nashville. It is not surprising that Boyd viewed the Publishing Board as a private enterprise independent of the National Baptist Convention and that he was loath to cede any control over it. Instead he insisted that he and the board of directors could take any actions they deemed necessary to preserve and extend the business, including using the current property as collateral to fund future growth.

Boyd's position was weakened, however, by his close relationship with agencies of the National Baptist Convention. For example, Boyd was at the head of the Home Mission Board of the National Baptist Convention, an agency he used largely as a means to advertise and distribute publications coming from the Publishing Board. Through such schemes, it appeared that Boyd was using the denomination for his personal benefit, a charge that had considerable ethical merit, despite Boyd's canny legal maneuvers to protect the independence of his publishing house. Boyd also maintained twenty-eight-year copyrights on Sunday-school commentaries in his name, allowing him to profit personally from selling religious literature to black churches. Convention leaders asked Boyd to transfer his copyrights to the National Baptist Publishing Board in 1912. Boyd refused, claiming that the organization had not created the Publishing Board but that he and the eight other members of the board of directors had initiated it as a private enterprise affiliated with the convention but not controlled by it.

Wrangling for control of the Publishing Board began in earnest in 1905 and continued over the next ten years. The ensuing series of skirmishes stalled the functioning of black Baptist national bodies. In 1915 the controversy exploded at that year's National Baptist Convention meeting in Chicago, attended by more than 15,000 delegates. Denominational leaders allied with longtime convention president Elias Camp Morris, who sought to assert the organization's legal authority over the publishing house as well as the Home Mission Board, which Boyd headed and ran more or less as a publicity agency for the Publishing Board. After Boyd's attempt to stop the regular convention session failed, he bolted from the meeting hall and reconvened his supporters at a large church on Chicago's South Side. The Boyd forces took from the convention the records of the Publishing Board as well as $10,000, which white southern Baptists had contributed to the Home Mission Board as part of their yearly donation to missionary efforts among black Baptists. This action set off another legal battle and led to a permanent split of the nation's black Baptists. The National Baptist Convention, led by Arkansas minister and president Morris, incorporated itself as the National Baptist Convention, U.S.A., in 1915, while Boyd's followers established the National Baptist Convention, Unincorporated, now known as the National Baptist Convention of America.

The battle for control over the Baptist publishing house raged for the next five years. A white arbiter, hired to untangle the legal knot, argued that the various boards of the National Baptist Convention held property "in trust, for the uses and benefit" of the organization and suggested that the convention create an executive board to transact its business.[10] The Boyd faction, however, claimed that Morris and his followers wanted to gain personal control over the publishing house because it had demonstrated financial stability, whereas other denominational agencies never managed to secure a sound funding base. Boyd contended that Baptist conventions were merely voluntary associations from which individuals and groups could withdraw whenever they wished. He accused the Morris faction of pursuing a "strong centralization form of government, a permanent organization with the property rights vested in a central body."[11] Boyd, in essence, objected to turning the denomination into a modern nonprofit corporation, a move that would diminish his personal success story—the growth of his publishing firm—and wrest from him the crown jewel of his business empire.

In 1918, at the request of some of the black disputants on both sides of the controversy, white southern Baptists attempted to referee the fray. Orren Luico Hailey, a white Baptist who in 1924 was instrumental in the opening of the American Baptist Theological Seminary for black Baptists in Nashville, headed the committee of white arbiters.

Some black ministers questioned why whites should be trusted to resolve this dispute when "Negroes are lynched and burned right under some of these white commissioners' noses and not one word spoken or protest uttered against it." Such evils, an ally of Boyd's suggested, were "more dangerous and damnable than all the dissension the race can create among themselves."[12] The committee of white arbiters, under the leadership of Hailey, favored Morris's philosophy of denominational control of all convention agencies and failed to resolve the dispute. As a result, the division between the Boyd and Morris factions persisted, as each convention developed constituent churches and agencies.

While Boyd's entrepreneurial spirit contributed to the bitter split among black Baptists, his political and business activities in Nashville resulted in the creation of institutions that served the city's black population through much of the twentieth century. Among his first business ventures was the One-Cent Savings Bank and Trust Company established in January 1904. Boyd and his partners, including James Carroll Napier, a lawyer and close friend of Booker T. Washington's, and funeral home director Preston Taylor, vowed to use the bank to instill "racial confidence, racial fidelity, racial patriotism, and racial love" in African Americans and teach them thrift and frugality.[13] Boyd insisted that the bank would practice fiscal conservatism to protect depositors. The bank, he wrote, was established "not for the purpose of investing and accumulating money for the stockholders, neither for the purpose of paying salaries to the officers, but for the purpose, first, of restoring confidence in the already industrious colored citizens and training young men in financial dealings."[14] Boyd's strategy included making only "safe" loans to institutions and individuals, providing modest salaries to bank employees, and encouraging stockholders to reinvest their dividends in the bank. He insisted that the bank be able at all times to meet the demand of its depositors, a policy that allowed it to survive through difficult years, including the Great Depression. The One-Cent Savings Bank and Trust Company, now known as the Citizen's Bank, continues to serve black residents of Nashville.

Perhaps Boyd's most important business venture was the launching of the *Nashville Globe* in 1906. Boyd and his eldest son, Henry Allen Boyd, started the newspaper to publicize and organize a black streetcar boycott. In the early twentieth century, Nashville began enforcing laws requiring segregated streetcars. Appalled by the inferior accommodations provided for black patrons, Boyd, along with other black busi-

nessmen and ministers, helped to organize a streetcar boycott in 1905–
1906. Boyd's fellow Nashville Baptist ministers Sutton Griggs and Edward W. D. Isaac were active in raising money and urging black
Nashvillians who had means of transportation, such as wagons, to make
them available to transport black residents. In 1905, Boyd also participated in the formation of the Union Transportation Company, a black-
owned streetcar enterprise. Boyd used the basement of the National
Baptist Publishing Board to install his own dynamo and generator to
run electric trains purchased with the proceeds from the sale of stock in
the Union Transportation Company, for which he served as purchasing
agent. The streetcar boycott and the black-owned Union Transportation Company eventually failed. The company's first vehicles, which
were steam driven, were not powerful enough to negotiate Nashville's
hills. A tax imposed on electric streetcars, levied by the city in 1906
specifically to combat the Union Transportation Company's fledgling
endeavor, finished off the undercapitalized business.

While the streetcar boycott collapsed in late 1906, the *Nashville
Globe* survived and thrived. By the late 1920s some 20 percent of the
city's black families subscribed to the paper, which promoted black businesses, publicized police abuses, and provided a forum for black protest
thought. After Boyd's death in 1922 his son Henry Allen took charge of
the paper, and the *Globe* continued to serve as the major voice of black
Nashville until Henry's death in 1959.

In addition to the *Globe*, Richard Henry Boyd also founded the
National Negro Doll Company in 1911. Funded with money from the
Publishing Board profits, Boyd's company manufactured and distributed black dolls. Although Marcus Garvey and the Universal Negro
Improvement Association are often credited with popularizing black dolls
in the years following World War I, Boyd was in fact the first to market
mass-produced black dolls to African American consumers. He initiated the National Negro Doll Company after he tried to purchase dolls
for his children but could find none that were not gross caricatures of
African Americans.[15] Beginning in 1908, Boyd distributed black dolls
that he had purchased from a European manufacturer, until he launched
his own company. An advertisement for the dolls, which ran in the
Nashville Globe, other black newspapers, and Boyd's Sunday-school publications, illustrates how Boyd marketed them to instill racial pride and
self-respect. "These toys," the advertisement proclaimed, "are not made
of that disgraceful and humiliating type that we have been accustomed

to seeing. . . . They represent the intelligent and refined Negro of today, rather than that type of toy that is usually given to the children, and as a rule used as a scarecrow." The dolls, Boyd explained, were to "teach the people that they may teach their children how to look upon their people."[16] The doll enterprise did not turn a profit, however. By about 1915, Boyd had phased out this portion of his business, in part because his National Baptist Church Supply Company had become so successful in selling pews, pulpits, choir robes, heaters, furnaces, and carpets to black churches throughout the country.

Pointing to his own lucrative career as a black businessman, Boyd embraced Booker T. Washington's racial advancement philosophy, which fostered racial solidarity and economic self-sufficiency. Like Washington, he urged African Americans to stay in the South, insisting that the region offered them "the very best opportunity to make money with which to buy property, and to speculate in legal business ventures."[17] Boyd also pursued this strategy as vice president of the National Negro Business League, dominated by Washington and his allies, which first met in Nashville in 1903.

Although Boyd, like Washington, did not advocate social equality, he was a vocal critic of racism. In 1917 he responded to an article in the *Georgia Christian Index*, a white denominational newspaper, that suggested that African Americans had been "well managed" in the South. Boyd bristled, "we do noᴛ like the idea of being 'managed.' " The "Negro problem," he insisted, was a dilemma created by whites through "mob violence, starvation wages, peonage, shameful educational neglect, Jim Crow laws, enforced segregation, miscarriage of justice in the courts, brutal police relations, inadequate housing, . . . disfranchisement, [and] mistreatment of our women and girls."[18] Nor did Boyd spare white northerners in his critique of racism. He and other black Republicans harshly criticized the Republican Party's move to "lily-white Republicanism" and blasted Theodore Roosevelt's deliberate snubbing of black Nashvillians when he visited the city in 1907.[19]

At a time that represented, in the words of Rayford W. Logan, the "nadir of race relations" in the post-Civil War South, Boyd forged strategic alliances with southern whites to foster black business enterprises. Similar to Washington, Boyd advocated accommodationism in the interest of achieving economic self-sufficiency, which he hoped would provide the members of his race not only with necessary capital but also with a sense of dignity and pride. Although Boyd was willing to work within the confines of segregation, he was not willing to accept racism and frequently exposed it in his publications. Indeed, Boyd's success as an entrepreneur called into question white racist claims that African Americans were inherently inferior.

Notes

1. It is unclear why he picked the name Richard Henry Boyd.

2. General Baptist State Convention of Texas *Minutes*, 1894, 20–32, on microfilm at the Southern Baptist Historical Library and Archives, Nashville, Tennessee.

3. Ibid.

4. Paul Harvey, *Redeeming the South: Religious Cultures and Racial Identities among Southern Baptists, 1865–1925* (Chapel Hill: University of North Carolina Press, 1997), 3.

5. L. C. Garland, "Why We Should Use the Sunday School Literature Published at Nashville, Tennessee," *National Baptist Magazine* (September 1901): 352–57. The *National Baptist Magazine* was a forum for black Baptist church leaders that, while short-lived, proved crucial in articulating the emerging separatist consciousness of that era.

6. Lewis G. Jordan, *The National Baptist Convention, U.S.A., Inc.* (Nashville: Publishing Board of the National Baptist Convention, 1935), 250.

7. Southern Baptist Convention *Annual*, 1897, Appendix B, LXXIV, part of Annual Proceedings of the Southern Baptist Convention at the Southern Baptist Historical Library and Archives, Nashville.

8. *National Baptist Union*, July 19, 1902.

9. National Baptist Convention *Journal* (1900), Report of the Publishing Board and the Home Mission Board, part of Annual Proceedings of the Southern Baptist Convention at the Southern Baptist Historical Library and Archives, Nashville.

10. "Statement of the Causes of Confusion," National Baptist Convention *Journal* (1915): 33–34. An executive committee of this sort would have solved a recurring problem of Baptist conventions, namely, that "conventions" legally existed only during the period of their annual meeting. Outside of those few days, they had no legal existence. An executive committee appointed by the convention to transact business could maintain the legal life of the convention through the remainder of the year, thus avoiding legal difficulties such as the publishing house controversy.

11. National Baptist Convention of America *Journal* (1916): 61–135, gives Boyd's side of the controversy. The National Baptist Convention of America was commonly referred to as the "unincorporated convention," though it was, in fact, incorporated.

12. M. F. R. Chapman, "The Baptist Difference as Seen by a Texan," *National Baptist Union Review* (April 5, 1919).

13. Quoted in Bobby L. Lovett, *A Black Man's Dream: The First 100 Years. Richard Henry Boyd and the National Baptist Publishing Board* (Jacksonville, FL: Mega Corporation, 1993), 151.

14. *Nashville Globe*, January 12, 1912, quoted in Christopher M. Scribner, "Nashville Offers Opportunity: *The Nashville Globe* and Business as a Means of Uplift, 1907–1913," *Tennessee Historical Quarterly* 54 (Spring 1995): 58.

15. *National Baptist Union*, October 24, 1908, and December 19, 1908.

16. Quoted in Samuel Shannon, "Tennessee," in Lewis Suggs, *The Black Press in the South, 1865–1979* (Westport, CT: Greenwood Press, 1983), 332.

17. *National Baptist Union Review*, June 20, 1908.

18. Ibid., July 28, 1917.

19. Lovett, *A Black Man's Dream*, 142 and 162.

Suggested Readings

A detailed account of Boyd's life can be found in Bobby L. Lovett, *A Black Man's Dream: The First 100 Years. Richard Henry Boyd and the National Baptist Publishing Board* (Jacksonville, FL: Mega Corporation, 1993). For a discussion of black life in Jim Crow Tennessee, see Bobby L. Lovett, *The African-American History of Nashville, Tennessee, 1780–1930: Elites and Dilemmas* (Fayetteville: University of Arkansas Press, 1999); Lester C. Lamon, *Black Tennesseans, 1900–1930* (Knoxville: University of Tennessee Press, 1977), 12–14, 184–85; and Faye Wellborn Robbins, "A World-Within-a-World: Black Nashville, 1880–1915" (Ph.D. diss., University of Arkansas, 1980), 249–50. For information on black religious life and the history of black Baptists see James Melvin Washington, *Frustrated Fellowship: The Black Baptist Quest for Social Power* (Macon, GA: Mercer University Press, 1987), and Paul Harvey, *Redeeming the South: Religious Cultures and Racial Identities among Southern Baptists, 1865–1925* (Chapel Hill: University of North Carolina Press, 1997).

5

Anna Julia Cooper
Educator, Clubwoman, and Feminist

Jacqueline M. Moore

Born into slavery shortly before the outbreak of the Civil War, Anna Julia Cooper lived for more than a century to witness the emergence of the modern civil rights movement. Coming of age in the post-Civil War South, she was free, yet as an African American and a woman she lived with the dual burden of racism and sexism. Determined to challenge both, Cooper became an outspoken proponent of racial and gender equality. Jacqueline Moore traces Cooper's long life and her struggle for a society without racial and gender barriers.

Growing up in the late nineteenth century, Cooper, like many former slaves, embraced education as the means to improve herself and her status in society. She attended a freedmen's school, graduated from Oberlin College in Ohio, and eventually earned a Ph.D. from the Sorbonne in Paris. Her pursuit of education, however, was not only a search for personal fulfillment. Education, she believed, could help her race achieve equality. Thus, she chose a lifelong career in teaching.

Cooper spent much of her professional life in Washington, DC, where she worked as teacher and principal at the Preparatory High School for Colored Youth, later known as M Street and Paul Laurence Dunbar High School. Under her leadership the school gained a national reputation for academic excellence. Insisting that blacks should pursue an education based on their ability without being limited by racial barriers, Cooper succeeded in placing many of her students at prestigious universities,

Likewise, Cooper challenged gender barriers. The struggle for racial equality, she reminded black men, would have to include demands for gender equality. As an ardent supporter of women's suffrage, Cooper also reminded white women to consider the unique situation of black women who were fighting against both gender and racial discrimination.

Cooper's concerns about the status of black women in American society also led to her involvement in the women's club movement. She immersed herself in the Colored Woman's League, the National Association of Colored Women's Clubs, and the "Colored" Young Women's Christian Association, which provided a variety of social services to black women who had moved to cities during the industrial revolution of the late nineteenth century. Cooper's lifelong struggle to end racial as well as gender discrimination exemplifies the plight of all black women who carry the twin burdens of racism and sexism.

In the course of Anna Julia Cooper's life she fought continuously for the rights of African Americans to equal treatment, particularly for the rights of black women. At times teacher, school principal, graduate student, and university president, she led a life that revolved around education and the ways in which it could serve to uplift the race. Born a slave, Cooper became, at the age of sixty-five, only the fourth African American woman to obtain a Ph.D.[1] With her charitable work she typified a generation of black middle-class women who came to prominence at the turn of the century and began the clubwomen's movement. As lecturer and representative of black women at major national and international conferences, woman's editor, and author, Cooper took every chance she could to speak out for equal rights for women. In the course of her struggles to champion the rights of African Americans, she faced controversy and opposition from both whites and blacks and remained as outspoken as ever.

Anna Julia Haywood was born on August 10, 1858, in Raleigh, North Carolina, the daughter of Hannah Stanley, a slave, and the property of George Washington Haywood. Although he never acknowledged the fact, Haywood was most likely her father. Haywood and his family owned a large number of slaves, 271 according to one census, but because he lived in the city and not on a plantation he did not work all the slaves himself; rather, he hired them out to other families in the city. At the time of Anna's birth, her mother was working as a nurse to a prominent Raleigh attorney, and her two older brothers worked in other businesses for the Haywoods. As a child, Anna never really had a father figure or a stable family life. Fifty years later, in response to a survey of black college graduates, she wrote of her parents: "I owe nothing to my white father beyond the initial act of procreation. My mother's self-sacrificing toil to give me advantages she had never enjoyed is worthy of the highest praise and undying gratitude."[2] It was probably this self-sacrifice that demonstrated to Anna the strength of black women.

Although it was not uncommon for masters to free slaves with whom they had borne children, or to free the children themselves, Anna and her mother did not become free until the Thirteenth Amendment abolished slavery in 1865. As freedpersons in a major southern city, Anna and her family took advantage of charitable endeavors that white philanthropists set up to help former slaves. During Reconstruction many white and black northerners organized within their churches to do missionary work among freedpersons. They raised money from northern businessmen to subsidize schools in the South as well as colleges and universities that would admit black students. Howard University in Washington, DC, and Fisk University in Nashville were products of such philanthropy.

Courtesy of the Moorland-Spingarn Research Center, Washington, DC

In Raleigh, members of the Episcopal church helped to establish St. Augustine's Normal School and Collegiate Institute, a school for African Americans designed to train teachers for the freedpersons. Since Anna and her mother attended the local Episcopal church they were able to enroll Anna in the school at the age of nine. Anna excelled at St. Augustine's where she was a student for the next ten years. She demanded a rigorous course of study and became increasingly frustrated when the school seemed to favor the male students over the female students who were studying to become teachers. She lodged a formal protest with school officials after the faculty told her she could not take a Greek course because it was reserved for male theology students. As a result of her protest the school allowed Anna to enroll in the Greek class. She left

St. Augustine's in 1877 primarily because she felt that it had little more to offer her but also because she married a fellow student and teacher of Greek, George A. C. Cooper, in that year.

Cooper, a native of Nassau, British West Indies, was one of the school's favored theology students and was training to become an Episcopal priest. Nearly fourteen years Anna's senior, George shared her convictions that education provided the key to racial uplift and that teaching was a noble cause. He and Anna both worked in the community in local charities while pursuing their studies. On June 21, 1877, the couple married, and in July 1879, George became a priest. On September 27, 1879, two months after George was ordained and two years after he and Anna married, George died from the stress of overwork, leaving Anna a widow at the age of twenty-one. There is next to no surviving record of their relationship to tell us of the emotional effect that George's death had on her, but Anna J. Cooper never remarried. Ironically, her status as a widow enabled her to continue a career in education. Most school districts forced women to retire at marriage, deeming it unsuitable for a wife to work. As a widow, however, Cooper could do so and still appear respectable by Victorian standards of propriety.

After George's death it was to this career that Cooper turned in earnest. She spent two years teaching in various Raleigh schools, including St. Augustine's, and finally saved up enough money to pay for room and board to go to college. In 1881 she enrolled in Oberlin College in northeastern Ohio. Oberlin was one of the few northern colleges that had accepted blacks before the Civil War, and it had the reputation of strong involvement with the abolitionist movement. It was also one of the first colleges to admit black women to its regular "Gentlemen's" course, and in 1862 graduated Mary Jane Patterson, the first black woman to receive a B.A. degree from an accredited college. Like Cooper, Patterson was from Raleigh, and although it is uncertain if they knew one another while living in the South, they both ended up teaching in the Washington, DC, school district, and it is likely that Patterson blazed the trail for Cooper to follow.

Cooper entered Oberlin with two other black women students, Ida A. Gibbs and Mary Eliza Church, the daughter of Robert R. Church of Memphis, one of the first African American millionaires. Gibbs and Church had attended Oberlin's preparatory school and roomed together throughout their years at the college. Cooper was twenty-three and a widow at the time she arrived and did not fit in easily with the other students. She roomed with a family off campus and concentrated almost entirely on her studies. Yet the paths of these three women would cross repeatedly throughout their lifetimes.

In 1884, Cooper, Gibbs, and Church graduated with B.A. degrees and all three went into teaching. In fact, teaching was one of the few professions considered respectable for women to enter and one of the few fields in which women could gain some independence. Teachers were in high demand in the black community, particularly in the South where blacks of all ages were rushing to gain a basic education denied them under slavery. The black community accorded high social status to teachers who, they understood, were helping the next generation of African Americans to succeed where their parents could not. Like many other black teachers, Cooper saw teaching as her duty to her race.

In 1884, Cooper accepted a position teaching at Wilberforce College in Ohio, as did Mary Church. After one year, however, family concerns brought Cooper back to St. Augustine's where she taught Latin and Greek for the next two years at a substantially lower salary. Teachers often did not earn high salaries, and many had to teach summer school or night school while others worked as waitresses in summer resorts to make ends meet. Cooper accepted the lower pay because she wanted to be near her mother, who needed her support. Meanwhile, Church and Gibbs went on to live in Washington, DC, where Church began teaching Latin in the Preparatory High School for Colored Youth. Back in Raleigh, Cooper continued the charitable work she had begun with her late husband, George. She started an outreach program from St. Augustine's into the larger community. She established Sunday schools to teach basic literacy as well as provide mission services such as food and clothing for the poor. In 1887, Oberlin College awarded Cooper an M.A. degree for teaching three years at the college level.

By the mid-1880s, Cooper had already begun to take on the second of her careers, perhaps to supplement her income, but also because she had begun to develop strong ideas about education and its importance for African Americans. She began to give public lectures about education for blacks and the achievements of black women. In 1886 she lectured before one of the foremost black intellectuals in the country, the Reverend Alexander Crummell of Washington, DC, arguing that the race could only progress as a whole if black women were lifted from the degradation they had suffered under slavery. Cooper also stressed the special qualities of black women that made them ideal ambassadors for their race. She noted that only a black woman could say: "when and where I enter, in the quiet dignity of my womanhood, . . . then and there the whole *Negro race enters with me*."[3] She made a plea for an end to white exploitation of black women as workers and sexual objects and demanded respect from black men. This early paper reflected her philosophy, which she continued to elaborate in later writings. While in Washington, Cooper also made friendships that would lead her to move to the nation's capital in the following year.

In 1887 the Washington school board wrote to Oberlin requesting recommendations for more graduates to teach in the capital's segregated public schools. Oberlin recommended Cooper, who came to teach Latin at Washington's Preparatory High School for Colored Youth. She was preceded there by fellow Oberlin graduates Ida Gibbs, Mary Church, and Mary Jane Patterson, who had served as the school's principal between 1871 and 1884.

Washington's black high school had a unique history. It had opened in 1870, one year before the white high school in the District, and was the nation's first high school for black youth. The school had more college graduates teaching there than at any other school in the city, black or white. There was a large middle- and upper-class black community in Washington with a long history of supporting education for its children, at first privately, then through the public schools. Black city residents were helped in this endeavor by the fact that three African Americans customarily sat on the city's school board.

Although black teachers received lower salaries than white teachers, compared to other segregated systems the Washington school district paid relatively well. While African Americans resented segregation in public education, they welcomed the opportunity to supervise their schools, which were administered under a black superintendent. Such self-regulation appealed to the black community, which insisted on high standards for its teachers and children. As a result, some of the best-qualified black teachers in the country came to teach in the District's segregated schools, including its black high school, which gained a national reputation for excellence. In 1891 the District's black Preparatory High School moved from its original location in the basement of the Fifteenth Street Presbyterian Church to a new building and became known as the M Street High School. In the course of its history, M Street and its later incarnation, Paul Laurence Dunbar High School, which opened in 1917, graduated some of the most notable African Americans in the country, including Benjamin O. Davis, the first black general; William H. Hastie, the first black federal judge; and Robert C. Weaver, the first black cabinet member.

Cooper fit in well at M Street. She advanced to teaching senior Latin in the same department with Mary Church. By 1899 she was serving as assistant principal under Robert H. Terrell, former Latin teacher and early graduate of the high school and suitor to Mary Church, who ultimately married him in 1891. As assistant principal, Cooper launched a series of weekly talks to instruct female students about the values of personal and social improvement.

In the meantime, Cooper was enhancing her reputation as an educational expert on the lecture circuit and through her publishing activities. In 1890 she had become editor of the Women's Department of a new journal, *The Southland*, which Cooper claimed was the first black magazine in the United States. In the same year the American Conference of Educators, a national black organization, invited Cooper to address its annual meeting on the subject of higher education for women. In her speech she again stressed the importance of women to racial uplift: "The earnest well-trained Christian young woman, as a teacher, as a home-maker, as wife, mother, or silent influence even, is as potent a missionary agency among our people as is the theologian."[4]

In 1892, Cooper published *A Voice from the South by a Black Woman of the South*, a collection of her lectures and essays. The book is now widely recognized as one of the first theoretical statements of the black feminist position. The essays challenged black men to pay more attention to the needs of black women in the struggle for racial equality and urged white women to consider the plight of black women in their struggle for gender equality. The book also addressed the larger context of race relations and the concerns of the black community as a whole.

A Voice from the South received strong positive reviews in the black press and sympathetic white press, and earned Cooper a national reputation as a black intellectual and spokesperson for black women. In 1893, Cooper was one of the prominent black educators and intellectuals invited to speak, along with educators Booker T. Washington and W. E. B. Du Bois and clergyman Francis Grimké, at the first annual Hampton Conference. Held at Hampton Institute in Virginia, an industrial training school for blacks, these conferences discussed whether African Americans should pursue vocational training or liberal arts in their struggle for racial uplift. Cooper, asserting that "we can't all be professional people," supported industrial education, which emphasized training students for practical work such as domestic service along with providing the basic Three Rs.[5] Ironically it would later be Cooper's championing of classical education that generated great controversy.

In 1893 the World's Congress of Representative Women, held in conjunction with the Columbia Exposition in Chicago, invited Cooper to be one of three black women, along with clubwomen Fannie Barrier Williams and Fannie Jackson Coppin, to address the assembly. The women all rose to the challenge and received high praise for their efforts. In 1900, Cooper achieved similar intellectual recognition on an international level. That year she was one of only two black women to speak for African Americans at the Pan-African Congress in London. While in Europe she made her first visit to France to see the Paris Exhibition, where she was gratified to see on display at the "Negro Exhibit" a scale model of M Street High School as a symbol of black educational excellence. Cooper continued to write essays and lecture on the rights of black women through the 1920s. Thereafter, she turned to academic reflections on race issues, concentrating largely on education and black history. In her personal and professional life, however, Cooper was perpetually outspoken as a feminist and ever quick to challenge gender discrimination.

While Cooper was building her teaching career and intellectual reputation, she was also heavily involved in community work and the women's club movement. Just as Cooper believed that it was her duty to teach, so did she believe that it was her duty to help those less fortunate than herself. These beliefs typified those of an entire generation of black middle-class women who joined together in ceaseless efforts to uplift the race as they improved their own lives. Inspired by their churches and aided by white philanthropists, these women first used their organizational skills to help the freed slaves in the South. By the late 1800s they had created a national network of women's clubs dedicated to charity work, particularly focusing on the plight of African Americans in the new urban slums that had emerged as a result of industrialization. Similar to white women who became involved in charitable work, black women used their immense talents to better the lives of black urban residents.

The efforts of black women's clubs were important, because by the late 1890s white charities were no longer willing to work with poor blacks. This attitude reflected a rise in racism that had led to racial segregation in the South. Pseudoscientific theories produced at white southern universities by racist scholars claimed that blacks were not capable of equal mental activity, that they were not able to progress beyond the level of menial workers, and that any attempts to improve their lot were pointless. Faced with such arguments, many white charity workers, who had never really embraced working with poor blacks, welcomed the excuse to concentrate on poor whites instead. In such an environment the work of the black women's club movement became vitally important in obtaining social services for impoverished blacks.

Cooper was actively involved in the creation of a settlement house in the poor black neighborhoods in Washington, DC. Moreover, she was instrumental in launching the National Association of Colored Women (NACW), which established the first national network of black clubwomen. As the nineteenth century came to a close, black women increasingly found themselves the objects of racist attacks, particularly aimed at their moral character. White scholars claiming to be experts on racial matters asserted that black women were promiscuous and blamed sexual relationships between masters and slaves on this alleged promiscuity. Cooper's support of women's rights was in part a response to these growing attacks on the character of black women. In Washington, clubwomen such as Cooper and Mary Church Terrell joined in 1892 to create the Colored Woman's League, an organization that promoted education and uplift for black women and sought to coordinate women's reform efforts in the District. The League soon decided to take on affiliates nationwide, and in 1896 it merged with a similar group of women from Boston to create the NACW. The organization chose as its motto "Lifting As We Climb," which demonstrated that these women envisioned their charitable work as part of their own identity and a duty to the less fortunate members of their race. Cooper remained active with the organization and Terrell became the group's first president.

Cooper was also one of the first lifetime members of the "Colored" Young Women's Christian Association (YWCA) in the District, named for Phillis Wheatley, an eighteenth-century black poet. The story of the Wheatley YWCA is interesting. Organized in 1905, before the city's white branch was established, the Wheatley YWCA should have become the central branch for the District. White women, however, refused to subordinate themselves to black women, and the Wheatley never affiliated with the national YWCA. Its organizers, who included Cooper, Terrell, and black charity worker Mary Cromwell, were amazing workers and fund raisers. Initially occupying merely one floor of the Miner Institute, the former home of a teacher training school, the Wheatley had come to occupy the entire building within three years. Over the next four years the women purchased their own building and raised enough money to pay off the mortgage. The Wheatley offered speakers, sewing lessons, a free library, and a dormitory for newcomers to the city and provided positive role models for young black girls. Cooper served as chair of Girls' Programs and helped to organize the first group of Camp Fire Girls. During World War I she worked with the YWCA's War Work Council, providing travelers' aid to black soldiers in transit.

While Cooper remained active in her charitable activities, the first decades of the twentieth century also brought her great personal turmoil. During that time she became involved in a national controversy over education that exploded between Booker T. Washington and W. E. B. Du Bois. In 1903, Du Bois published *The Souls of Black Folk*, an analysis of race relations and the problems African Americans faced in the United States. In the book he attacked Washington, who advocated that industrial education was the key to racial uplift. Du Bois argued that vocational training would keep blacks in inferior positions, doing manual labor. Instead, he urged blacks to focus on training a "Talented Tenth" who would become teachers, doctors, lawyers, and other professionals, and who, after having achieved positions of importance, could then uplift the rest of the race. Du Bois angered many whites with his outspoken demand for equal rights and an end to segregation. These people preferred Booker T. Washington's gradualist approach and his public insistence that if blacks could attain economic self-sufficiency, they did not need to mingle socially with whites. Washington had used his gradualist rhetoric to gain the confidence of many white philanthropists and politicians, including President Theodore Roosevelt, who consulted him regularly about black political appointments. Washington, as a result, was probably the most powerful black man in the country, and many African Americans owed their livelihood to his influence. He did not take Du Bois's challenge lightly and used all of his influence to try to defeat Du Bois and his allies.

Cooper, in fact, had been a strong supporter of industrial education and Booker T. Washington. Yet she also shared Du Bois's belief that those blacks who were capable of succeeding in higher education should not face any racial barriers. In 1901 she became principal of M Street High School, an institution that was committed to educational excellence and whose students were children of the "Talented Tenth" whom Du Bois had championed. She immediately began to work on improving opportunities for her students, including ensuring that they would be accepted directly into northern colleges rather than be required to attend an additional preparatory school prior to admission. Under her administration, students gained entrance to Harvard, Dartmouth, Princeton, and other prestigious universities.

Such success for a "colored" school in the segregated city of Washington was certain to bring out racist opposition. In 1900 the District's black schools had suffered a blow to their independence. That year the city reorganized its school board, placing the black and white schools under separate assistant superintendents who answered to a white superintendent of schools. To make matters worse, the city's black and white high schools now came under the control of a white director, forcing Cooper to answer directly to a white supervisor. Not surprisingly, the white administration favored an industrial curriculum for the black schools, and Cooper's efforts to maintain a classical curriculum at M Street struck the white administrators and members of the school board as, at best, undesirable.

Cooper further agitated the white administrators in the winter of 1902–1903 when she invited W. E. B. Du Bois to speak at M Street on the importance of maintaining high standards in black education and resisting industrializing of the curriculum. By taking such action, Cooper also antagonized many people in the District's black community who owed their political appointments or jobs in various government departments to Booker T. Washington's influence. One such antagonist was Robert H. Terrell, who, as a result of Washington's recommendation, had been appointed the first black municipal judge in the District. His wife, Mary Church Terrell, would soon become one of the three black members of the city's school board. With such powerful opposition, it was inevitable that Cooper would face a challenge to her authority.

In 1904 the white director of high schools, Percy M. Hughes, accused Cooper of insubordination for seeking college scholarships for M Street students who he claimed were ineligible. He also recommended that M Street offer more industrial education classes so that its students could learn the "dignity of labor" and be "better educated men and women and therefore better fitted to win out in life's battle if properly trained in the use of tools as well as books."[6] In addition, Hughes accused Cooper of lack of discipline and inefficient management. M Street students, he stated, were performing poorly because Cooper was running the school without regard to the needs of its students or teachers. The House of Representatives investigated the charges and exonerated Cooper in 1905. During the investigation, which lasted one year, the school board did whatever it could to prevent Cooper from defending herself, including forcing her and her supporters to wait in a hallway during a board meeting until after midnight, before allowing her to state her case.

In 1906 the District commissioners reorganized the school district again, in the process appointing two Booker T. Washington allies, including Mary Church Terrell, to the school board. In the wake of the reorganization, the school board took the position that it was within its power not to reappoint teachers and administrators who had received poor performance evaluations. Invoking its power, the board refused to reappoint fifty teachers and four principals, among them Cooper and her foster son. The four principals and teachers engaged legal representation to challenge the board's authority and were advised to act as if they still held their positions. As a result, Cooper showed up for work at M Street when school began in September 1906, only to be turned away by a police officer. The board ultimately reappointed most of the teachers and principals, except Cooper and her foster son, whom they dismissed officially in late September. Cooper was replaced with a Booker T. Washington ally.

Cooper suffered defeat largely because the Washington/Du Bois controversy had divided the black community, allowing white administrators to take advantage of the situation and assert control over the black schools. Cooper was forever embittered by the experience and, not surprisingly, hostile toward Terrell, who had failed to defend her before the board. Cooper and Terrell had been acquaintances for most of their adult lives, but they had never been close friends. Terrell knew that her husband owed his position as the District's first black municipal judge to Booker T. Washington's influence. Thus, she could not side with Cooper, who appeared to be supporting Du Bois. Cooper, rather than accept a position as principal of an elementary school, which the board half-heartedly offered her as compensation, decided to teach Greek and Latin at Lincoln Institute in Jefferson City, Missouri. She later remarked that she "suffer[ed] to this day the punishment of the damned from both the white masters & the colored understrappers."[7]

Cooper stayed in Missouri for four years but ultimately missed Washington and her friends and returned there in 1910, once again to teach Latin at M Street. The controversy never left her, however, and on several occasions when she was due for promotions or other considerations, the school administration placed barriers in her way. Beginning in 1911, Cooper traveled to France in the summers and took courses in

French. In 1914 she enrolled as a doctoral student at Columbia University. Nonetheless, Cooper never completed her Ph.D. at Columbia because she was unable to fulfill the university's one-year residency requirement. She could not obtain a leave of absence from her teaching job at M Street and had family responsibilities that kept her at home.

In 1915 she had become the foster mother to five children, aged six months to twelve years, when their mother, Cooper's niece, died. With no children of her own, Cooper thrived on caring for her new family. She purchased a house in Washington that required many repairs and began the process of creating a true home for herself and her family. With these new responsibilities, Cooper found little time to devote to her studies, and it was not until the 1920s that she once again turned toward her goal of completing her doctorate.

Faced with the barrier of a year's residency at Columbia, Cooper decided to transfer to a school that required a shorter stay. The Sorbonne, the University of Paris, where she had taken summer courses, offered the same degree but required only a fifty-day residency. Cooper had to retake some courses in order to be admitted but became an official doctoral candidate in 1923. She began work in earnest on her dissertation, an examination of French attitudes toward slavery between 1789 and 1848. By 1924, Cooper had completed all requirements except the residency. She applied several times for a leave of absence from teaching but was denied, perhaps as a result of lingering hostilities. Believing she had received permission, however, she went to France only to have a friend cable her that she was in danger of losing her job if she did not return within sixty days. She completed her residency and returned five minutes before classes started on the sixtieth day. She finished her dissertation in an alcove at the Library of Congress and again could not get permission to return to France to defend it. Finally, in March 1925, at the age of sixty-five, Cooper went to Paris during her spring vacation and defended her dissertation, returning to the United States as the fourth African American woman to receive a Ph.D. In December 1925, Cooper officially received her degree in a ceremony at Howard University, since she was unable to return to the Sorbonne.

Cooper's last years of teaching were not without continued controversy. Despite her academic accomplishments and obvious dedication to her work, she was denied a final promotion, which would have made a substantial difference in the amount of her retirement benefits. Her application for promotion was rejected on the basis of poor examination results, which may have been due to her taking extra time away from the written exam during the lunch break in order to find a restaurant that served African Americans. Despite claims that her examination results were insufficient to warrant a promotion, officials granted promotions to those whose scores were lower than hers.

When Dr. Cooper retired from teaching in 1930, she had served over forty years in the District schools. She was not idle in her retirement, however. She continued to publish essays on race topics and wrote a brief memoir of her time at the Sorbonne. Yet she devoted most of her energies to a new educational endeavor, serving as president of Frelinghuysen University. Established in 1906, Frelinghuysen was designed as a school for working blacks who could not attend traditional daytime classes and offered both academic and professional courses. Unfortunately, at the time Cooper became president of Frelinghuysen in 1930, the school was experiencing numerous problems. With no central campus, classes met in various homes and businesses around the city. Its teachers received no pay except from tuition, which, because of the economic status of the students, was very little. Moreover, the professional branches wanted to dissociate from the main school. Cooper, trying to save expenses, moved some of the academic branches of the school into her own home, rent free. In reality, Cooper was fighting a losing battle with finances. In 1937, at age seventy-nine, she applied for a job with the Works Progress Administration, one of the New Deal agencies established by President Franklin D. Roosevelt, hoping to use the income for the school. She was, however, turned down, probably because of her age. In the same year the school lost its accreditation. In 1940, Cooper stepped down as president to become registrar and in an early version of her will left her house for the school's use. Despite Cooper's best efforts, by the late 1940s lack of students and funding forced Frelinghuysen to close.

Cooper lived to witness the emergence of the modern civil rights movement but died in February 1964 at the age of 105. She was buried in Raleigh, North Carolina, after a brief service at St. Augustine's College where she had begun her formal education. Few people can say they dedicated nearly a century to the cause of education, but Anna Julia Cooper left such a legacy. She was an outspoken proponent of black rights and an uncompromising challenger of discrimination. She was an early advocate of black feminism and a tireless worker on behalf of members of her race who were less fortunate than herself. Educator, clubwoman, and feminist, Cooper was in many ways a most remarkable woman, yet she was also typical of an entire generation of black middle-class women who together accomplished a great deal for racial uplift.

Notes

1. The previous three women were Georgiana Rose Simpson and Eva B. Sykes, both of whom taught at M Street High School; and Sadie Tanner Alexander, who attended M Street as a student. Anna Julia Cooper, *A Voice from the South by a Black Woman of the South* (New York: Oxford University Press, 1988), xxxix n.

2. "Questionnaire Survey of Negro College Graduates" [1932], folder 1, box 1, Anna Julia Cooper Papers, Moorland-Spingarn Research Center, Howard University, Washington, DC.

3. Anna J. Cooper, "Womanhood: A Vital Element in the Regeneration and Progress of a Race," in Charles Lemert and Esme Bhan, eds., *The Voice of Anna Julia Cooper* (Lanham, MD: Rowman and Littlefield, 1998), 63.

4. Cooper, "The Higher Education of Women," in *The Voice of Anna Julia Cooper*, 87.

5. Quoted in Louise Daniel Hutchinson, *Anna J. Cooper, A Voice from the South* (Washington, DC: Smithsonian Institution Press, 1981), 61.

6. Report of the Board of Education, 1903–04, in U.S. Congress, *Annual Report of the Commissioners of the District of Columbia* (Washington, DC: Government Printing Office, 1904), 187–88.

7. "Survey of Negro College Graduates."

Suggested Readings

The most complete published biography of Cooper is Louise Daniel Hutchinson, *Anna J. Cooper, A Voice from the South* (Washington, DC: Smithsonian Institution Press, 1981), and the most comprehensive collection of her writings along with analysis of her philosophy is Charles Lemert and Esme Bhan, eds., *The Voice of Anna Julia Cooper* (Lanham, MD: Rowman and Littlefield, 1998). The Schomburg Center for Research in Black Culture, New York Public Library, has reissued as part of its series on nineteenth-century black women Cooper's *A Voice from the South by a Black Woman of the South* (New York: Oxford University Press, 1988), which includes a good analytical essay on Cooper and her life by Mary Helen Washington. For a more expanded discussion of the M Street controversy and a general description of black life in Washington at the turn of the twentieth century, see Jacqueline M. Moore, *Leading the Race: The Transformation of the Black Elite in the Nation's Capital, 1880–1920* (Charlottesville: The University Press of Virginia, 1999). For more on the Washington-Du Bois debate, see Louis R. Harlan, *Booker T. Washington: The Wizard of Tuskegee, 1901–1915* (New York: Oxford University Press, 1983); and David Levering Lewis, *W. E. B. Du Bois: A Biography of a Race, 1868–1919* (New York: Henry Holt and Company, 1993).

In recent years there has been much new scholarship on the clubwomen's movement including Dorothy Salem, *To Better Our World: Black Women in Organized Reform, 1890–1920* (Brooklyn, NY: Carlson Publishing, 1990), and Evelyn Brooks Higginbotham, *Righteous Discontent: The Women's Movement in the Black Baptist Church, 1880–1920* (Cambridge, MA: Harvard University Press, 1993).

6

Noble Drew Ali
Popular Religion in the Promised Land

A. J. Scopino Jr.

Since the days of slavery, black southerners had looked to the North as the "Promised Land"—the land of freedom and opportunity. In the decades following the Civil War, however, only a few of them made the move to the North. While many black southerners were anxious to abandon the segregation, racial violence, and poverty that characterized their lives in the Jim Crow South, they had no money to pay for the move. That changed when World War I created a labor shortage in the industrial centers of the North. The war triggered an increase in defense production but also reduced the size of the work force, as the number of immigrants dropped and the U.S. Army drafted millions of men for military service. Northern industries now looked elsewhere to replenish their workforce and sent labor recruiters, armed with railroad tickets and work contracts, to the South. The promise of employment and hope for a better future attracted thousands of rural black southerners and set into motion the Great Migration. Between 1910 and 1930 an estimated 1.5 to 2 million blacks left the cotton fields of the South and headed for the factories of the North.

As black migrants flocked to the "Promised Land," they soon discovered that the cities of the North did not greet them with open arms. White fears of labor competition sparked race riots, and housing conditions for African Americans deteriorated as a result of the influx of the newcomers. The black migrants, new to city life and removed from their familiar surroundings, felt a sense of alienation and disillusionment. Searching for meaning, comfort, and solace, many of the migrants turned to the black churches. Others sought spiritual, emotional, and psychological support from the large number of black religious groups that emerged in the urban ghettos of the North.

Timothy Drew's Moorish Science Temple of America, founded in 1913, was one of the many groups that appealed to the displaced black migrants. Drew, who had migrated from North Carolina to New Jersey, rejected Christianity as the white man's religion. He fashioned a distinct African American religion that combined elements of orthodox Islam, Orientalism, and black nationalism with the symbolism and rituals of Freemasonry. A. J. Scopino Jr. traces the origins of Drew's religious philosophy and explains its popularity, particularly among urban blacks. By 1929, the year Drew died, Moorish Science had attracted a following of 30,000 members, and it continued to flourish even after the prophet's death. While Moorish Science, like other alternative black religions, has often been dismissed as an escapist cult or sect, Scopino demonstrates that it served an important purpose. It provided psychological sustenance for those who were adrift in the "Promised Land" by encouraging them to create a world of their own—a world that was not defined by white society. Its emphasis on racial identity and consciousness also paved the way for other separatist groups that fused religion with black nationalism, such as the Nation of Islam.

Noble Drew Ali was born Timothy Drew in North Carolina in 1886. He was the son of former slaves, but little else is known about his early life. In 1913, Drew founded the Moorish Science Temple of America, a curious brand of Islam that contained elements of Orientalism, Freemasonry, Christianity, orthodox Islam, and black nationalism. The circumstances leading to Drew's knowledge of Islam are shrouded in myth and legend. One account explains that in the 1880s the Drew family moved to Newark, New Jersey, where Timothy had the good fortune to study Islam with the visiting scholar Jamal al-Din al-Afghani (1838–1897). Another story holds that he acquired the knowledge while employed as a traveling magician. A still more imaginative, but unlikely, tale is that he was introduced to Eastern religions while serving as a merchant seaman sometime before 1912. On one of his journeys in Egypt, the sixteen-year-old seaman was blindfolded by a high priest of an ancient cult, who abandoned him in the pyramid of Cheops. Drew's ability to find his way out earned him the respect of the priest, who conferred on him the name Sharif (Noble) Abdul Ali. Further travels supposedly took him to the Middle East where he increased his knowledge of Islam.[1]

More trustworthy evidence suggests that Drew's contact with Islam was in closer proximity to his birthplace in North Carolina. Recently scholars have documented that remnants of African culture, as well as some elements of orthodox Islam, survived not only the transatlantic journey from Africa to the New World but also the transition from slavery to freedom. In the Carolinas and Georgia, particularly the coastal Sea Islands, which had few white residents but large and relatively isolated slave populations, scholars have found evidence for the survival of some aspects of African culture and religion well into the nineteenth century. This evidence includes Muslim names and artistic expressions along with Arabic writing.[2] Muslim slaves, these scholars argue, perpetuated their faith in spite of Christianizing efforts by masters and missionaries. Although Islam may not have survived as a coherent system of faith, its elements persisted. Drew matured at a time when the "children and grandchildren of these earlier Muslims were, at the very least, highly cognizant of their Islamic heritage."[3] Therefore, it is probable that Drew obtained his most elementary knowledge of Islam in familiar surroundings.

Courtesy of the Moorish Science Temple of America Photograph Collection, Photographs and Prints Division, Schomburg Center for Research in Black Culture, The New York Public Library, Astor, Lenox and Tilden Foundations

Autobiographies, diary entries, slave narratives, Arabic documents, and other writings suggest that some measure of Islam may have been more commonplace among southern blacks than once believed. One of the most informative and revealing documents is the *Autobiography* of Umar Ibn Said, written in Arabic and discovered in 1831 in Fayetteville, North Carolina—Drew's home state. Moreover, nineteenth-century travel accounts tell of encounters with African Muslim slaves throughout the South. Other sources indicate that Christian masters provided Korans for Muslim slaves as late as the 1830s. In addition, Africans, both free and nonfree, who served as sailors on crews of slave ships often remained in contact, however limited, with African Islam. Finally, although interviews conducted with former slaves during the 1930s suggest the incorporation of Christian elements into Muslim beliefs, many black American and Caribbean cults continue to use practices widespread in popular Islam, including herbal medicine, amulets, animal sacrifices, prayers, and incantations.[4] In light of these findings it is likely that Drew acquired his first knowledge of Islam while growing up in the South.

When Drew established Moorish Science in the urban North, his first audiences were black migrants from the South. Southern blacks began migrating to the cities of the North in the late nineteenth and early twentieth centuries. Initially the number of migrants was relatively small, since most black southerners lacked the financial resources to move to the North. This situation changed, however, with the outbreak of World War I in 1914. When the European nations mobilized for war, their increased demands for manufactured goods triggered an economic boom in the United States. Although the American government proclaimed neutrality, the nation's industries were eager to meet the European demands. Increased production in the industrial centers of the North created new employment opportunities that attracted an ever-growing number of black migrants.

African Americans were eager to flee the Jim Crow South, where economic opportunities were limited. Most southern blacks labored as sharecroppers or tenants and were thus locked into a state of economic dependency. "They did the dirty work of southern society, and most lived on the edge of poverty."[5] At the same time, white southerners disfranchised blacks through intimidation, the poll tax, the literacy test, and the "grandfather clause." The Supreme Court's decision in *Plessy v. Ferguson* (1896), upholding the "separate-but-equal" doctrine, further supported on the national level what already had become law throughout the southern states. Hard pressed politically and economically, southern blacks were also threatened with physical violence at the least provocation. After the 1890s lynching figures rose dramatically in the South, where 90 percent of the victims were people of color. Seeking to escape the racially oppressive climate of the South and attracted by employment in the North, African Americans headed for the "Promised Land."

In 1917, when the United States entered World War I and drafted millions of men into military service, the demand for labor became acute. Agents for northern industries offered incentives to black workers and paid the fare for many rural southerners willing to go North. Black newspapers, like the *Chicago Defender*, encouraged the exodus of African Americans by printing train schedules, advertising transportation discounts, and providing information on jobs and housing.

Although economic opportunities and the promise of a better future attracted many rural migrants to the northern cities, urban life in the North presented its own challenges. Racism, though more subtle than in the South, forced the migrants to settle in urban ghettos. The small number of black northerners who already resided in the ghettos observed the arrival of the rural southern migrants with some concern. The black neighborhoods were unable to absorb the large influx of new residents, which created overcrowding, health and sanitation problems, and a shortage of recreational facilities. Afraid that the physical deterioration of the black ghettos would reflect poorly on all members of the race, some black northerners rushed to assist the migrants, while others distanced themselves from the rural newcomers.

As black migrants left the rural farmsteads and cities of the South, urban centers in the North became "the critical arena" in the struggle for a better life.[6] The Great Migration was not only a tremendous demographic watershed for blacks in American history but also affected their religious life. African American religious bodies assumed a central role in interpreting the new experience. Following their congregants to the urban North, transplanted churches from the South helped to cushion the migrants' transition from rural southern to urban northern life. The church, as the primary social institution in black life, now shouldered the burden of providing meaning, comfort, and solace to a displaced population. As a result of the changes, the religious life of blacks became more diversified and complex.

In addition, numerous new religious groups emerged that catered to the spiritual and psychological needs of the migrants. These new "black gods of the metropolis," according to sociologist Arthur Huff Fauset, offered social panaceas and religious salvation to the new urban dwellers.[7]

Among these groups, often derisively labeled "cults" and "sects," were Father Divine's Peace Mission movement, Daddy Grace's United House of Prayer for All, the followers of the Prophet F. S. Cherry, and Black Jews as well as Pentecostal churches, faith healers, and spiritualist enclaves. Competing with mainline Christian denominations such as the Baptists, Methodists, and Episcopalians, these rival religions glutted the black ghettos of the urban North in the first half of the twentieth century. Several Islamic groups, including Timothy Drew's Moorish Science Temple of America, also vied for converts.

In 1913, at age twenty-seven, Drew took his unique brand of Islam to Newark, New Jersey. Drew's message was foreign to most black migrants from the South, but soon he attracted a large following. Shrewd and capable of mastering an audience, Drew, who now referred to himself as Noble Drew Ali, proclaimed himself to be the last prophet of Islam. This designation earned him the admiration and awe of his urban converts but also initiated charges of heresy from the followers of orthodox Islam. In traditional Islam, Mohammed is held to be the last prophet. Drew Ali claimed that he had been prepared by Allah to redeem the "Asiatic" peoples of North America, as he referred to African Americans, from their sinful ways.[8] Blacks in North America, Ali announced, were really descendants of the ancient Moabites who had made their way to Africa, specifically Morocco. From there, they were taken into slavery by whites and, as a result, the "Moors" were left without a homeland and nationality. To add luster to these "revelations," Ali issued nationality cards to his followers, proclaiming their new Moorish identity. Converts indicated their transformation by adding the suffix "Bey" or "El" to their surnames.

In 1928, Drew Ali provided his followers with sacred scripture called the *Holy Koran of the Moorish Science Temple of America*, a work not to be confused with the Koran of traditional Islam. The *Holy Koran* was a slender volume of sixty-four pages, the first half of which was copied, with very minor alterations, from Levi H. Dowling's *The Aquarian Gospel of Jesus Christ*. Published in 1908, Dowling's work recounted the travels of Jesus Christ in India. The remainder of the *Holy Koran* discussed ethical concerns, Ali's role as prophet, the prediction of his coming by "Back to Africa" promoter Marcus Garvey, and the Asiatic origins of America's black population.

The *Holy Koran* also served as a catechism for temple members, prescribing dietary guidelines and a specific dress code. The eating of pork and certain other foods was proscribed. Men were required to wear the red fez with yellow robes, while women donned headdresses and flowing gowns. The use of cosmetics for women and the shaving of beards for men were banned. Services were conducted in a quiet, subdued manner. Congregants gained entrance to meetings and services by a secret password and signal borrowed from Ali's Masonic background.

The most controversial part of the *Holy Koran* dealt with race. Islam, claimed Noble Drew Ali, was the true religion of the Moors. Christianity was the white man's religion. It was time for the Asiatic peoples or Moors, he announced, to return Christianity to the white man and embrace Islam, their true religion. While Ali was careful to avoid any racist pronouncements, the central position of race in Moorish Science was obvious.

Ali's message appealed to many black migrants, particularly those who had become disillusioned with life in the "Promised Land." The wartime economic boom, which had lured them to the cities of the North, was short lived. When World War I ended in November 1918, black employment opportunities dwindled, and labor competition with white workers increased. Numerous race riots erupted in 1919, further crushing the hopes of African Americans that their home-front support and military participation would help improve race relations. Living in overcrowded urban ghettos and faced with growing job competition and heightened racial tensions, many disillusioned blacks embraced Moorish Science. It provided them with an opportunity to escape, through religious redemption, the abuse and discrimination that they had suffered at the hands of white society. For the first time in their lives, they were presented with something distinctly their own: a religion, a nationality, and a history as a people.

Moreover, in contrast to Christianity, which promised compensation in an afterlife, Moorish Science offered an affirmation of life experiences. It provided the spiritual, social, and psychological backbone for a people caught in a continuing struggle. Moorish Science, for many ghetto residents, was a means of becoming healed and made whole. As African Americans adopted Islam, they became involved in what psychologist Robert W. Crapps has termed a "religion of becoming," a faith that offered hope and affirmation in their lived experiences.[9] For the Moors, Allah was effecting radical changes in their lives. This "religion of becoming" was a means to realize a better life through a faith that concentrated on the here and now. The prophet Ali himself was not a remote entity, but one who was intimate and who spoke the language of a suffering people. Moorish Science allowed its followers to create their environment rather than be subjected to it. It provided tangibles, through inventive fashion in dress, different forms of prayer, elaborate rituals, and social support, that contributed to the well-being of African Americans. While there were many new religions emerging in the northern cities, Moorish Science was visibly and exotically different. It advanced a unique message, a clear promise, and a more meaningful self-understanding that cultivated hope for a displaced and oppressed people.

Noble Drew Ali, after establishing his first Moorish Science Temple in Newark, New Jersey, moved to Chicago in 1925. In the Windy City he appeared in vacant lots and on street corners, introducing his religion to any who would listen. It was not long before Moorish Science had gained a foothold in the cities of the Midwest and other parts of the country. Drew Ali was not only successful at winning converts, but also in amassing a small fortune. Some calculate that he collected $35,000 in one year through the sale of charms, herbal medicines, bath oils, brooms, pajamas, and other Moorish wares. At the time of his death in 1929, there were seventeen temples throughout the country with 30,000 members.[10]

In the spring of 1929, as the organization was enjoying success in Chicago and elsewhere, a peculiar series of events unfolded that threatened to ruin Moorish Science. Apparently the success of the group had ignited internal division. One member, Claude D. Greene, became embroiled in a power struggle with Drew Ali. A Tuskegee graduate, Greene had come to Chicago twenty years earlier and had worked in the city as a chauffeur, interior decorator, and real estate promoter. He was also involved in local politics and ran excursions to southern cities during the summer months. The rift between Drew and Greene erupted in March 1929, when the prophet arrived at the organization's headquarters located at 3140 Indiana Avenue and found his furniture and office equipment removed. Greene, it appeared, had taken charge of the Moors.[11]

In the following weeks the power struggle between Ali and Greene escalated and turned violent. On May 15, 1929, Greene's corpse was discovered at the Moorish headquarters on Indiana Avenue. He had died from gunshot and knife wounds. Allegations surfaced that Drew had called for Greene's death. According to one account, Drew Ali had offered one of his followers, John Small Bey, $1,000 to kill Greene. Even though the prophet was reportedly not in town at the time of the murder, he and a handful of his advisers were arrested.

While the case dragged on, City Coroner Herman Bundesen took charge of the investigation. Frustrated about what the *Chicago Defender* called an "indifferent" investigation conducted by city police, Bundesen directed the probe himself. Rumors of graft, the failure of police in apprehending Moor Ira Johnson Bey, who was wanted by authorities for questioning, and allegations regarding the withholding of vital information alarmed the coroner.[12]

Meanwhile, Moorish Science temples around the country contributed to the defense of the prophet. While incarcerated, Noble Drew Ali sent word to his faithful, stating: "Though I am now in custody for you and the cause, it is all right and it is well for all who still believe in me and my father, God. I have redeemed all of you and you shall be saved, all of you, even with me. I go to bat Monday, May 20, before the Grand Jury. If you are with me, be there. Hold on and keep faith, and great shall be your reward. Remember my laws and love ye one another. Prefer not a stranger to your brother. Love and truth and my peace I leave all."[13] This statement was the prophet's last official proclamation. Awaiting his trial, Drew died mysteriously at his home at 3603 Indiana Avenue, on July 20, 1929. Ali's sudden death, as well as the internal power struggle that had preceded it, gave rise to several rumors. Some of his followers claimed that the prophet had been poisoned, while others held that Drew had died as the result of a police beating while in custody. Still others believed that the supporters of Greene had killed him.

Drew's funeral was elaborate and well attended. "Shrouded with the royal raiment" and encased in a $1,000 metallic casket, the body of Noble Drew Ali lay in state at Frank Edwards's undertaking parlor at 4136 Michigan Avenue for five days. During that period, thousands of people paid their last respects to the prophet. An hour-long funeral service was held at the Pythian Temple on 37th Place and State Street. Ali's lieutenant Charles Kirkman Bey performed an Eastern burial ritual. "Whatever he was saying in connection with this ceremony," claimed a reporter for the *Defender*, "was as foreign to the audience as Caesar is to a fourth grade pupil." Moorish officer William Mealy read the obituary, and representatives from various temples presented resolutions. Aaron Payne, assistant city prosecutor and business manager for the Moorish Science Temple, delivered the principal eulogy. One elderly woman was overheard to have said that since the prophet's work was done, he had laid his head on the lap of one of his successors and "passed out." Some members believed that the spirit of the prophet would enter the body of his successor. The two-mile funeral procession moved south on State Street en route to Burr Oak Cemetery where Ali's body was interred.[14]

Although death silenced the voice of the founder and prophet of the Moorish Science Temple, it did not put to rest the organization's internal power struggle. Nearly two months after Ali's death the Moorish annual convention was held in Chicago. Photographs in local newspapers depicted Moors from temples around the country, bedecked in flowing robes and headdresses and waving American flags. The otherwise quiet event, however, was marred when violence erupted again. This time two policemen and one Moor died. On September 25, 1929, the headlines of the *Chicago Defender* screamed, "Chicago Policeman Slain in Moorish Society Riot," in what the paper called the "bloodiest mission since St. Valentine's day" the same year, when mobsters murdered seven members of a rival gang.[15]

The violence began when Charles Kirkman Bey, Ali's successor in Chicago, was kidnapped and taken to the 4137 South Parkway apartments. This was done supposedly at the behest of Moor Ira Johnson Bey, who sought to obtain important organization documents that he believed to be in the possession of either Kirkman or Aaron Payne. The police cordoned off an entire block on South Parkway and called every squad on the South Side to the scene where an hour-long gun battle ensued between the authorities and the Moorish abductors. Eventually, police hurled tear gas through second-floor apartment windows and gained access. Inside the building a shoot-out cost the lives of one policeman and one Moor. A second policeman died of his wounds the following day. Kirkman Bey was rescued and the abductors eventually brought to justice.[16]

In the aftermath of the bloody encounter, rival Moorish leaders, one even claiming to be Noble Drew Ali reincarnated, collected their followers and retreated to their respective temples. Some scholars suggest that one of Ali's disciples, a man by the name of Wallace D. Fard, began to gather his own following in Detroit. During the 1930s, Fard's group grew, particularly under the leadership of his successor, Elijah Muhammad, and came to be known as the Nation of Islam. Meanwhile, Moorish Science temples throughout the country turned inward and rallied around their various leaders, none of whom was apparently able to replace the charismatic Ali. Moorish Science lost much of its vitality with the death of Ali, but it did not wither and continues to maintain several temples in the United States.

Noble Drew Ali's message appealed largely to the black urban underclass, which had become disillusioned and disenchanted with life in the "Promised Land." Black ghetto residents, caught in the grips of discrimination, displacement, and poverty, embraced Moorish Science because it allowed them to understand themselves and their environment. It encouraged them to create a world of their own and define their identity without the racist limits imposed by white society. Ali's efforts to create a race-based history and identity through myth, legend, lore, and rituals were powerful and imaginative attractions. Laying claim to a distinct and separate heritage engendered at once race consciousness and race pride among his followers. Moreover, the prophet himself, Noble Drew Ali, the son of slave parents, was one of their own. While contemporaries often ridiculed Ali's curious and exotic blend of Islam as escapist, it inspired many African Americans in the first decades of the twentieth century to seek more knowledge about themselves and their race.

Notes

1. Peter Lamborn Wilson, *Sacred Drift: Essays on the Margins of Islam* (San Francisco: City Lights Bookstore, 1993), 16.

2. See Michael A. Gomez, "Muslims in Early America," *Journal of Southern History* 60 (November 1994): 671–710; Allan D. Austin, *African Muslims in Antebellum America: Transatlantic Stories and Spiritual Struggles* (New York: Routledge, 1997); and Sylvaine A. Diouf, *Servants of Allah: African Muslims Enslaved in the Americas* (New York: New York University Press, 1998).

3. Gomez, "Muslims in Early America," 709.

4. See "Omar Ibn Said, A Slave who Wrote an Autobiography in Arabic," *Journal of Negro History* 39 (January 1954): 58–63; "A Trading Trip to Natchez and New Orleans, 1822: Diary of Thomas S. Teas," *Journal of Southern History* 7 (February–November 1941): 388; and Diouf, *Servants of Allah*, 110–16, 188, and 201.

5. Carole Marks, *Farewell—We're Good and Gone: The Great Black Migration* (Bloomington: Indiana University Press, 1989), 61.

6. Milton C. Sernett, *Bound for the Promised Land: African American Religion and the Great Migration* (Durham, NC: Duke University Press, 1997), 3.

7. See Arthur Huff Fauset, *Black Gods of the Metropolis: Negro Religious Cults in the Urban North* (Philadelphia: University of Pennsylvania Press, 1971).

8. *The Holy Koran of the Moorish Science Temple of America* (n.p.: n.p., 1927), 59.

9. Robert W. Crapps, *An Introduction to the Psychology of Religion* (Macon, GA: Mercer University Press, 1986), 311.

10. For the historical background of Moorish Science, see Wilson, *Sacred Drift*; Yvonne Haddad and Jane Idleman Smith, *Mission to America: Five Islamic Sectarian Communities in North America* (Gainesville: University of Florida Press, 1993); C. Eric

Lincoln, *The Black Muslims in America* (Grand Rapids, MI: Wm. B. Eerdmans Publishing Company, 3d edition, 1993); and E. U. Essian-Udom, *Black Nationalism: A Search for an Identity in America* (Chicago: The University of Chicago Press, 1971).

11. *Chicago Defender*, March 23, 1929.
12. Ibid., May 18, 1929.
13. Wilson, *Sacred Drift*, 35.
14. *Chicago Defender*, August 3, 1929.
15. Ibid., October 12, 1929.
16. Ibid.

Suggested Readings

The most comprehensive account of the life of Timothy Drew is Peter Lamborn Wilson, *Sacred Drift: Essays on the Margins of Islam* (San Francisco: City Lights Bookstore, 1993). The history of Moorish Science is recorded in Yvonne Haddad and Jane Idleman Smith, *Mission to America: Five Islamic Sectarian Communities in North America* (Gainesville: The University of Florida Press, 1993), which discusses the scriptures and teachings of the group. Recent scholarship tracing the lasting influences of Islam in America includes Allan D. Austin, *African Muslims in Antebellum America: Transatlantic Stories and Spiritual Struggles* (New York: Routledge, 1997), and Sylvaine A. Diouf, *Servants of Allah: African Muslims Enslaved in the Americas* (New York: New York University Press, 1998). For a discussion on the role of religion during the Great Migration, see Milton C. Sernett, *Bound for the Promised Land: African American Religion and the Great Migration* (Durham, NC: Duke University Press, 1997). Still useful in the examination of black urban sects and cults is Arthur Huff Fauset's *Black Gods of the Metropolis: Negro Religious Cults in the Urban North* (Philadelphia: University of Pennsylvania Press, 1971). Richard Brent Turner's *Islam in the African American Experience* (Bloomington: Indiana University Press, 1997), provides a broad treatment of the influence of Islam in America. The *Chicago Defender*, one of the leading black newspapers during the 1920s, carried articles on Moorish Science, including Drew Ali's funeral. Finally, the declassified Federal Bureau of Investigation (FBI) files provide another look into Moorish Science, particularly the organization's alleged relations with Imperial Japan before and during World War II.

7

Ma Rainey
Mother of the Blues

S. Spencer Davis

While the 1920s have often been characterized as the Jazz Age, the decade was also the heyday of the blues. Unlike jazz, which was a product of urban culture, blues had its roots in the late nineteenth-century rural South. Despite its country origins, the blues enjoyed tremendous popularity among urban audiences. In particular, African Americans who had left the rural South and migrated to the cities of the North during World War I longed to hear the down-home sound of the blues. Eager to meet the demand, the Theater Owners' Booking Agency (TOBA), which united over thirty theater owners during the 1920s, recruited large numbers of black performers. TOBA provided black audiences with black entertainment and black entertainers with steady employment. One of TOBA's headliners was Ma Rainey.

Like many other black performers of the early twentieth century, Ma Rainey started her career in southern minstrel shows. These traveling black variety shows included singers, dancers, comedians, and other entertainers who performed on portable stages in tents. Ma Rainey moved from the rural tent-show circuit to national stardom when record companies tried to capitalize on the African American demand for "race music." In 1923, Ma Rainey made her first recording, "Moonshine Blues," for Paramount Records in Chicago. Although Rainey was not the first black blues singer to record an album, her performance struck a chord with audiences and soon she came to be known as the "Mother of the Blues."

S. Spencer Davis traces the life of Ma Rainey, who rose from touring minstrel performer to become one of the nation's first professional female blues singers. Rainey was at the peak of her career during the 1920s, when she recorded ninety-three songs, many of which she had also composed. By the end of the decade, however, the radio and the talking movies started to push Rainey out of the limelight. The onset of the Great Depression further undermined Rainey's career. At the time of her death in 1939, the "Mother of the Blues" had been all but forgotten.

This essay originally appeared in Donald W. Whisenhunt, ed., *The Human Tradition in America between the Wars, 1920–1945* (Wilmington, DE: Scholarly Resources, 2002), 47–58.

Gertrude "Ma" Rainey is remembered today as second only to Bessie Smith among blues vocalists—a judgment that is at once accurate in the minor sense and yet inadequate as a full understanding of Rainey's career. She was the first professional singer to incorporate blues numbers into her act, and as an entertainer she was the greatest crowd-pleaser of the women singing blues. But even these substantial "firsts" are not the full measure of her achievements.

Gertrude Pridgett was born in Columbus, Georgia, in 1886, the second of the five children of Thomas and Ella Pridgett. Columbus was a town of 7,000. With its industry and location on the Chattahoochee River, it had attracted Thomas and Ella to migrate from their native Alabama.[1] No evidence beyond a baptism record describes Gertrude's youth, but un-

The singer circa 1923. *Courtesy of the Hulton| Archive by Getty Images, New York*

doubtedly she was singing at church and school events. At fourteen she sang in a local group called "The Bunch of Blackberries." Soon afterward, she must have begun to sing professionally. At eighteen she married William "Pa" Rainey, the manager and a performer in the Rabbit Foot Minstrels. They immediately worked together in the show as "Pa" and "Ma" Rainey, with an act combining comedy, singing, and dancing. Since Pa Rainey was substantially older than his eighteen-year-old bride, the match must have been as much professional as romantic.[2]

The situation of black entertainers in the first years of the last century was complex. A life of constant travel brought them into collision with the absurdities and indignities of segregation. Within the black community many religious believers frowned on secular music and looked on entertainers as Satan's assistants. The tangled cultural life of the nation put black entertainers in the dilemma of seeing their culture derided by Anglo-Saxon supremacists while their works were being adopted—or stolen—by white performers.[3]

Charles Dudley Warner, Mark Twain's coauthor of *The Gilded Age*, toured the South in 1888 and recorded his impressions in *On Horseback: A Tour in Virginia, North Carolina, and Tennessee*. In Asheville, North Carolina, Warner and a crowd of both races were entertained by Happy John. Once a slave of Wade Hampton, one of the largest and most famous slaveowners, and now appearing in Uncle Sam costume and black-face make-up, Happy John sang and told stories. According to Warner, Happy John received the biggest response, from blacks in the audience as well as from whites, when his jokes were at the expense of his race. Warner, perhaps momentarily troubled by the situation, reached a conclusion that did not entirely disguise his anxiety. "I presume none of them analyzed the nature of his infectious gayety, nor thought of the pathos that lay so close to it, in the fact of his recent slavery, and the distinction of being one of Wade Hampton's [slaves], and the melancholy mirth of this light-hearted race's burlesque of itself."[4] The possibility of double-meaning in this stereotyped humor did not occur to Warner.

Happy John may not have been performing in the minstrel format, but there were similarities. The minstrel show is a strange American creation. White minstrel shows first appeared in the 1840s and created a sensation among white audiences. Most of them focused on plantation life, and many or most of them purported to depict "authentic" slave life. How white Americans could believe that is difficult to understand, given the fact that the actors were white people using burnt cork to blacken their faces. Their exaggerated physical movements helped to establish stereotypes that have persisted to this day.

By the middle of the 1850s black actors began to appear as minstrels, and they became firmly established as a part of the show business tradition by the 1870s. Showmen such as Charles Callender and J. H. Haverly were instrumental in making minstrels an integral part of show business. Black-owned companies also formed in the 1860s. Among the more important ones were the Brooker and Clayton Georgia Minstrels, a group that was very popular in the Northeast. Minstrels succeeded partly because they appealed to an essentially illiterate society, but their popularity was not limited to the unlettered. Prominent people, including Abraham Lincoln, reportedly found them very entertaining.

By the 1870s a separation occurred between black and white minstrels. Because black minstrels had the aura of authenticity, especially with "real Negroes," white shows moved away from portrayals of "realistic" plantation and black life to more lavish productions. They became more professional as well but continued to use African American culture as a major focus. Black minstrels flourished in the later decades of the nineteenth century and the first few decades of the twentieth.[5]

Thomas L. Riis, in his study of jazz, suggests a plausible explanation for the popularity of minstrels among whites and blacks alike. People have wondered why blacks would participate in and attend minstrel shows when portrayals were racist, degrading, and grotesque. He suggests that the actors and audiences of the day may not have seen them in the way that contemporary society does. In fact, he explains the low educational level of the country at the time and the importance of oral-cultural entertainments. In an oral culture, he believes, exaggeration and grotesque portrayals are necessary and are common in most nonliterate or semiliterate cultures. The exaggerations are needed to deliver the message, and the audience does not see the performances as degrading.[6]

Such was the minstrel tradition that Ma Rainey joined when she became a performer. Whether she was conscious of the subtleties of its historical and cultural significance is a moot point. She was essentially illiterate herself; and, if one accepts Riis's conjecture, she might not have seen it as degrading at all. Perhaps the Rabbit Foot Minstrels had no such figure as Happy John in their cast in 1904 when Ma Rainey joined the troupe, but minstrel shows, though they typically had black casts by that time, retained their stereotypes and the indignity of blackface. In the 1870s black minstrel shows and white minstrel shows had begun to diverge; the black entertainers included spirituals as well as stereotypes.[7] To play within yet rise above the stereotypes was a difficult feat.

The Rabbit Foot Minstrels played only in the South, traveling in their own railroad car and playing one-nighters in their gigantic tent. The program included acrobats and a contortionist; eventually Ma Rainey was the star of the show. The Rabbit Foot Minstrels usually spent the winter in New Orleans, which gave her the chance to perform with some of the greats of New Orleans music such as Joe Oliver, Louis Armstrong, Sidney Bechet, and Kid Ory. In 1914, 1915, and 1916 she toured with Tolliver's Circus and Musical Extravaganza with the billing of "Rainey and Rainey, Assassinators of the Blues." In 1917 she created her own traveling show, Ma Rainey and Her Georgia Smart Set.

There is a fairly detailed account of that show. Rainey was short and heavy-set; she had diamonds in her hair, gold-capped teeth, and heavy jewelry. In order to lighten the tone of her skin she used a great deal of skin cream and powder. Her humor, warm smile, and open sexuality compensated for her lack of classic features. Rainey played to all-black, segregated, and all-white audiences. If the audience was segregated, whites were seated on one side of the tent and blacks on the other side. Her show began with a band number followed by several numbers by male and female dancers. Next came two skits of ethnic humor, the first portraying a Japanese character and the second a black man stealing chickens. A fast number featuring the soubrette and the dancers was followed by another comedy routine. Then Ma Rainey came on stage, began with some comedy, sang half a dozen numbers including "Memphis Blues" and "Jelly Roll Blues," and ended with her specialty, "See See Rider Blues." The show closed with all the cast on stage for the finale.[8]

By this time, Rainey had been singing blues in her performances for a decade and was the preeminent female blues artist. She claimed that while she was working a tent show in Missouri in 1902, she overheard a young woman singing a strange lament about the man who left her. Taken by the unique sound, she learned the song and put it in her act. When asked what kind of song it was, she replied "the blues" and thus named the genre. It is unlikely that Rainey was in Missouri before 1904 and, therefore, equally unlikely that, in a moment of inspiration, she invented the label. But as an explanation of how Rainey became the first professional singer to put blues in a minstrel show, the story is more credible.[9]

The first sheet music with "blues" in the title was published in 1914 by a white band leader from Oklahoma, but the blues genre began almost certainly in the 1890s, almost certainly in the Mississippi Delta, and quite certainly among rural blacks. Defining the blues is more difficult. Blues began in the 1890s (or perhaps a little earlier) in the Delta—the heart of share-cropping, cotton-producing, rural Mississippi. The typical blues artist was a man singing and playing the guitar. The typical blues form was a twelve-bar, three-line stanza with the second line repeating the first (AAB) and the third line ending with the rhyme word. Blues singers drew on familiar lines from earlier songs, added their own, and used filler words or moans to complete lines. Blues numbers could change from one rendition to the next as lines were changed, or formulas from other numbers were added, or new stanzas were improvised. Blues lyrics focused on personal problems such as unfaithful lovers, whiskey, debts, and trouble with the law. The leading study of these original down-home blues finds surprisingly little social protest in them.[10]

Down-home blues were sung at picnics, on the porch, at the depot, and outside the barbershop. But to fit into the structure of the minstrel and tent shows, changes had to be made. Instrumental soloists could improvise, but too much improvising by vocalists would upset the band.[11] Rainey had to standardize the lyrics, but accompaniments had to be worked out for the band or small group.

In the late 1910s, Rainey's act changed. Pa Rainey, always a dim figure, dropped out of the picture. Ma Rainey was then a singles act. She may have spent a year in Mexico, but that is not confirmed. Within a year, however, she was back, entertaining southern black audiences. In 1922 and 1923 she worked with a pianist, usually Troy Snapp, accompanying her.[12] By this time the first recorded blues, Mamie Smith's "Crazy Blues," had appeared, and no doubt Rainey changed to keep up with the popularity of recorded blues—keep up, but never totally imitate. She remained closer to down-home blues than any of the other women recording classic (or vaudeville) blues in the 1920s.

On her own, Ma Rainey performed with many others, but she also befriended and assisted struggling entertainers. One of the most famous was Bessie Smith, who would overshadow Rainey in fame and popularity. In the beginning, however, Rainey gave her a start in the business. Their relationship may have been more than that. Smith later was well known for her bisexuality, and Rainey may have been bisexual as well. *Completely Queer* indicates that Rainey was a lesbian and that she introduced Bessie Smith to lesbian love. "Rainey was one of a number of legendary women singers associated with the Harlem Renaissance who were known to prefer women over men." This reference work also indicates that her nickname, Ma, referred to "the affection and nurturing she lavished on those around her."[13] Whatever her personal affairs may have been, her career flourished in the 1920s.

In 1920, Mamie Smith recorded "Crazy Blues" for Okeh Records. Its success persuaded record companies that there were profits to be made in "race records." Other vaudeville singers who had the clear tone and distinct pronunciation of Mamie Smith were rushed into studios to record blues. In 1921 about fifty race records were released; by 1927 the number had soared to five hundred.[14] These blues—classic or vaudeville blues—were neither the down-home kind nor the blues of tent show veterans such as Ma Rainey and Bessie Smith. But, in 1923, both Smith and Rainey were recorded.

The phenomenal growth of radio in the 1920s created a crisis for the music industry. Record sales continued to decline throughout the decade. Since music could now be disseminated even to the most rural and unsophisticated audiences, record companies began to look for other entertainers who performed less well-known "folk" music. Company scouts fanned out across the country, especially the South, to find singers who would sound good on wax and whose talents could be promoted. One of the pioneers in this development was Ralph Peer, the man who first recorded Mamie Smith in 1920, but he became better known because he soon focused on recording country singers, including Jimmie Rodgers.

Mamie Smith's records for Okeh were successful and offered a potential new market for black singers—African Americans themselves who preferred to hear people of their own race perform music from their own culture.[15] Several recording companies created separate listings for songs designed for other races—meaning, almost always, African Americans. These became known as "race records." The term "race" in the 1920s was a badge of pride in the black community. "Although race records included spirituals, instrumentals, comedy, sermons, and even occasional classical arias, the biggest money was in the blues."[16] Okeh, Columbia, and Paramount set the pace for race records in the 1920s. Paramount had a black talent scout and recording director, J. Mayo Williams, who aggressively recruited black entertainers.[17]

In December 1923, at age thirty-seven, Rainey went to Chicago to record eight songs at Paramount Records. Despite its array of talent, Paramount was limited when compared to Columbia Records. Paramount recorded Rainey acoustically, "a crude process in which she sang into an enormous horn," and the results were primitive and disappointing.[18] That first session produced one hit, "Moonshine Blues." Rainey did most of her recording for Paramount in Chicago, where she kept an apartment, but in 1924 she had two Paramount recording sessions in New York. The back-up musicians were among the stars of the jazz world: Fletcher Henderson, a leading New York band leader, on piano; Charlie Green on trombone; and, for the second session, Louis Armstrong on cornet. Of these six tracks, "See See Rider Blues" was the most important.[19]

With recording success came the opportunity to move from tent shows to the stages of the Theater Owners' Booking Agency (TOBA), the black vaudeville circuit. TOBA had been around since about 1907, but it really came into its own in the 1920s. The shows were targeted to black audiences, but on Thursday nights a separate performance was given for whites. The "Midnight Ramble" was a standard—a late show featuring the blues—unlike the regular performances, which were more like white vaudeville in that various types of entertainment were provided. The typical TOBA show might include "comedy, circus acts, dramatic scenes, and pure vaudeville hokum as well as singing and dancing."[20] While TOBA stood for Theater Owners' Booking Agency, the performers often referred to it as "Tough on Black Artists," or, in more crude moments, "Tough on Black Asses." Even so, and despite low pay, hard work, and poor working conditions, TOBA offered regular employment for hundreds of black entertainers who would have had a difficult time arranging bookings for themselves.[21]

For her TOBA act, Rainey worked with Tommy Dorsey, a prominent musician in years to come, as pianist and music director. He put together and rehearsed a five-piece group, the Wildcats Jazz Band.[22] Evidently "jazz," like "blues," was an elastic and even indefinite term. The publicity photo of Rainey, Dorsey, and the rest of the Wildcats put them in awkward poses that nevertheless captured some of Rainey's energy.

Dorsey defined the connection between jazz and blues in several ways that help place Ma Rainey's music. He described jazz as music played at the better clubs; blues was played in Chicago in the back of saloons, at rent parties [held to raise funds to pay rent], and at buffet flats (unlicensed clubs set up in apartments and patronized by working-class people). Jazz was blues speeded up, a faster and flashier music; blues maintained a slower tempo to fit its sad mood.[23] Dorsey also described slowing down or dragging out popular tunes of the day to suit the taste of couples who wanted to "slow drag" or "shimmy" late at night.[24] Rainey's power over the audience is given in Dorsey's words:

> When she started singing, the gold in her teeth would sparkle. She was in the spotlight. She possessed her listeners; they swayed, they rocked, they moaned and groaned, as they felt the blues with her. A woman swooned who had lost her man. Men groaned who had given their week's pay to some woman who promised to be nice, but slipped away and couldn't be found at the appointed time. By this time she was just about at the end of her song. She was "in her sins" as she bellowed out. The bass drum rolled like thunder and the stage lights flickered like forked lightning. . . . As the song ends, she feels an understanding with her audience. Their applause is a rich reward. She is in her glory. The house is hot. . . . By this time everybody is excited and enthusiastic. The applause thunders for one more number. Some woman screams out with a shrill cry of agony as the blues recalls sorrow because some man trifled with her and wounded her to the bone. [Ma Rainey] is ready now to take the encore as her closing song. Here she is, tired, sweaty, swaying from side to side, fatigued, but happy.[25]

Rainey's record sales and TOBA bookings were very successful through 1928, but at the end of that year conditions changed abruptly. Paramount decided not to renew her recording contract. The competition from sound movies, introduced in 1927, had sent the TOBA theaters into a steep decline, and in May 1929, Rainey quit the circuit with wages owed her. Thereafter came a series of desperate moves to keep her career going, but the Great Depression took its toll on her as it had on many other black performers. Still she persevered, taking whatever engagements she could find. She toured with some of the tent repertory companies, but the depression was destroying more prestigious careers than hers. Paramount Records went bankrupt in the early 1930s, black vaudeville died, and Ma Rainey quit the business.

In 1935 she returned to Georgia to her hometown of Columbus after the death of her sister Malissa; her mother died during the same year. Rainey purchased two theaters in Rome. During this time, she joined the Friendship Baptist Church where her brother, Thomas Pridgett, was a deacon. Her life in Georgia is not well known today, but clearly she dropped out of entertainment except for owning the theaters, and she essentially was forgotten in blues circles.

Rainey died on December 22, 1939, and was buried in Porterdale Cemetery in Columbus. She was only fifty-three years old; the cause of death was reported to be heart disease—not unexpected considering her lifestyle and weight. Her death went entirely unnoticed by the black press or by any other news medium. It seems especially ironic that her death certificate listed her occupation as housekeeping. One wonders if her neighbors were aware of her career in entertainment.[26]

Ma Rainey was a black woman and a professional entertainer. She played minstrel shows, tent shows, circuses, carnivals, clubs, theaters, and even a Texas cattle show. Wherever engagements were offered, she took them until, in the Great Depression, there were none. When wealthy white folks in Jackson, Mississippi, hired her, she serenaded at their homes. When black sharecroppers in Alabama were flooded out, she organized a fund-raising concert. She sang blues, popular tunes, and comedy numbers; she danced; she told jokes, often at her own expense and often ribald; she worked with partners in comedy routines. At times, she managed her road shows. She composed about one-third of the numbers she recorded, or, more accurately, she was listed on the copyright forms as composer or co-composer. She paid her musicians on time, treated them well, and never missed an engagement.

For all her versatility, Ma Rainey was most successful singing traditional blues—that is, songs employing many of the formulas and the loose organization of down-home blues but performed by a vocalist and small group as were vaudeville blues. In his poem celebrating the power of Ma Rainey over her audience, Sterling A. Brown tells how her rendition of "Backwater Blues" so perfectly expressed the tribulations of the audience that heads bowed and tears flowed.[27] Brown explained her appeal: "Ma Rainey was a tremendous figure. She wouldn't have to sing any words; she would moan, and the audience would moan with her." She dominated the stage. "She had them in the palm of her hand. I heard Bessie Smith also, but Ma Rainey was the greatest mistress of an audience."[28]

Her commanding presence was also reported by Jack Dupree: "She was really an ugly woman, but when she opened her mouth—that was it! You forgot everything. She knew how to sing those blues, and she got right into your heart. What a personality she had. One of the greatest of all singers."[29] Almost everyone who saw her perform agreed that she was a "blues queen" who, like so many others, acted the part. Strong, unpredictable, and "volcanic," she spoke her mind. She was "soft-hearted and generous; but she was a tigress when roused."[30]

In her recorded blues, Rainey touched upon all the causes of heartache and anguish—unfaithful lovers, violent men, poverty, debt, jail time, alcoholism—of women abandoned, betrayed, or overpowered by life's problems. But in some of her numbers she portrayed aggressive, violent, lustful women—those sinning rather than those sinned against. Thus, in "Bared Home Blues," written by Louie Austin, Rainey's "Mama" matches "Papa," vice for unblushing vice.[31] In "Black Dust Blues," she is a woman who has stolen another one's man but pays the price through the effect of the voodoo potion placed in her house.[32]

In his path-breaking analysis of French folk tales, Robert Darnton discovered a world of constant poverty, death, hunger, starvation, injustice, and cruelty. The poor survived only by tricking others; in such a world the eradication of personal and social problems was inconceivable.[33] Reading the lyrics to Ma Rainey's blues can create the same sense of global despair. But when we turn from the lyrics on the printed page to the recordings, the power of her voice and the gusto in her delivery come into play. The sadness and hurt do not disappear but undergo a transformation. The sheer waste and inwardness of suffering are overcome; artistry gives meaning to the pain of a world we must take as we find it. For Ralph Ellison this was the outrageous, inexplicable truth of

African American culture.[34] Many artists represent Ellison's insight as
well as Ma Rainey, but none represents it better.

Notes

1. Hattie Jones, *Big Star Fallin' Mama*, rev. ed. (New York, 1995), 19–21.

2. Sandra Lieb, *Mother of the Blues* (Amherst, MA, 1981), 4–5.

3. W. C. Handy, *Father of the Blues* (New York, 1969). Chapters 1–4 describe the
conflict between religion and secular music.

4. Quoted in Alton Hornsby Jr., ed., *In the Cage: Eyewitness Accounts of the Freed
Negro in Southern Society, 1877–1929* (Chicago, 1971), 140–42; quote on 142.

5. Lieb, *Mother of the Blues*, 4–7; Thomas L. Riis, *Just before Jazz: Black Musical
Theater in New York, 1890–1915* (Washington, DC, 1989), 4–5.

6. Riis, *Just before Jazz*, 5–7.

7. Lieb, *Mother of the Blues*, xiii, 5.

8. Ibid., 10–13.

9. Ibid., 3–5.

10. Jeff Todd Titon, *Early Downhome Blues*, rev. ed. (Chapel Hill, NC, 1994).

11. For the problems created by an improvising soloist in Mahara's Minstrel Show
see Handy, *Father of the Blues*, 40–41.

12. Lieb, *Mother of the Blues*, 18–25.

13. Steve Hogan and Lee Hudson, *Completely Queer: The Gay and Lesbian Encyclopedia* (New York, 1998), 471.

14. Titon, *Early Downhome Blues*, 200.

15. Bill C. Malone, *Country Music U.S.A.*, rev. ed. (Austin, TX, 1985), 34–35.

16. Lieb, *Mother of the Blues*, 21.

17. Ibid.

18. Ibid., 22.

19. Ibid., 10, 26, 178.

20. Ibid., 27.

21. Ibid., 26–27.

22. Paramount Records talent man J. Mayo "Ink" Williams paired Dorsey with
Rainey. Lieb, *Mother of the Blues*, 29; Michael W. Harris, *The Rise of Gospel Blues* (New
York, 1992), 86–87.

23. Harris, *Rise of Gospel Blues*, 53.

24. Ibid., 59.

25. Ibid., 89–90.

26. Darlene Clark Hine, ed., *Black Women in America: An Historical Encyclopedia*,
2 vols. (Brooklyn, NY, 1993), 960; John A. Garraty and Mark C. Carnes, eds., *American National Biography* 18 (New York, 1999), 80.

27. Sterling A. Brown, "Ma Rainey," in *The Collected Poems of Sterling A. Brown*,
ed. Michael S. Harper (Evanston, IL, 1980), 62–63.

28. Quoted in Derrick Stewart-Baxter, *Ma Rainey and the Classic Blues Singers*
(New York, 1970), 42.

29. Ibid.

30. Ibid.

31. Angela Y. Davis, *Blues Legacies and Black Feminism* (New York, 1998), 200–201. Davis provides the words to all the songs of Rainey and Bessie Smith, a tremendous aid to scholars, but the interpretive section of her book is another matter.

32. Ibid., 203.

33. Robert Darnton, *The Great Cat Massacre* (New York, 1984), chap. 1.

34. Ralph Elllison, in *Collected Essays*, ed. John Callahan (New York, 1995).

Suggested Readings

Albertson, Charles. *Bessie.* New York, 1982.

Armstrong, Louis. *Satchmo.* New York, 1986.

Cohn, Lawrence, et al. *Nothing But the Blues.* New York, 1993.

Davis, Angela Y. *Blues Legacies and Black Feminism.* New York, 1998.

Falkenburg, Carole van, and Christine Dall. *Wild Women Don't Have the Blues.* San Francisco: California Newsreel, 1989, videorecording.

Floyd, Samuel A., Jr. *The Power of Black Music.* New York, 1995.

Handy, W. C. *Father of the Blues.* New York, 1969.

Lieb, Sandra. *Mother of the Blues.* Amherst, MA, 1981.

Malone, Bill C. *Country Music U.S.A.* Rev. ed. Austin, TX, 1985.

Morgan, Thomas L., and William Barlow. *From Cakewalks to Concert Halls.* Washington, DC, 1992.

Oliver, Paul. *The Story of the Blues.* Boston, 1997.

Oliver, Paul, et al. *The New Grove: Gospel Blues and Jazz.* New York, 1986.

Riis, Thomas L. *Just before Jazz.* Washington, DC, 1989.

Southern, Eileen. *The Music of Black Americans.* 3d ed. New York, 1997.

Stewart-Baxter, Derrick. *Ma Rainey and the Classic Blues Singers.* New York, 1970.

Titon, Jeff Todd. *Early Downhome Blues.* Rev. ed. Chapel Hill, NC, 1994.

8

Addie W. Hunton
Crusader for Pan-Africanism and Peace

Christine Lutz

The struggle for racial equality changed dramatically when the United States entered World War I in 1917. Prior to the war, African Americans had focused much of their energies on improving conditions in the United States. In the aftermath of the war a growing number of African Americans argued that the fight for racial equality in this country was linked to the struggle of colored people against racial oppression throughout the world. Pan-Africanists fostered cooperation among all people of African descent in the fight against racism and colonialism. Initial efforts to provide a forum for the people of the African Diaspora to discuss their common problems had resulted in the first Pan-African Congress in 1900. Not until after World War I, however, did the Pan-African Congress movement reach its heyday.

World War I heightened African American interest in international affairs, as black American soldiers were fighting alongside colonial troops on the battlefields of Europe, and the black press in the United States regularly reported their exploits. Black military participation, as well as President Woodrow Wilson's pledge "to make the world safe for democracy," raised the hopes of many African Americans that U.S. victory in the war would alleviate racial oppression throughout the world. Thus, African Americans rallied behind the nation's war effort.

Among them was Addie W. Hunton, who went to France on behalf of the Young Men's Christian Association (YMCA) and organized social, recreational, and educational programs for the black troops. Addie had been involved in YMCA work prior to the war as a result of her marriage to William A. Hunton, the father of the black YMCA movement. In addition to assisting her husband's effort to establish YMCAs for African Americans, she had been active in the Young Women's Christian Association (YWCA) and the National Association of Colored Women. Her work in both organizations allowed her to pursue her dual interest in racial advancement and women's rights.

As Christine Lutz demonstrates, World War I radicalized Addie W. Hunton. Before the war, Hunton had been willing to work for racial uplift within the segregated YMCA and YWCA. After the war she was less willing to accommodate and challenged racism in the United States as well as colonialism abroad. She became a salaried field officer for the National Association for the Advancement of Colored People, the nation's leading civil rights organization, and an uncompromising advocate of black women's suffrage. Hunton's wartime work also propelled her into the Pan-African and international peace movements. In the postwar years, she sought to forge a global alliance between African Americans and other nonwhite people by helping to organize several Pan-African Congresses as well as the International Council of Women of the Darker Races. After witnessing the carnage of World War I, Hunton also became a vocal proponent of world peace and joined the Women's International League for Peace and Freedom.

B orn in Norfolk, Virginia, Addie Waites Hunton was the oldest of three children of Jesse and Adelina Lawton Waites.[1] Jesse, the owner of a wholesale oyster and shipping business and operator of an amusement park for African Americans, prospered after the Civil War. Adelina, a former slave, died at an early age, and Addie was raised by an aunt in Boston. Following her high school graduation in 1884, Addie taught school in Portsmouth, Virginia. Meanwhile, Addie's father had become acquainted with William Alphaeus Hunton, a black Canadian, who had moved to Norfolk to take charge of the city's "colored" Young Men's Christian Association (YMCA) in 1888. By 1890, Hunton had fallen in love with Addie Waites. Instead of rushing into marriage, Addie accepted a teaching post at the State Normal and Agricultural College in Normal, Alabama, while William remained in Norfolk. For the next three years they courted almost daily through correspondence. In June 1893, William and Addie married. The couple had two children: Eunice, born in 1899, and William Alphaeus Jr., born in 1903.

During the initial years of her marriage, Addie assisted her husband in his pioneering efforts to organize black YMCA branches. In 1891, William had become the nation's highest-ranking black YMCA official when the International Committee of the YMCA employed him to supervise the association's work with African Americans throughout the United States. William's work required frequent travel, and Addie decided to find "new avenues of satisfying usefulness."[2] Like many other educated African American women, Addie became involved in the black women's club movement. In 1895 she became a charter member of the National Association of Colored Women (NACW), the premier organization for black women at the turn of the century. The NACW sought to improve the lives of African American women through a variety of programs. Local affiliates provided child care, sponsored scholarships, hosted musical and literary groups, and offered health and nutrition classes as well as vocational training and other educational courses. In addition the NACW served as an outlet for civic reform, political protest, and social activism. Its members advocated woman suffrage, supported antilynching legislation, and challenged racism, discrimination, and segregation while fostering racial advancement. The NACW's motto, "Lifting As We Climb," illustrated the group's dual goal of racial solidarity and community uplift. Hunton remained a powerful force in the NACW for much of her life.

Addie Hunton is in the second row, first on the left, at a 1916 conference. *Courtesy of the Library of Congress*

While Addie started to play an active role in the struggle to improve racial conditions in the United States, she also became interested in the plight of nonwhite people throughout the world. William's work had taken him to Europe and Asia and he was eager to extend YMCA services to Africa. Addie later recalled, "Again and again we had talked about Africa."[3] In 1899 the Huntons moved to Atlanta, where Addie helped her husband organize the first Negro Young People's Christian and Education Congress. Convening in Atlanta in 1902, the Congress featured many speakers from African missions. This experience further stimulated Addie's interest in the world's colored people, as did her acquaintance with Jesse Max Barber, who co-edited with John Wesley Bowen, a friend of the Huntons, the *Voice of the Negro*. The monthly journal, with a circulation of several thousand, denounced segregation in the United States, expressed sympathy for socialism, and called attention to the conditions of nonwhites around the world. Many prominent African Americans contributed to the *Voice*, including poet D. Webster Davis, militant editor and novelist Pauline Hopkins, civil rights activist W. E. B. Du Bois, African-born educator J. E. Kwegyir Aggrey, Atlanta businessman Henry Rucker, and socialist Reverdy Ransom as well as NACW leaders Mary Church Terrell and Margaret Murray Washington. The *Voice* also provided coverage of international affairs, especially the struggle of people of color who were fighting to gain political and economic independence. Addie read the *Voice* and wrote several articles for the journal, and thus developed a global perspective on racial issues.

In 1906, in the wake of the Atlanta race riot, the Huntons left Georgia and moved to Brooklyn, New York. The location of their new home placed William near the national headquarters of the YMCA and afforded Addie with ample opportunity to pursue her social and political activism. In New York, Addie became acquainted with the Young Women's Christian Association (YWCA) through her husband's work for the YMCA. She became friends with Grace Dodge, a white liberal philanthropist and leading board member of the YWCA, whose husband, William Earl Dodge Jr., had been a longtime financial supporter of the YMCA.

The year the Huntons moved to New York, the YWCA consolidated its local associations and established a National Board. The status of black YWCA branches, however, remained unresolved. In 1907, Grace Dodge, president of the new National Board, called for a meeting to discuss the future of the YWCA's "colored work" and formulate a racial policy. Sixty southern white women, but no representatives of black YWCAs, gathered in Asheville, North Carolina, on June 7–17, 1907. The white participants had no interest in encouraging association work among black women in the South, but acknowledged existing black YWCAs.

Perhaps as a result of Dodge's insistence, the YWCA's National Board hired Addie Hunton as a consultant to survey the extent of association work among black women. Between September and December 1907, Addie visited black colleges and cities throughout the South. She found that only four black city branches were ready to affiliate with the national YWCA. She discovered, however, that black students had launched numerous college associations on their campuses. Addie urged the National Board to hire a permanent staff member to assist the fledgling black associations. In 1908 the YWCA's National Board hired Elizabeth Ross Haynes, a Fisk University-trained sociologist, to supervise the work of black branches.

Upon Addie's return from Germany, where she had attended Kaiser Wilhelm University in Berlin for one and one-half years, the YWCA rehired her to cooperate with Ross. Confronted with frequent queries about the administrative status of black branches within the YWCA, Hunton pressured the National Board to formulate a racial policy. In 1910 the National Board recommended that in any southern city in which separate black and white YWCAs existed, the white branch was to serve as the city's central association, while any black branches were to be placed under the control of the all-white National Board in New York. While the YWCA's 1910 policy acknowledged segregation, in order to avoid alienating the association's southern white members, it also committed the National Board to assist black women in their efforts to establish branches. Hunton's work eventually resulted in the addition of black staff to the YWCA's headquarters and programs for black industrial workers. Hunton helped lay the foundation for a network of black YWCAs that provided many African American women with social, educational, and recreational services. Perhaps more important, though, black YWCAs served as an arena in which African American women could hone their leadership skills and fight for civic reforms.

Hunton's work as a YWCA consultant also allowed her to maintain her ties with the NACW, since the local membership rosters of both organizations were often identical. Indeed, between 1906 and 1912, Hunton served in a dual capacity as YWCA consultant and NACW national organizer. Traveling throughout the country, Hunton visited thirty cities in twenty states and was instrumental in establishing more than fifty NACW clubs as well as numerous state federations. Although black middle-class women had founded the NACW primarily to improve the conditions of black women in the United States, Hunton urged its members to adopt a global perspective. In 1908, when the NACW gathered for its biennial meeting in Brooklyn, Hunton helped to develop a conference program that included African dancers and a speech by a NACW member who had recently returned from Liberia. In 1910, at the NACW's next national convention, Hunton reported about her own international experiences while visiting Germany in 1908–9.

By the early twentieth century, Hunton had established a national reputation as a leader of her race. In June 1916, Joel Spingarn of the National Association for the Advancement of Colored People (NAACP), the nation's leading civil rights organization, invited Hunton to attend the Amenia, New York, conference, a leadership summit of African Americans slated for August that year. The goal of the conference, W. E. B. Du Bois, editor of the NAACP's monthly journal the *Crisis*, wrote, "was to bring about as large a degree as possible of unity of purpose among black leaders." Hunton, who was one of seven women attending the meeting of about five dozen distinguished African Americans, was hopeful that the conference would result in "harmonious thinking and acting, with an inspiration to really do things."[4] Participants agreed to work for civil rights and fight for the abolition of lynching in the United States.

Any plans Addie Hunton may have had to implement the Amenia resolutions, however, were put on hold by the death of her husband and America's entry into World War I. On November 26, 1916, William A. Hunton died after a two-year battle with tuberculosis. Addie had little time to grieve. In April 1917, Congress declared war on Germany, and President Woodrow Wilson pledged "to make the world safe for democracy." Wilson's declaration raised the hopes of many African Americans that black support of the war effort would secure them democratic rights in the United States.

The recently widowed Hunton resolved to do her part in support of the nation's war effort. She joined a handful of black men and women who were employed by the YMCA to organize leisure-time activities for African American soldiers stationed in France. When the war ended in November 1918, Hunton remained in France where she worked in one of the two segregated holiday resorts that the YMCA had established for black soldiers on leave. Hunton served with the black troops until their demobilization and return to the United States in the spring of 1919. Despite military segregation and incidents of racial discrimination, the wartime work emboldened Hunton. The black YMCA workers, she later recalled, "were crusaders on a quest for Democracy."[5]

In the years following World War I, Hunton pursued her quest for democracy in the global arena. Witnessing the horrors and destruction of modern war, Hunton worked for international peace, "a real peace, born of knowledge . . . blotting out hate and its train of social and civil injustices."[6] Determined to establish global peace, Hunton sought to implement President Wilson's pledge and strove to unite people of color throughout the world in the fight against racism and sexism. Thus, Hunton's war work propelled her into the international peace and Pan-African movements.

Pan-Africanism had emerged in Africa in response to the European partition of most of the continent during the late nineteenth century. Native Africans, resentful of the colonial powers, staged several revolts in an effort to drive out the Europeans. Black newspapers and magazines in the United States publicized the demands of native Africans and reported their efforts to gain autonomy. Some African Americans, particularly members of the intellectual elite, realized that the struggle against colonialism in Africa was linked to their campaign for racial equality in the United States. The first efforts to provide a forum for Africans and those of African descent to discuss their common problems were made in Europe. In 1900, Henry Sylvester-Williams, a West Indian barrister living in London, organized the first Pan-African Congress. Conference participants, including W. E. B. Du Bois, issued an appeal "To the Nations of the World" to acknowledge and protect the rights of people of color.[7]

Following World War I, Du Bois resurrected the Pan-African Congress when he and the NAACP called for a conference to take place in Paris in February 1919. World leaders were gathering at nearby Versailles to draft a peace treaty, and Du Bois believed that "one of the surest methods of calling the attention of the Delegates at the Peace Table to the condition of colored people everywhere will be to make an issue of the future status of the African colonies." Congress participants paid close attention to President Woodrow Wilson's Fourteen Points peace proposal, particularly the fifth point, which addressed the future of the former German colonies and called on European nations to assist colonial people on the road to independence. Among the fifty-seven black delegates—from Africa, the West Indies, and the United States—were several prominent African Americans, including Morehouse College president John Hope, feminist Ida Gibbs Hunt, editor and publisher Charlotta Bass, and Addie Hunton. Addressing the Congress, Hunton pointed out "the importance of women in the world's reconstruction and regeneration of today" and urged conference participants to consider "the necessity of seeking their cooperation and counsel." The Congress adopted several resolutions calling for the international protection of African natives and an end to their economic exploitation.[8]

While the Pan-African Congress failed to influence the colonial powers represented at Versailles, participants agreed to reconvene. In March 1921, Hunton was one of twelve men and women who signed the call for a second Pan-African Congress. Financial and health reasons, however, prevented Hunton from joining the 113 delegates who met in London in August 1921 and one month later in Brussels. Delegates, about one-quarter of whom were American, denounced imperialism in Africa and racism in the United States and demanded "absolute race equality" and suffrage "based on educational qualifications alone." Furthermore, they insisted on "the duty of the world to assist in every way the advancement of backward and suppressed groups of mankind."[9]

Despite the failure of these international gatherings to produce any lasting results, Hunton continued to support the Pan-African Congress when it reconvened for a third time in 1923. That year, Hunton organized the Circle for Peace and Foreign Relations, a small group of black women "who believe in the universality of the race problem."[10] The Circle raised money to pay for Du Bois to attend the third Pan-African Congress, which met in two separate sessions in London and Lisbon in 1923. Delegates stated their support for African self-determination, acknowledged the right to armed self-defense, and demanded equality before the law and equal access to education for all nonwhite people. They called for an end to the economic exploitation of Africa and Africans and the abolition of segregation and lynching in the United States. Finally, they requested that the League of Nations implement their demands to no avail.

Undeterred by the lack of success, Hunton pushed for another conference. In 1927, after consulting with Du Bois, the Circle issued a call for a Fourth Pan-African Congress, to be held in New York City in August of that year. The NAACP endorsed the group's effort but left the fund-raising, organization, and direction of the event in the hands of Hunton and the Circle. The Fourth Congress attracted a record number of 208 representatives from the West Indies, South America, Africa, and the United States. Gathering for the first time on American soil, delegates reiterated their previous demands, urged African Americans to "vote with their eyes fixed upon the international problem of the color line," and reminded white workers "that no program of labor uplift can be successfully carried through . . . so long as colored labor is exploited and enslaved." Congress participants, including Hunton, condemned U.S. control of Haiti and white minority rule in South Africa and called for an international reorganization of capital and labor relations.[11] Like their predecessors, however, delegates to the Fourth Pan-African Congress lacked political clout and failed to effect any change in the status of colonized nonwhite people or African Americans.

For Hunton, however, the measure of success was that the Pan-African Congresses had led "toward a wider acquaintance of the leaders among people of the colored race and of the oppressed classes throughout the world."[12] The meetings had provided them with a forum that fostered global communication and collaboration and raised international awareness of colonialism and racism. Following the Fourth Congress of 1927, supporters of Pan-Africanism suspended future meetings, largely because of the financial crisis caused by the onset of the Great Depression.

While Hunton focused much of her postwar energies on stimulating dialogue and cooperation among the nonwhite people of the world, she also continued her advocacy of black women's rights. Even prior to World War I, Hunton had urged black women in the United States to consider the plight of colored women everywhere. Following the war, she was more determined than ever to forge global alliances between women of color. In 1922, Hunton agreed to chair the NACW's Peace and Foreign Relations Department, and she and her daughter Eunice brought "distinguished foreign women" to that year's biennial meeting. Among them was Adelaide Casely-Hayford, an educator from Sierra Leone, who "held the vast audience spellbound as she pleaded the cause of African womanhood." Hunton also chaired the NACW's Programs and Literature Department between 1924 and 1926. In that capacity she distributed hundreds of pieces of literature on international relations, at least once at her own expense.[13]

Another outlet for Hunton's postwar activism was the International Council of Women of the Darker Races (ICWDR). In 1922, Hunton and other leading members of the NACW had established the ICWDR to foster international cooperation among women and children of "the darker races." Margaret Murray Washington, widow of Booker T. Washington, served as the group's president until her death in 1925. Hunton, who initially served as vice president, succeeded her that year and remained at the helm of the organization until 1928. The ICWDR's constitution called for a membership of 200 women of color, with no more than 75 percent coming from the United States. Hunton was enthusiastic about the group's effort to attract a global membership. In August 1923 she proudly wrote to the NAACP that "this movement is the first attempt to organize the colored women of different countries into a body."[14] Yet logistical problems, such as travel distance and expenses, frequently prevented the regular participation of foreign women. In the 1920s the ICWDR launched several international research and education projects. It investigated and compiled reports on the status of women and children in Haiti, Cuba, the Virgin Islands, West Africa, and India and designed black history courses for teachers and community leaders.

The ICWDR continued to meet annually during the 1920s, but in the following decade gatherings became more erratic and less frequent, and in 1940 the group folded.

Although Hunton had helped launch the ICWDR as an organization composed exclusively of women of color, she also fostered interracial cooperation in her quest for global democracy. Following the war, she joined the Women's International League for Peace and Freedom (WILPF), a group that shared many of her ideals and goals. Established in 1919, the WILPF had grown out of the woman's suffrage movement, the Women's Peace Party, and a 1915 meeting of European women who had gathered in the Netherlands and demanded an immediate end to World War I. The WILPF, composed of European and American women, sought to establish a "permanent peace" and advocated universal disarmament, human rights, and gender equality as well as social and racial justice. In 1926, Hunton was part of a WILPF delegation that toured Haiti to investigate living and working conditions on the island since the invasion of U.S. Marines in 1915. After a three-week visit, Hunton and another WILPF leader, Emily Greene Balch, coauthored an essay on race relations in Haiti. Published in the WILPF's *Occupied Haiti*, the essay was a harsh indictment of the United States: "Haiti constitutes a clear challenge to all who believe in the fundamental principle upon which the United States is founded, that government should rest upon the consent of the governed. The United States is at a parting of the roads. There has been for some time a drift toward imperialism, a movement veiled and therefore the more dangerous, dangerous to the liberty of our own neighbors, dangerous to our own democracy."[15]

Hunton's involvement in the women's peace movement also led her to Europe in the fall of 1929. She attended a summer "peace school" near Budapest where she lived for one week with women from fifteen countries. While in Hungary she delivered four speeches that emphasized the international links between oppressed people of color and the women's peace movement. Subsequently, she attended an international peace conference of women in Prague, which gave her "a new faith and a new zeal." She addressed the body and was a welcome guest at luncheons and dinners hosted by groups from different European nations. Hunton spoke French and German, and she patiently tried to interpret to the "women leaders of the Old World the position of the American Negro."[16] Hunton's years in the WILPF were troubled ones. The organization was controlled by white women who, at times, were insensitive to colonialism and racial discrimination in the United States. Hunton became increasingly disillusioned with the WILPF because the white rank-and-file members failed to embrace interracial cooperation. Not until 1929 did her own New York City branch sponsor its first interracial activity, a program about India, attended by white and black women. Frustrated with the WILPF's lack of commitment to interracial cooperation, Hunton resigned in 1934. She later explained her decision to Dorothy Detzer, a white WILPF leader, stating that "for a year or so I have felt less and less sure of the fact that the organization was really ready for an interracial program."[17]

Hunton's lack of faith in white women was compounded by her experience with the National Woman's Party (NWP) during the postwar years. Following the ratification of the Nineteenth Amendment in 1920, which gave women the right to vote, Hunton became embroiled in a controversy with white suffrage leaders. Reports about southern states refusing to register black women voters poured into the NAACP. Hunton, who worked as a salaried NAACP field organizer, often heard angry complaints of black women who had attempted to register and been rejected by white clerks. During a 1920 trip to Virginia, Hunton reported to the NAACP that many black women were losing their patience: "One of the strongest proofs of the enormity of the humiliation and injustice to which the women were subjected is the vehement freedom with which they recite their grievances and the desire not only for redress but in many cases, vengeance."[18] She described two women as "murderous" and noted that "the temper of the colored people, the most conservative of them, is high."[19]

Hunton tried to pressure white suffrage leaders to support black women who wanted to exercise their constitutional right to vote. Many white leaders of the suffrage movement, especially Alice Paul of the powerful NWP, had expressed their sympathy with African American women. Yet the NWP refused to help the NAACP bring the issue to Congress or to a federal court. Hunton collaborated with Ella Rush Murray, a white suffragist, to introduce a motion before the NWP Advisory Council urging the organization to lobby Congress to investigate violations of black women's voting rights. The motion was defeated. Hunton and others then plotted secretly to request a floor hearing of Murray's motion at the NWP's 1921 convention in order to publicize the South's franchise violations and to "challenge" the NWP "to uphold the principles upon which it is founded." Paul found out about this plan and attempted to avert the imminent public relations crisis. She asked NACW leader Hallie Q. Brown to read the motion before the Resolution Committee, hoping to prevent a public discussion. Hunton advised Brown, her good friend, to sidestep this maneuver. "Miss Paul," she wrote, "is not a bit interested in the question of suffrage as it relates to the colored woman and I am afraid she has given us the opportunity of having you before the Resolutions Committee because she knows that it will be a nice burying ground for anything that we want to do."

Hunton found herself in "a sharp contest of words" with Paul and was delighted to "have the National Woman's Party in a corner." She decided to press for all-out media exposure and led sixty black women from twelve states into a "thoroughly hostile" meeting with Paul. The women reiterated their request to read a resolution from the floor at the NWP's upcoming convention. Paul was disinclined to bend. Yet, when "every movie camera in town" filmed the delegation's exposure of racial prejudice in the NWP, other party officers became concerned and begged Hunton to compromise. Hunton, however, stood her ground, assuring James Weldon Johnson, her supervisor at the NAACP, that "I feel merciless and want this to be a success." Hunton did succeed, and Mary Church Terrell, lifetime president of the NACW, read aloud the resolution at the NWP's 1921 convention, proclaiming: "Five million women in the United States cannot be denied their rights without all the women of the United States feeling the effect of that denial. No women are free until all women are free." Hunton had won a major victory. She had exposed voting rights violations in the South as well as racism in the NWP. Proud of her achievement, Hunton wrote to Mary White Ovington, chair of the NAACP's board of directors: "we harassed them very thoroughly and succeeded in bringing our issue to the floor of the Convention. We distributed nearly one thousand of our disfranchisement pamphlets and gained many friends."[20]

Yet, Hunton also made many enemies, particularly in the American government. As a result of her consistent advocacy of racial equality in the United States and her involvement in the Pan-African and international peace movements, Hunton became the target of a government investigation. During and after World War I, the U.S. Military Intelligence Division (MID), the Department of Justice, and other federal agencies spied on black political and social activists, including Hunton, in an effort to expose their alleged seditious and subversive activities. According to an MID agent, supporters of Pan-Africanism were especially dangerous because their "agitation goes far beyond the redress of the alleged grievances of our Negro group. It aims at Pan-Negroism and a combination of the other colored races of the world." The agent warned that Pan-African efforts to unite the nonwhite peoples of the world represented "a transfer of leadership from the more conservative leaders to others of a radical type."[21]

Federal officials also claimed that these "radical" black activists posed a threat to U.S. economic interests in Central and South America and undermined diplomatic relations with Great Britain.[22] In 1921, J. Edgar Hoover of the Department of Justice, in a "very secret and confidential" memorandum entitled "British Espionage in the United States," claimed that the British government maintained an "extensive secret force" in the country to spy on 100,000 "Negro rebels," in an effort to uncover their connection to the growing political unrest in the colonies of America's wartime allies.[23] After an initial pursuit of Hunton, the Justice Department closed down its investigation of her in 1921, apparently because the agent-in-charge found his assignment to be absurd.[24] Yet federal agents continued to watch, and even hound, Hunton's friends and associates who were affiliated with the Pan-African and peace movements. Hunton remained relatively secure from persecution until the 1930s, when she attracted the attention of the Federal Bureau of Investigation because of her involvement in the American League against War and Fascism, an organization deemed subversive.[25]

Despite government efforts to document her alleged "un-American" activities, Hunton remained committed to her quest for global democracy during the last decade of her life. She continued to insist that "the problem of the colored group in the United States is but a part of the great world urge for the suppression and exploitation of the weak by the strong." African Americans, she admitted, had pressing problems, particularly because the Great Depression had resulted in high unemployment rates and a resurgence of lynchings. Yet, Hunton reminded blacks in the United States not to forget that "we are still a part of the world order." Horrified "at the flagrant violation of rights of darker peoples," she insisted "that unless we speedily build a bridge of justice and cooperation the chasm of misunderstanding and distrust may become too wide to be spanned." Hunton called on African Americans to join the ranks of those who were "struggling desperately to . . . establish a world wherein Truth and Justice shall be supreme and a will to live in unity . . . is the basic principle in the sacredness [of] life."[26]

Hunton's efforts to secure a permanent peace—based on social and racial justice, gender equality, and the respect for human rights and the dignity of all people—failed. When she died of diabetes on June 21, 1943, the world was embroiled in yet another global war. Her crusade for Pan-Africanism, however, had helped to increase African American international awareness and laid the foundation for the anticolonial movement of the post-World War II era. Several Africans who had been involved in the Pan-African movement, including Ghana's Kwame Nkrumah, Nigeria's Nnamdi Azikiwe, and Kenya's Jomo Kenyatta, led their nations to political independence in the 1950s and 1960s.

Hunton's political activism and commitment to public service also influenced her children, Eunice and Alphaeus, who carried on their mother's work. Eunice Hunton Carter served on the YWCA's National Board and collaborated with her mother in publicizing the causes of Pan-Africanism, anticolonialism, and black women. In 1935, Eunice, a lawyer and Republican Party activist, became New York State's first black woman district attorney and a charter member of the National Council of Negro Women. In 1945 she attended the founding of the United Nations in San Francisco and remained an accredited UN observer until 1952. Her son, Lisle Carter, brought his concerns as a civil rights attorney to the administration of President Lyndon B. Johnson, where he was the highest-placed African American working for Johnson's Great Society.

Addie Hunton's son Alphaeus gained notoriety as a result of his involvement in the National Negro Congress, which mobilized African Americans in the fight against fascism in the 1930s, and the Council on African Affairs, which advocated the political liberation of colonized African nations during and after World War II. Like his mother, Alphaeus became the target of government investigations because of his allegedly subversive activities. In 1951 he served six months at a segregated prison for contempt of court, when he refused to divulge the names of those who had contributed to a bail fund. A victim of the cold war Red scare, Alphaeus had difficulty in finding employment in subsequent years. Though he had earned an M.A. from Harvard and a Ph.D. in literature from New York University, he worked as an unskilled laborer in the late 1950s. In 1960, Alphaeus left the United States for Guinea, where he taught English, and then moved to Ghana, where he worked with W. E. B. Du Bois on a planned *Encyclopedia Africana*. Alphaeus lived out his days in Zambia, where he died in 1970.

Notes

1. Addie Hunton was less than frank about her birthdate. She was born June 11 and on different occasions claimed to have been born in 1866, 1868, and 1875. Jesse Waites spelled his name differently; at times it appears in records as Jessie Waits.

2. Addie W. Hunton, *William Alphaeus Hunton: Pioneer Prophet of Young Men* (New York: Association Press, 1938), 27.

3. Ibid., 167.

4. W. E. B. Du Bois, *The Autobiography of W. E. B. Du Bois* (New York: International Publishers, 1968), 264–65; Addie Hunton to Joel Spingarn, June 27, 1916, Joel Spingarn Papers, Folder 226, Box 95–6, Manuscript Division, Moorland-Spingarn Research Center, Howard University, Washington, DC (hereafter cited as Spingarn Papers). See also National Association for the Advancement of Colored People, *Freeing America: Seventh Annual Report of the National Association for the Advancement of Colored People* (New York: NAACP, 1917), 8–10; and W. E. B. Du Bois, *The Amenia Conference, An Historic Negro Gathering* (Amenia, NY: Troutbeck Press, 1925).

5. Addie Hunton and Kathryn Johnson, *Two Colored Women with the American Expeditionary Forces* (Brooklyn, NY: Brooklyn Eagle Press, 1920; reprint, New York: AMS Press, 1971), 11–12, 116, 148, 157.

6. Ibid., 239.

7. W. E. B. Du Bois et al., "To the Nations of the World" (1900), *Black Protest Thought in the Twentieth Century*, ed. August Meier, Elliott Rudwick, and Francis L. Broderick (Indianapolis: Bobbs-Merrill, 1971), 55–58.

8. [NAACP] *Branch Bulletin*, December 1918; W. E. B. Du Bois, "The Pan-African Congress," *Crisis* 16 (April 1919): 273–74; Richard B. Moore, "Du Bois and Pan-Africa," *Freedomways* 5 (1st Q, 1965): 179–80; and NAACP, *Tenth Annual Report of the National Association for the Advancement of Colored People, for the Year 1919* (New York: NAACP, 1920), 65–67.

9. "The Second Pan-African Congress," "The Pan-African Association Declared the 8 December 1921 Statutes," "To the World: Manifesto of the Second Pan-African Congress," and "The Pan-African Association Declared the 8 December 1921 Statutes," in Herbert Aptheker, ed., *A Documentary History of the Negro People in the United States: From the N.A.A.C.P. to the New Deal* (New York: Citadel Press, 1973; reprint, Carol Publishing, 1990), 335–47; "Pan-African Congress," [NAACP] *Branch Bulletin*, October 1921; NAACP, *Twelfth Annual Report of the National Association for the Advancement of Colored People, for the Year 1921* (New York: NAACP, 1922), 70, 73; and "Demands Race Equality," *New York Times*, August 30, 1921.

10. Circle for Peace and Foreign Relations, "About the Fourth Pan-African Congress," in Aptheker, *A Documentary History*, 548.

11. "Press Service of the NAACP," in Aptheker, *A Documentary History*, 548–49.

12. Circle for Peace and Foreign Relations, "About the Fourth Pan-African Congress," 546.

13. "Minutes of the Twelfth Biennial Convention of the National Association of Colored Women," in Lillian Serece Williams, ed., *Records of the National Association of Colored Women's Clubs, Inc., Part 1* (Bethesda, MD: University Publications of America, 1994), microfilm reel 1; Elizabeth Lindsay Davis, *Lifting As They Climb* (Washington,

DC: National Association of Colored Women, 1933; reprint, New York: G. K. Hall, 1996), 39–40, 50–54, 63–67; *National Association* [NACW] *Notes* 23, nos. 1–3 (Fall 1920); [NACW] *National Notes* 25 (January 1923), 27 (July 1924), 28 (July 1926), 28 (September–October 1926), and 28 (December 1926); Charles Harris Wesley, *The History of the National Association of Colored Women's Clubs: A Legacy of Service* (Washington, DC: NACW, 1984), 99; Monroe N. Work, ed., *The Negro Year Book: An Annual Encyclopedia of the Negro, 1921–22* (Tuskegee, AL: Negro Year Book Publishing, 1922), 17–18; Floris L. B. Cash, "Womanhood and Protest: The Club Movement among Black Women, 1892–1922" (Ph.D. diss., State University of New York, 1986), 15.

14. Addie Hunton, "Report for June, July, August, 1923," in Mark Fox and Randolph Boehm, eds., *Papers of the National Association for the Advancement of Colored People: Part 1, 1909–1950* (Frederick, MD: University Publications of America, 1981), microfilm reel 16 (hereafter cited as *Papers of the NAACP*).

15. Emily Balch and Committee, "Preface," *Occupied Haiti,* ed. Emily Greene Balch (New York: Writers Publishing, 1927), v–viii; and Harriet Hyman Alonso, *Peace as a Women's Issue* (Syracuse, NY: Syracuse University Press, 1993), 114.

16. *Crisis* (August 1924); and Addie Hunton to Joel Spingarn, October 5, 1929, Spingarn Papers, Box 95–6, Folder 227.

17. Alonso, *Peace,* 103–5, 148, 267; Addie Hunton to "Mrs. Olmstead," in *The Papers of Mary Church Terrell* (Washington, DC: Library of Congress Photoduplication Service, 1977), microfilm reel 4.

18. Addie Hunton to Mary White Ovington, October 25, 1920, in *Papers of the NAACP: Part 4, Voting Rights Campaign, 1916–1950* (Frederick, MD: University Publications of America, 1986), microfilm reel 2.

19. Ibid.

20. The incident can be traced through correspondence in the *Papers of the NAACP: Part 4,* microfilm reel 2. See also Ella Rush Murray, "The Woman's Party and the Violation of the 19th Amendment," *Crisis* (April 1921): 259; Addie Hunton to Mary White Ovington, March 25, 1921, in *Papers of the NAACP: Part 1,* microfilm reel 16; and "How Did the National Woman's Party Address the Issue of Enfranchisement of Black Women, 1919–1924?" in Kathryn Kish Sklar and Thomas Dublin, eds., *Women and Social Movements in the United States, 1830–1930* (Binghamton: State University of New York, 1997–2001), womhist.binghamton.edu/

21. John Trevor to Director, Military Intelligence, April 5, 1919, in Theodore Kornweibel, *Federal Surveillance of Afro-Americans, 1917–1925: The First World War, the Red Scare, and the Garvey Movement* (Frederick, MD: University Publications of America, 1986), microfilm reel 21 (hereafter cited as *Federal Surveillance*).

22. For two of many examples, see Major Norman Randolph to W. L. Hurley, U.S. Department of State, May 22, 1920, in *Federal Surveillance,* microfilm reel 18; and Military Intelligence Director, New York City, to Director, U.S. Military Intelligence, May 2, 1919, in *Federal Surveillance,* microfilm reel 22.

23. J. Edgar Hoover, Department of Justice, to Major W. W. Hicks, Military Intelligence Division, February 21, 1921, in *Federal Surveillance,* microfilm reel 22.

24. Marshall E. Tucker to J. Edgar Hoover, January 19, 1921, in *Federal Surveillance,* microfilm reel 7.

25. See Mark Naison, ed., *Department of Justice Investigative Files, Part II: The Communist Party* (Bethesda, MD: University Publications of America, 1989), microfilm reels 7, 8, 9, 15, 22, 23, and 24.

26. "Excerpts from the Speech Made by Mrs. Addie Hunton at the 23rd Annual Conference of the National Association for the Advancement of Colored People, Washington, DC, May 17–22 [1932]," in *Papers of the NAACP: Part 1*, microfilm reel 9.

Suggested Readings

Addie W. Hunton's personal papers are inaccessible; however, her correspondence, reports, and speeches can be found in the following collections: *Papers of the National Association for the Advancement of Colored People: Part 1, 1909–1950*, ed. Mark Fox and Randolph Boehm (Frederick, MD: University Publications of America, 1981); *Papers of the National Association for the Advancement of Colored People: Part 4, Voting Rights Campaign, 1916–1950* (Frederick, MD: University Publications of America, 1986); *Records of the National Association of Colored Women's Clubs, Inc., Parts 1 and 2* (Bethesda, MD: University Publications of America, 1994), ed. Lillian Serece Williams; *The Papers of Mary Church Terrell* (Washington, DC: Library of Congress Photoduplication Service, 1977); and *The Papers of W. E. B. Du Bois, 1803 (1877–1963) 1979* (Sanford, NC: Microfilming Corp. of America, 1994). Hunton was also the author of numerous articles, the most noteworthy of which can be found in the NAACP's magazine the *Crisis* and the monthly journal *Voice of the Negro*.

For biographical information about the Hunton family, see Addie W. Hunton, *William Alphaeus Hunton: Pioneer Prophet of Young Men* (New York: Association Press, 1938); Sylvia Dannett, *Profiles of Negro Womanhood* (New York: Educational Heritage, 1966); Dorothy Hunton, *Alphaeus Hunton: The Unsung Valiant* (Richmond Hill, NY: D. K. Hunton, 1986); Nina Mjagkij, *Light in the Darkness: African Americans and the YMCA, 1852–1946* (Lexington, KY: The University Press of Kentucky, 1994); and Christine Lutz, " 'The Dizzy Steep to Heaven': The Hunton Family, 1850–1970" (Ph.D. diss., Georgia State University, 2001). For Addie W. Hunton's experience in Europe during World War I, see Addie W. Hunton and Kathryn M. Johnson, *Two Colored Women with the American Expeditionary Forces* (Brooklyn, NY: Brooklyn Eagle Press, 1920; reprinted, New York: AMS Press, 1971).

For a discussion of the National Association of Colored Women's Clubs and Hunton's involvement in the organization, see Ruby Kendrick, " 'They Also Serve': The National Association of Colored Women, Inc.," *Negro History Bulletin* 17 (March 1954): 171–74; Maude T. Jenkins, "The History of the Black Women's Club Movement in America" (Ph.D. diss., Columbia University Teachers College, 1984); Elizabeth Lindsay Davis, *Lifting As They Climb* (Washington, DC: National Association of Colored Women, 1933; reprint, New York: G. K. Hall, 1996); Charles Harris Wesley, *The History of the Na-*

tional Association of Colored Women's Clubs: A Legacy of Service (Washington, DC: National Association of Colored Women, 1984); Floris Loretta Barnett Cash, *African American Women and Social Action: The Clubwomen and Volunteerism from Jim Crow to the New Deal, 1896–1936* (Westport, CT: Greenwood Press, 2001); and Stephanie Shaw, "Black Club Women and the Creation of the National Association of Colored Women," in Darlene Clark-Hine, Wilma King, and Linda Reed, eds., *"We Specialize in the Wholly Impossible": A Reader in Black Women's History* (Brooklyn, NY: Carlson Publishing, 1995), 433–47.

For black women's involvement in the Young Women's Christian Association, see Dorothy Salem, *To Better Our World: Black Women in Organized Reform, 1890–1920* (Brooklyn: Carlson Publishing, 1990), 137–50; Judith Weisenfeld, *African-American Women and Christian Activism: New York's Black Young Women's Christian Association, 1905–1945* (Cambridge, MA: Harvard University Press, 1997); Nina Mjagkij and Margaret Spratt, eds., *Men and Women Adrift: The Young Men's Christian Association and the Young Women's Christian Association in the City* (New York: New York University Press, 1997); and Anna Rice, *History of the World's Y.W.C.A.* (New York: Woman's Press, 1948).

W. E. B. Du Bois wrote extensively on Pan-Africanism in the *Crisis* and numerous other periodicals. A good introduction to Du Bois's influential views can be found in *The Autobiography of W. E. B. Du Bois* (New York: International Publishers, 1968). Other useful studies of Pan-Africanism include Aubrey Bonnett and G. Llewellyn, eds., *Emerging Perspectives on the Black Diaspora* (Lanham, MD: University Press of America, 1990); Joseph E. Harris, ed., *Global Dimensions of the African Diaspora* (Washington, DC: Howard University Press, 1993); Elliott Skinner, *Afro-Americans and Africa: The Continuing Dialectic* (New York: Urban Center, Columbia University, 1973); Collin Legum, *Pan-Africanism: A Short Political Guide* (New York: Praeger, 1962); Olisanwube P. Esedebe, *Pan-Africanism: The Idea and the Movement* (Washington, DC: Howard University Press, 1982); and Immanual Geiss, *The Pan-African Movement: A History of Pan-Africanism in America, Europe, and Africa* (London: Methuen and Co., Ltd., 1974); and Tony Martin, *The Pan-African Connection: From Slavery to Garvey and Beyond* (Cambridge, MA: Schenkman Publishing, 1983). For a discussion of the growing African American interest in international affairs, see Brenda Gayle Plummer, *Rising Wind: Black Americans and U.S. Foreign Affairs, 1935–1960* (Chapel Hill: The University of North Carolina Press, 1996), and Penny M. Von Eschen, *Race against Empire: Black Americans and Anticolonialism, 1937–1957* (Ithaca, NY: Cornell University Press, 1997). The microfilm collection, *Federal Surveillance of Afro-Americans, 1917–1925: The First World War, the Red Scare, and the Garvey Movement* (Frederick, MD: University Publications of America, 1986), compiled by Theodore Kornweibel, is invaluable for understanding the U.S. government's view of Pan-Africanists such as Hunton as well as other black internationalists, including Marcus Garvey, A. Philip Randolph, and W. E. B. Du Bois.

Useful histories that consider the issue of race in the international women's movement are Harriet Hyman Alonso's *Peace as a Women's Issue* (Syracuse, NY: Syracuse University Press, 1993), and Leila Rupp's *Worlds of Women: The Making of an International Women's Movement* (Princeton, NJ: Princeton University Press, 1997). Elinor Hinton Hoyt's article, "International Council of Women of the Darker Races: Historical Notes," a short but astute account of the ICWDR, appeared in *Sage* 3 (Fall 1986): 54–55.

9

Lester A. Walton
A Life between Culture and Politics

Susan Curtis

Lester A. Walton was a reporter, songwriter, journalist, drama critic, and political activist who fought to expose racism in the world of theater and television while raising public awareness of the work of black entertainers. He challenged discrimination against African American performers, sought to enhance their employment opportunities, and helped to formulate professional standards for black actors.

At the core of Walton's struggle was his effort to end the stereotypical racist portrayals of African Americans on stage and television. Walton was convinced that the casting of black actors in roles that reinforced racist stereotypes, or having whites in blackface, undermined the black struggle for equality. White Americans, he believed, would continue to deny African Americans equal rights as long as racist portrayals on stage and television helped to perpetuate white popular perceptions of blacks as racially inferior. Struggling to convince white theater owners and television executives to cast black entertainers in diverse roles, Walton showcased the work of black performers and helped shape an African American aesthetic in popular entertainment.

Susan Curtis demonstrates that Walton saw the interplay between culture and politics as central to the black struggle for equality. Combining his cultural vision with political activism and relying on his journalistic skills, Walton used the press to expose racism, discrimination, and segregation on stage and television. Moreover, he lobbied the white entertainment industry to end its practice of casting black performers in roles in which they were perceived as racially inferior, which served as the main justification for the white denial of black civil rights. Ultimately, Walton's crusade to alter the portrayal of African Americans in popular culture served the political goal of achieving racial equality.

In the 1950s, Lester A. Walton initiated a campaign to shape the new medium of television to promote racial equality in the United States. He wrote the script for a program entitled "Tenth Citizen, U.S.A." designed as a showcase for history, interviews, cultural expression, and talent in the African American community. He approached executives of Pepsi-Cola Company to see if they would sponsor this program or others like it. Finding no encouragement there, Walton turned directly to two of the national broadcasting companies—CBS and NBC—suggesting ways that television programs featuring African American progress and achievement could be both profitable and educational. In 1953 he lobbied Stockton Hellfrich of NBC to provide the public with "a larger opportunity to know more about the remarkable advancement the Negro is achieving, due to vision, initiative and enterprise, also co-operation and integration." A year later he pressed Lawrence W. Lowman of CBS to consider airing weekly or monthly programs on African Americans to give "facts and figures on Negro progress" and to engender "a more favorable attitude at home and abroad in the area of inter-racial relations." In the following years, having failed to persuade either company to adopt his plan, Walton continued to badger the executives about their failure to tap into the pool of African American talent. At the dawn of the television age, Walton insisted that the new medium could serve effectively his political agenda of achieving full citizenship for African Americans in the United States.[1]

Walton's campaign to gain access to American living rooms with educational entertainment was the culmination of a five-decade career. Throughout much of his adult life he had seen the interplay between culture and politics as central to the black struggle for full citizenship. Although he could not have anticipated the shocking effect that newscasts of white violent responses to civil rights marches would have on the consciousness of black and white Americans in the 1960s, he had long understood that social justice demanded new ways of thinking, seeing, and appreciating ability across the color line just as much as it required legislation, law enforcement, and the Supreme Court. Even more remarkable than Walton's insight is the general lack of awareness about this talented man. An examination of Walton's life illuminates the ways that African American leaders perceived culture as politics, and politics as culture.

Lester Aglar Walton was born in St. Louis on April 20, 1882. His father, Benjamin Walton, had migrated from Arkansas to the Gateway City, where he had worked his way up to the position of head bellman at the Lindell Hotel. His mother, Ollie May Walton, was a teacher and proudly had traced her family tree back to Madagascar, where her grand-mother had been born. Lester, one of six children, learned from the example of his parents the importance of education and middle-class respectability. His father, though not well schooled, served as a Sunday-school teacher, class leader, and superintendent of the church the family attended. Letters exchanged between Walton and his mother reveal her commitment to education, political engagement, fiscal responsibility, and community involvement. In the family home at 4265 Cottage Avenue, Walton grew up in the shadow of Sumner High School, where he earned a diploma in 1900.

Walton also grew up in the shadow of Jim Crow, the South's social, political, legal, and economic system of racial segregation. He was part of the generation of freeborn African Americans who came of age in the 1890s, a decade regarded widely by historians as the "nadir" of black life in the United States. The number of grisly public lynchings of African Americans soared throughout the decade. Court-sanctioned segregation of public facilities, including schools, hotels, and railroads, solidified the line that separated blacks socially from whites. State after state throughout the former Confederacy passed laws that effectively denied African Americans the

From "Liberia's New Industrial Development," *Current History* (April 1929): 108.

right to vote. Even in entertainment, minstrel shows and so-called coon songs provided an unflattering image of African Americans as lazy, thieving, violent, and potentially dangerous. By the time Walton left Sumner High School in 1900, he entered a society that harbored both fear of and loathing for people of color and in which the range of opportunities for members of the race was narrowing. Although born free he was limited by the culture of racism and the denial of political involvement.

Walton could neither escape nor ignore these restrictions, but with his parents' support he refused to be dispirited by them. When the state university system in Missouri refused to admit him, Walton studied business with a private tutor his father hired. He also enjoyed the company of talented black entertainers such as Charlie Turpin, Sam Patterson, and Louis Chauvin, who became headquartered at the Rosebud Cafe in St. Louis and who were pioneers of ragtime, the musical craze that was sweeping the nation. Instead of going into business, Walton began working as a reporter for the St. Louis dailies, the *Globe-Democrat* and the *Post-Dispatch*. Because of his obvious talent as a writer and his genial personality, he became friendly with white reporters Herbert Bayard Swope and Irving Dilliard, who would play crucial roles in his life in the 1920s and 1930s. Most important, Walton's association with rising stars in the field of African American entertainment and his work on white dailies sharpened his consciousness of the need for cultural as well as political change and allowed him to launch a career in which he pursued both.

While working as a news and sports reporter for the *Globe-Democrat*, Walton began writing songs with friends in the community, entering what seemed a promising avenue for advancing an African American aesthetic. He met Ernest Hogan, one of the few widely known black entertainers, who was passing through St. Louis on a national tour. In 1903 the two collaborated on four songs, which Hogan incorporated into his popular "Rufus Rastus" show. In the same year, Walton published "The Future of the Negro on the Stage" in *The Colored American Magazine*, celebrating the achievements of performers such as Hogan, George Walker, and Bert Williams. In the next couple of years, Walton copyrighted at least four more songs before deciding to move to New York, the heart of the music business and home to an increasingly visible black entertainment community.

It was in Harlem that Walton began in earnest to combine his cultural vision with political activism. In 1908 he became the drama editor for the *New York Age*, an influential black weekly edited by Fred R. Moore. Every week, Walton directed his readers' attention to stage productions and musical performances he deemed worthy of praise. He wasted no time in establishing his criteria for excellence. Performances had to meet a high standard of execution and had to reflect positively on African American life. He praised dancers who showed precision and originality in their routines, actors who projected and enunciated their lines and thoughtfully delineated their characters, singers who strove for clarity and rich vocal tones, and comedians who understood the importance of timing. Unlike some of his contemporaries, Walton commented extensively on the content of black shows, noting the ways that entertainment might lead to political rewards. The variety of black types portrayed on stage, he hoped, would counteract white acceptance of a single stereotype of the race, which was often used to justify political disfranchisement and second-class citizenship.

As a drama critic, Walton linked the performances by African Americans to the ongoing debates about the nature and condition of the American stage. In 1914, for example, Walton commented on a play called *America* staged at the New York Hippodrome. Produced by Lee Shubert, an influential white impresario, *America* cast whites in all of the black parts. Walton stormed in protest:

> With many theatrical managers allowing their conscious and unconscious prejudices to blind them to such an extent that they are blocking the progress of dramatic art, it seems that the American stage is likely to suffer dire consequences until they have been emancipated from their absurd notions with respect to one-ninth of the entire population of the United States—a people who have been on this soil for hundreds of years and whose life is one of the chief fabrics of our American civilization. It is a difficult task to produce native plays and wholly leave out the colored American, and when portrayed the character should be the real thing and not a cheap imitation.[2]

Essential to Walton's analysis of the interplay between culture and politics was his insistence that blacks were Americans. In one review after another, Walton claimed for his race the birthright of American.

Walton recognized the limits of his journalistic protests against racist entertainment and segregation on stage, since his readers by and large were black subscribers to the *New York Age*. Thus, he decided to push his agenda beyond the confines of Harlem and the black community. In 1908, for example, he and leading black entertainers proposed forming "The Frogs," an organization whose purpose was to promote "social intercourse between the representative members of the Negro theatrical profession and those connected directly or indirectly with art, literature, music, scientific, and liberal professions and the patrons of the arts." They planned to establish a library consisting of histories of African Americans and other material documenting "all worthy achievements . . . in which the Negro has participated."[3] They hoped to create an organization similar to the Lambs or the Players, white organizations that gave their members greater public visibility and a venue for social intercourse, mutual support, and collective action. Less than a month later, "The Frogs" found themselves embroiled in a heated legal battle over the right to incorporate under New York State law. A state judge refused to approve the petition for incorporation of the group on the grounds that art and frogs should not be coupled. Walton fired off an angry reply: "It could be possible that it was not the combination of art and frogs that appeared so incongruous to the learned Judge as it was the combination of Negro and art."[4]

Walton and the other founding members resolved to fight the ruling, using the courts to assert their rights as citizens. Walton's charge of racism elicited a swift denial from the judge, which provided Walton with an opportunity to make political hay out of the conflict. He urged "the powers that be to assist the race in all endeavors that tend to elevate and instruct" and that "make us better citizens" because "to be a good citizen—regardless of color—means that much more to this country, for the higher the development of citizenship the higher is the status of the United States."[5] On August 18, 1908, "The Frogs" won their right to incorporate when a new justice assigned to read the petition approved it.

In the next year, perhaps encouraged by this minor victory, Walton used his editorial office as a clearinghouse for cases of discrimination against black theater patrons. He urged the wronged parties to take matters to the courts, and he reported regularly when African Americans won their cases. But individual cases like these, while important, did not have the same effect as more organized appeals on behalf of his race. In 1913, Walton sent a letter to the Associated Press asking its members to capitalize the "N" in Negro. Uncapitalized, the term was an affront, and alternatives such as "black" or "Afro-American," Walton argued, were not accurate descriptions of the vast majority of American Negroes. "I feel certain," he concluded, "that if the influential papers connected with the Associated Press would [capitalize the "N" in Negro] they would materially aid a struggling people in their efforts to advance and become a credit to themselves and to the Nation."[6] A frosty reply indicating that the time was not right for such a change did little to discourage Walton. He continued to raise the issue publicly and privately with individual editors as well as with the Associated Press until, by the early 1930s, capitalizing Negro had become the convention among journalists.

As Walton entered his thirties he had achieved a great deal of which he could be proud. His insightful columns in the *New York Age* had raised entertainment criticism to a new level in the African American community. His leadership in such organizations as "The Frogs" and the Colored Vaudevillian Benevolent Association had raised the consciousness of black performers and had contributed to the formulation of professional standards for black entertainers. His successful use of the courts to advance civil rights also warranted praise. On a personal level, Walton was managing and dramatic editor of one of the most influential black newspapers in the country, and he had married the boss's daughter, Gladys F. Moore, on June 29, 1912. Within two years, the Walton family had grown to four as two daughters, Marjorie and Gladys, were born. Walton's marriage to Gladys Moore resulted not only in more than fifty years of loving companionship and a close family life with his children but also introduced Walton to his father-in-law's extensive network of contacts with people in positions of power. Through Fred R. Moore, Walton met local municipal officials, leaders of the National Urban League and National Negro Business League, and prominent white philanthropists seeking to aid the struggle for full citizenship.

Walton might well have continued developing the critical linkages between culture and politics in the relative comfort and safety of Harlem, but America's entry into World War I in 1917 shattered whatever complacency he might have felt. During the war and in the decades that followed, Walton became ever more determined to challenge Jim Crow and second-class citizenship and ever more impatient with the color line.

In early 1917, as Americans anxiously watched the reports from the European battlefields, Walton was preoccupied with an equally momentous development at home. Along with many other critics in New York, Walton had learned that a group of whites—playwright Ridgely Torrence, producer Emilie Hapgood, and stage artist and director Robert Edmond Jones—planned to stage a production of three one-act plays about black life. The plays would be performed in a Broadway theater and interpreted by an all-black cast, including Inez Clough, Lottie Grady, Blanche Deas, Jesse Shipp, and Alexander Rogers. All spring, Walton followed the progress of the production and reminded black readers of the *New York Age* of the upcoming debut. In the week after opening night, April 5, 1917, Walton reviewed the plays on the newspaper's front page, declaring triumphantly that the "drama, America and the Negro will greatly profit by this daring and unique move in the interest of 'Art for art's sake.' "[7] After harping on the issue for nearly a decade, Walton must have been happy to see the race question addressed on Broadway, not just in Harlem. But his joy was short-lived. By the time Walton's comments were published the United States had declared war on Germany, cutting short the public discussion of the Torrence plays.

President Woodrow Wilson had pressed for war "to make the world safe for democracy." Not surprisingly, Walton saw this as an opportune moment to examine the status of African Americans and their exclusion from the democratic process in the United States. Like W. E. B. Du Bois, black editor of the *Crisis*, the monthly magazine of the National Association for the Advancement of Colored People (NAACP), who urged African Americans to "close ranks" and support America's war effort, Walton supported the war. Walton hoped that the valor of black soldiers and the patriotism of black civilians would awaken the white majority to the inseparability and interdependence of the races in the United States. Two events, however, dampened his optimism—the outbreak of a race riot in East St. Louis in July 1917; and his unrecognized service on the Commission on Training Camp Activities, the organization responsible for providing wholesome recreational and leisure-time services for soldiers.

The East St. Louis riot occurred just across the river from Walton's childhood home. Striking white ironworkers, who had refused to admit blacks to their unions, raged against the decision by their employers to hire African Americans who had recently arrived from Mississippi and Tennessee. Sporadic violence gave way to full-scale riot on July 2, 1917, and when order was finally restored, dozens, perhaps hundreds, of blacks were dead and property worth hundreds of thousands of dollars had been destroyed. Walton covered the silent march down Fifth Avenue, which the NAACP organized to protest the violence. According to Walton, nearly 10,000 men, women, and children staged a political drama as they proceeded wordlessly for more than thirty city blocks carrying banners that spoke loudly of patriotism and sacrifice. "Make America Safe for Democracy," one sign read; "The First Blood for American Independence Was Shed by a Negro—Crispus Attucks" read another.[8] In the face of the horror in East St. Louis and the somber parade in New York, Walton nevertheless made a plea for national unity. He sent a song entitled "All for One, One for All" to Emmett J. Scott, special assistant for Negro affairs to the secretary of war, hoping it would be approved for use by music directors in the army training camps.

Late in 1917 one member of the Commission on Training Camp Activities, Marc Klaw, asked Walton to serve as one of the committee heads to help organize entertainment for black soldiers in Camp Upton, New York. Walton leapt at the chance to showcase black talent in support of the war effort. He cast about for acts and performers, made countless trips to the camp on Long Island, organized rehearsals, and prepared for a show in the spring of 1918. After Klaw resigned in early 1918, however, Walton faced polite but consistent resistance to his work. In response, Walton resigned from his position in September.

Embittered by this experience, Walton returned to the familiar role of critic. He had written to Joseph Patrick Tumulty, secretary to Woodrow Wilson, in June to urge the president to speak out against lynching. Perhaps to appease Walton the president invited him to cover the peace talks in Versailles late in 1918. In October that year, Walton chided the editor of the *New York Times* for failing to capitalize the "N" in Negro. And as the end of the war approached, Walton used the drama page of the *New York Age* to attack the Committee on Public Information, the government agency responsible for America's wartime propaganda, for its failure to include the heroism of black soldiers in newsreels and war films.

In the decade following the war to make the world safe for democracy, Walton harbored serious doubts that the victory "over there" had improved the status of African Americans at home. Like many Americans who were disillusioned by the outcome of World War I, Walton wavered in his commitment to political action and withdrew into the theatrical world of make-believe. Between 1919 and 1922, he comanaged the Lafayette Theatre in Harlem with a white partner and toured the country with Ethel Waters, a rising entertainer in the black community.

Walton's withdrawal, however, did not last for long. Indeed, like many black intellectuals, writers, and artists, Walton became energized by the dramatic rise of the "New Negro," a term used by Howard University Professor Alain Locke in 1925 to describe the growing display of racial pride and celebration of black cultural accomplishments. Despite the outbreak of numerous race riots between 1917 and 1919, the war itself had accelerated migration of blacks from the rural South to the small towns, cities, and metropolises of the Midwest and North. The streams of people flowing northward pooled in places such as Harlem and Chicago's South Side, where black culture, religion, society, and music flourished. "The American mind must reckon with a fundamentally changed Negro," Locke wrote in *The New Negro*.[9] A younger generation of black artists working within their communities and with white collaborators pushed impatiently toward the center of American cultural life as jazz performers, blues singers, dancers, actors, poets, and playwrights. A few pioneers, Walton among them, abruptly abandoned the party of Lincoln and embraced the Democratic Party to declare their political independence in an age of new possibilities.

The new era for Walton began characteristically at the intersection of politics and culture. He was working as a journalist on the *New York*

World managed by his old friend from St. Louis, Herbert Bayard Swope. In 1922 the paper introduced Walton as a feature writer on black life in the city. In turn, Walton introduced the newspaper's primarily white readers to the experiences, aspirations, achievements, and thoughts of the people of color who were making Harlem the nation's black capital. In early 1923, for example, he attempted to ease white concerns about the continued arrival of black southern migrants in New York. He explained that African Americans came to New York with "sparkling eyes and faces wreathed in smiles . . . longing to live in a land where lynching is not a favorite pastime and where race discrimination in its various forms is not so pronounced."[10] Explaining black aspirations in terms that were familiar to the newspaper's white readers, Walton told "rags to riches" stories, hailed the benevolent activities of black churches, reported on exhibits at the Harlem branch of the New York Public Library, and sought to advance the common cultural ground established by the popularity of jazz and dance. Walton continued writing weekly features for the *New York World* until 1931, when the Great Depression forced the paper out of business.

While writing for the *World,* Walton also became active in party politics. In 1922, when he covered local elections in Harlem, he reported exuberantly on the impromptu celebration of a Democratic victory. As his headline indicated, blacks had become "soured" on the Republican Party, which increasingly took black voters for granted. Walton later saw 1922 as a turning point in his own political thinking and action. That year he campaigned for the Democrats and never returned to the Republican Party. Throughout the 1920s he became more deeply immersed in Democratic politics. In 1924 and 1928, Walton worked for the Colored Democrats in New York, putting his years as a journalist to good effect as director of publicity. It was Walton who helped craft the messages designed to dislodge blacks from the Republican Party. As publicity director, Walton also became a valuable source of information about black voters for Democratic candidates who tried to appeal to a new constituency.

Between journalism and Democratic Party politics, Walton had expanded his base of professional contacts and his influence considerably beyond Harlem. The drama critic of the 1910s, who helped shape an African American aesthetic in popular entertainment, was by the end of the 1920s affiliated with influential white journalists and immersed in a political process that would eventually realign the constituencies of the major parties in the United States. As Walton sought to introduce white Americans to the experience of African Americans, he also used political power to leverage first-class citizenship for members of his race. Linking culture and politics also broadened Walton's consciousness of race in an international context. The critic once isolated in Harlem now traveled in circles much closer to the center of economic and political power. In the 1920s, Walton met Harvey S. Firestone, who set him on a course that forever changed his life.

Firestone owned a tire-manufacturing plant in Akron, Ohio. In 1926, hoping to guarantee his own inexpensive source of raw material, Firestone negotiated an arrangement with the government of Liberia in West Africa allowing him to lease land for a rubber plantation. Founded in the 1820s by the American Colonization Society as a refuge for free blacks and former slaves, Liberia had struggled throughout its century-long existence to accommodate tribal and American-Liberian differences and to maintain its national autonomy and financial solvency. Firestone's presence offered some financial stability, but it also disrupted Liberian society. Firestone's employment of native workers provided many Liberians with a source of income but also interfered with tribal customs, making the "Rubber Baron" an early symbol of the "ugly American" abroad.

Firestone hired Walton to visit Liberia and publicize his venture to American readers—black and white. After his first trip, Walton published an article in *Current History* praising the progress toward modernization made in Liberia since the arrival of the Firestone rubber planters. But the politically conscious journalist recognized in his relationship with Firestone an even greater opportunity for advancing his political agenda at home. By showing how an African republic, ruled by black descendants of former slaves, could create a stable society and government, Walton hoped to instill in African Americans the confidence to push for political equality at home and to convince the white majority that people of color in the United States deserved civil rights.

Two major obstacles, however, partially blocked Walton's efforts. The first was an international scandal brought to light in the 1920s. Tribes in the interior of Liberia had engaged in labor practices that either bordered on or qualified as slavery. Young men were "pawned" to employers to generate income for their tribes, but the length of their servitude was not always clearly defined. Thus, Liberia, the nineteenth-century refuge from slavery for African Americans, had become a nation in the twentieth century that seemed to condone human bondage. African American scholars such as Charles Spurgeon Johnson and W. E. B.

Du Bois attempted to make sense of the scandal as the League of Nations investigated the charges. Johnson's *Bitter Canaan*, which offered a history of Liberia that placed slavery within the context of long-standing conflicts between native groups and American-Liberian settlers, contrasted sharply with Du Bois's bitter denunciation of western imperialism as oppressive and exploitative. As Du Bois saw it, European powers and American businessmen like Firestone had created social and economic hardships that pushed tribes to desperate actions. The controversy generated an intense debate among African Americans, making it difficult for Walton to find an audience for his laudatory assessment of Firestone's enterprise in West Africa.

Seeking to understand the Liberian situation, Walton made two additional trips to the country in the early 1930s. On those visits he became acquainted not only with the Firestone operation but also with Liberian government officials, missionaries working for American-based philanthropic organizations, and reformers and educators affiliated with the Booker T. Washington Institute in Monrovia, the capital. In 1933, Walton also went to Geneva to attend the League of Nations meeting at which a plan of international assistance for Liberia was adopted. From these contacts, Walton emerged as a prominent American well informed about conditions in West Africa. After the 1932 election ushered Franklin D. Roosevelt into the White House—an election in which Walton had played a key role in garnering black votes for the Democratic Party—the new administration considered reestablishing diplomatic ties with Liberia. Walton, the leading candidate for a diplomatic appointment, became U.S. minister and envoy plenipotentiary in 1935. He held the post until 1946.

Walton's tenure in Liberia occurred at a moment of great international turmoil. As war brewed in Europe and in the Pacific, independent republics in Africa fell prey to the designs of developed nations seeking land, resources, and strategic military bases. When Italy invaded Ethiopia in 1936, alarm spread in Liberia. Walton wrote his friend Thomas Jesse Jones of the Phelps-Stokes Fund that Liberians had taken the news of the "rape of Ethiopia" very hard and worried lest they be overrun as well. "Now all friends of Liberia must be alert," Walton wrote Jones, "and work together to keep this one spot in all Africa left from aggression by European powers."[11]

In response to the crisis, Walton pursued several strategies to maintain Liberia's autonomy and to advance the cause of equal rights for African Americans in the United States. He negotiated treaties that strengthened the ties between Monrovia and Washington and that guaranteed both financial and military commitments to guard against European encroachment. He also helped pave the way for the construction of a new port facility and an airbase, both of which made Liberia accessible to the American military as well as American businesses. He oversaw the construction of a modern new Legation, which symbolized the U.S. commitment to the country. While seeking to preserve Liberia's independence, he also sent official press releases and unofficial news stories to Claude Barnett, director of the Associated Negro Press, to cultivate awareness of and pride in African achievement and self-rule. Walton's tenure as minister in Liberia made him realize that racism in the United States existed within an international context defined by racial inequality. He came to believe that solidarity among people of color around the world could strengthen movements for social justice in nations where nonwhites were in the minority.

Walton's Pan-African racial ideas, however, were always limited by his deep attachment to American nationalism. A respected diplomat, Walton also served as a powerful cultural ambassador. Accustomed to a comfortable middle-class way of life, Walton insisted on bringing American goods and foods with him in order to maintain that standard. He shipped a Studebaker to Monrovia and ordered a radio and generator so he could hear favorite late-night broadcasts at times when Liberian power plants were not in service. Moreover, he ordered crates of American canned goods and clothing for himself and his wife. He also introduced Hollywood films to Liberian audiences. Thus, while Walton gained new international allies for the struggle against racism in the United States, he elevated American cultural life above that of other cultures around the world. This attitude placed him at odds with black intellectuals determined to think and act in explicitly transnational terms.

When Walton returned home in 1946, Liberia was a much more economically developed nation with ties to the United States that were stronger than they had ever been in the past. He was the senior African American in the diplomatic corps and had maintained good relations with many members of the Roosevelt administration. In 1936 and 1940, for example, Walton had returned to America to campaign for the Democratic Party and had helped to draw an increasing number of African American voters away from the party of Lincoln. Curiously, however, Walton struggled to find a position in Washington or New York where he could contribute to the emerging civil rights movement, which had gathered momentum as a result of black participation in World War II.

It took a few years for Walton to adjust to the new black militancy and the expanded range of strategies for attacking racial discrimination in America. His years in Liberia had removed him from the struggle for racial equality at a time when the New Negroes of the 1920s and 1930s had begun to translate their politically charged artistic endeavors into artful politics. Walton's first brush with the new race leaders had occurred in the early 1940s, when he accepted a special assignment from President Roosevelt to investigate black morale during the war. Walton reported that African Americans were deeply committed to the "Double V" campaign, which propagated victory for democracy overseas as well as victory over racial discrimination at home. He recommended that the administration "resort to all the media throughout the country" to combat discrimination against African Americans "in the armed services, war industries, civilian defense, housing, etc."[12] Without consulting prominent black leaders, such as A. Philip Randolph, Mary McLeod Bethune, Walter White, W. E. B. Du Bois, Ralph Bunche, and William Pickens, Walton proposed that he and two white members of the Roosevelt administration oversee a clearinghouse on racial affairs. When his proposal was leaked to the Black Cabinet, a group of unofficial African American advisers to the president, retribution and denunciation were swiftly delivered. Walton had reeled from the unforeseen opposition. From 1946 to 1955 he stepped out of the limelight of public service and worked to reintegrate himself into the African American struggle for equality.

Walton's involvement in the Negro Actors Guild of America went a long way toward integrating him into this struggle. He had been unanimously selected as one of twelve honorary vice presidents in 1939, but after his retirement from the diplomatic post in Liberia, he immersed himself in the Guild's activities. Walton became an advocate for the black entertainment community in an age of rapidly expanding mass media. Although primarily a social fraternity, the Negro Actors Guild of America aimed "to foster and promote the welfare of the Negro actor and actress in every branch of the theatrical profession" and to "promote Americanism, American ideals, good citizenship, good fellowship, and . . . the good and welfare of the theatrical profession."[13] Within a couple of years, however, these aims seemed too limited to Walton. In 1951 he spearheaded the initiative to create the Coordinating Council for Negro Performers (CCNP) as a separate entity to investigate cases of racial discrimination and to seek redress for injustices. As chair of the CCNP, Walton met top executives at NBC and CBS and kept pressure on them to increase the presence of blacks in their programming and to hire black personnel behind the scenes. He also became active in the NAACP, which during the war had increased its membership ninefold. In 1953, Walton wrote a song called "Jim Crow Has Got to Go," which was featured in a dramatic sketch for the NAACP's Great Night of Entertainment held in Madison Square Garden. Ed Sullivan served as master of ceremonies, and Lena Horne, the Ink Spots, Leslie Uggams, Cab Calloway, and Ossie Davis were among the black stars on the program.

Between working for the CCNP, supporting NAACP activities, lobbying television and radio executives, presenting lectures on Liberia and the progress in race relations in twentieth-century America, and dabbling once again in writing songs, Walton remained busily engaged in the political and cultural life of the African American community. But he longed to return to public service. In 1955, at age seventy-three, Walton got his wish. His old friend, Herbert Bayard Swope, assumed the leadership of the New York Commission on Intergroup Relations and named Walton as one of the commissioners. Mayor Robert Wagner charged the commission to deal with specific cases involving racial and religious discrimination and violations of civil rights, but Swope wondered just how much the commission was really empowered to accomplish. As he told the mayor in 1956, "This commission functions in the field of Opinion; in the application of Ethics; in the pursuit of an Ideal."[14] Swope put Walton in charge of public relations and information, a job for which he was well suited. Walton excelled at keeping race issues in the news and in providing specific information to researchers at Columbia University, writers at prominent magazines, and administrators of philanthropic institutions. Whereas Swope doubted the efficacy of such consciousness raising, Walton immersed himself in the work, because it reflected the position he had held for decades: cultural awareness was essential for political change.

As a commissioner, Walton eventually could do more than direct publicity. As a member of the Committee on Integration in Housing in 1961, Walton heard numerous cases involving discrimination against selling or renting homes to African Americans and Puerto Ricans. Transcripts from the hearings reveal an aging Walton no longer patient with recalcitrant landlords. He challenged defendants directly, incredulously asking them if they were aware that racial discrimination was illegal. Week after week, one case at a time, Walton pushed for fair play. Now, at nearly eighty, he could reflect on the distance he had come from attending the segregated schools of the 1890s to being an outside agitator on a black newspaper to occupying the seat of judgment in New York City.

As a new era of civil rights activism emerged in the late 1950s and early 1960s, Walton's strength began to wane. Crippled with arthritis and rapidly losing his eyesight, he attended the farewell party in his honor in a wheelchair. In 1965, one year after the passage of landmark civil rights legislation, Lester Walton died. Several years earlier, Marguerite Cartwright had prepared a brief biography of Walton for *The Negro History Bulletin*. She concluded the sketch by noting that Walton "claimed he had met with no hardships based on color in pursuit of his career" and "believed prejudice and discrimination to be on the wane." She rightly concluded that Walton could make such statements "because he, himself, has lived, worked, and is working among us."[15]

To put Walton's life in proper perspective it is important to note that his was but one vision of how a just society would look. Walton was an integrationist who badgered his white countrymen to expand the range of opportunities available to minorities and to share power and responsibility equally. Not everyone agreed with this vision; indeed, many black intellectuals whom he considered friends and allies believed that inclusion without substantial changes in value and practice fell short of the goal of reforming the nation. As an integrationist, Walton recognized clearly that inclusion would be neither easy nor restricted to politics. As his life illustrates, Walton saw the struggle for black citizenship and equality in the United States as one waged against both politics and culture.

Notes

1. Filmscript, "Tenth Citizen, U.S.A," n.d.; Walton to Walter M. Furlow, Pepsi-Cola Company, March 26, 1953; Walton to Stockton Hellfrich, NBC, June 8, 1953; Walton to Lawrence W. Lowman, February 12, 1954; and various letters between Walton and Robert E. Kalaidjian, 1954–1957, in Lester A. Walton Papers, Schomburg Center for Research in Black Culture, New York (hereafter cited as LAWPA).

2. Lester A. Walton, "Prejudice vs. Art," *New York Age*, February 12, 1914.

3. "Well-Known Performers Organize the 'Frogs,' " *New York Age*, July 9, 1908.

4. Lester A. Walton, "The Frogs," *New York Age*, August 6, 1908.

5. Lester A. Walton, "Judge Goff Heard From," *New York Age*, August 13, 1908.

6. Walton to The Associated Press, April 21, 1913, LAWPA.

7. Lester A. Walton, "Negro Actors Make Debut in Drama at Garden Theatre," *New York Age*, April 12, 1917.

8. Lester A. Walton, "Nearly Ten Thousand Take Part in Big Silent Protest Parade Down Fifth Avenue," *New York Age*, August 2, 1917.

9. Alain Locke, *The New Negro: An Interpretation* (New York: Arno Press, 1968), 8.

10. Lester A. Walton, "Negroes in Terror Fleeing the South; Whites Alarmed," *New York World*, January 14, 1923.

11. Walton to Thomas Jesse Jones, June 1, 1936, LAWPA.

12. Memo marked "Secret," March 16, 1942, LAWPA.

13. Lester A. Walton, "The Aims of the Guild," *The Negro Actors Guild of America, Inc. Newsletter* 8 (November 1949): 3, Schomburg Center for Research in Black Culture, New York.

14. Herbert Bayard Swope to Robert F. Wagner, September 4, 1956, LAWPA.

15. Marguerite Cartwright, "Lester A. Walton—Distinguished Diplomat," *The Negro History Bulletin* 19 (October 1955): 12–13.

Suggested Readings

No complete biography of Lester A. Walton exists, but for more detailed information about his connections to African American entertainment, see Artee F. Young, "Lester A. Walton: Black Theatre Critic" (Ph.D. diss., University of Michigan, 1980); Allen Woll, *Black Musical Theatre: From Coontown to Dreamgirls* (Baton Rouge: Louisiana State University Press, 1989); and Susan Curtis, *The First Black Actors on the Great White Way* (Columbia: University of Missouri Press, 1998). Two books provide valuable information about Walton's diplomatic career and about other black diplomats: Walter Christmas, *Negroes in Public Affairs and Government* (Yonkers, NY: Educational Heritage, 1966), and Jake C. Miller, *The Black Presence in American Foreign Affairs* (Washington, DC: University Press of America, 1978). For more information on Liberia in the 1920s and 1930s, consult Ibrahim K. Sundiata, *From Slaving to Neoslavery* (Madison: University of Wisconsin Press, 1996). Nancy J. Weiss in *Farewell to the Party of Lincoln* (Princeton, NJ: Princeton University Press, 1983), and Harvard Sitkoff in *A New Deal for Blacks*, vol. 1, *The Depression Decade* (New York: Oxford University Press, 1978), offer two interpretations of the process by which African Americans became part of the Democratic coalition. The following articles provide insight into the range of Pan-African visions, within which Walton's views can be located: Robin D. G. Kelley, " 'But a Local Phase of a World Problem': Black History's Global Vision, 1883–1950," *The Journal of American History* 86 (December 1999): 1045–77; Michelle A. Stephens, "Black Transnationalism and the Politics of National Identity: West Indian Intellectuals in Harlem in the Age of War and Revolution," *American Quaterly* 50 (September 1998): 592–608; and Nikhil Pal Singh, "Culture/Wars: Recoding Empire in an Age of Democracy," *American Quarterly* 50 (September 1998): 471–522.

10

Willard Townsend
Black Workers, Civil Rights, and the Labor Movement

Eric Arnesen

In the years following the Civil War the United States became increasingly industrialized as new technology gave rise to mass production and the need for a large unskilled work force. Attracted by employment opportunities, an ever-rising number of impoverished white American farmers and European immigrants flocked to the urban manufacturing centers. As a result of the growth of industrial production, America ceased to be a nation of farmers. By 1880 the majority of the population worked outside of agriculture.

While industrialization and urbanization characterized the experience of most white Americans and recent immigrants in the late nineteenth century, the overwhelming majority of African Americans remained in the rural South, where they continued to work as landless sharecroppers and tenant farmers. They did not join the industrial urban working class in significant numbers until World War I triggered an increase in defense production and a simultaneous decline in immigration. The resulting labor shortage forced northern industries to recruit black southern workers. During the Great Migration of World War I, nearly 400,000 rural black southerners moved to the manufacturing centers of the North.

White workers, fearing labor competition and the potential use of African Americans as strikebreakers, observed the arrival of the black migrants with concern and suspicion. Beginning in the nineteenth century, whites had sought to improve their wages and working conditions through the organization of labor unions. Viewing black workers as a threat to their economic security, whites generally excluded African Americans from membership. Barred from white labor organizations, African Americans launched their own all-black unions, but they also challenged white unions to end their exclusionary policies.

The 1935 founding of the Congress of Industrial Organizations (CIO) signaled a shift in the racial policies of the American labor movement. Unlike earlier unions, which had organized skilled workers by trade, the CIO sought to organize all workers by industry, including the substantial number of African Americans who had joined the ranks of the industrial working class. Soon, all-black unions affiliated with the CIO, including the United Transport Service Employees of America (UTSEA), which had been organized by

Willard Saxby Townsend to improve the working conditions of black baggage handlers operating in railroad terminals. In 1942, Townsend became the CIO's highest-ranking black official when the union appointed him to its executive board.

Using his influential position, Townsend continued to challenge discrimination in employment and the racist practices of white trade unions during and after World War II. Yet, as Eric Arnesen demonstrates, Townsend not only fought to end racial discrimination in the labor movement but also in all of American society. Indeed, Townsend maintained that the causes of labor and civil rights were inseparable.

A recent arrival in the city of Chicago at the outset of the Great Depression in 1930, thirty-five-year-old Willard Saxby Townsend struggled, like so many other Americans, white and black, to earn a living. His status as a World War I veteran meant little, as did his university degree, in his search for meaningful and well-paid work. As a black man in a glutted and racially discriminatory labor market, Townsend found himself relegated to poorly paid service labor. Among his various jobs was a position as an unskilled redcap in Chicago's Northwestern Railroad Terminal. Carrying the bags of passengers to and from trains, he was dependent upon their gratuities for his remuneration.

By the late 1930s, Willard Townsend found himself at the forefront of a trade-union campaign to organize and unify redcaps, not just in Chicago but across the United States. He helped to build the International Brotherhood of Red Caps (IBRC), which changed its name to the United Transport Service Employees of America (UTSEA) in 1940, into a viable independent union. The union played a crucial role in improving the working conditions of redcaps. In addition, Townsend and his union turned their energies to fight racial discrimination in the larger labor movement and in American society. When the UTSEA affiliated with the Congress of Industrial Organizations (CIO) in 1942, Townsend became the CIO's highest-ranking African American official. In less than a decade, then, Townsend had emerged as one of the nation's most visible black labor leaders. He was, black labor journalist George McCray suggested in 1942, "fast becoming the most powerful Negro leader in the country."[1] From his rise as a redcap organizer in 1936 until his death in 1957, Townsend insisted that the causes of labor and civil rights were inseparable.

Willard Townsend was born in Cincinnati, Ohio, in 1895, the same year that Booker T. Washington delivered his "Atlanta Compromise" speech abandoning the goal of black political and equal rights.

Townsend's great-grandfather was Hiram W. Revels, Mississippi's black Reconstruction-era senator; his grand-uncle was Samuel Mitchell, who at one point served as president of Wilberforce University; and his father was William Townsend, a Cincinnati building contractor. Like hundreds of thousands of other young African American men during

From the *Souvenir Journal of the Third Biennial Convention of the United Transport Service Employees of America*, May 17–19, 1942, located in the Department of Labor Library, Washington, DC

World War I, Willard served in the U.S. military, becoming a first lieutenant in the army's 372d Infantry in France. His postwar career revealed a thirst for education. With an eye on medicine, Townsend first
attended the University of Toronto and later the Royal Academy of Science. To pay for his education, Townsend turned to the railroad industry, working weekends and summers as a dining car waiter on the
Canadian National Railroad.

As secretary of a local affiliate of the Canadian Brotherhood of Railway Employees, he learned one of his first lessons in the divisive power
of race to stop union organizing.[2] "It was one grand happy family" in
the union local until an economic downturn threatened, Townsend later
recalled. "One morning when we pulled in from Montreal en route to
London, Ontario, where we stopped to pick up provisions, the platform man came in and said: 'Tomorrow after you have fed [the passen-
gers] breakfast, take off all of your things'. . . There hasn't been a black
waiter since." By 1926 the Canadian National Railroad had replaced
many of its African American waiters with whites, on the grounds that
black waiters provided unsatisfactory service. As critics of the move
charged, the railroad raised no complaints against black waiters until
they requested an equalization of their wages to the level of whites.[3]
Out of a job, Townsend made his way to Texas, where he briefly taught
in a black religious high school before marrying Consuelo Mann, a resident of Cincinnati. Relocating to Chicago, he worked as an assistant at
the Adler Psychological Laboratory, as a messenger to a bank president,
and, by 1930, as a redcap at the Northwestern Railroad Terminal.[4]

The American railroad industry in which Townsend found employment was marked by sharp racial divisions of labor from its inception in
the early nineteenth century through the 1960s. Black workers often
confronted abusive treatment on the job, a system of widespread employment discrimination that blocked occupational advancement and
kept them restricted to the lowest rungs on the job ladder, and the opposition of a significant number of white workers and white trade unions.
Until the 1960s most blacks found the jobs of conductor and engineer
completely closed to them, as were the jobs of fireman and brakeman in
the northern and western states. Their one relatively secure niche was in
the realm of service. White Americans and European immigrants avoided
the railroads' service sector for more lucrative and less demeaning positions, while railroad managers turned to African American men as a
source of cheap servile labor. On Pullman sleeping cars and dining cars,
white passengers expected to be catered to by attentive and obedient

black porters, cooks, and waiters, whose low wages were supplemented by the tips of white passengers.[5]

Redcapping fit comfortably into the tradition of African American service labor in the railroad industry. By the end of the nineteenth century, white passengers counted on redcaps to carry their luggage to and from the trains. America's largest railroad stations—Grand Central and Pennsylvania Stations in New York—employed hundreds of permanent and part-time redcaps, while smaller stations in Jackson, Mississippi, or New Haven, Connecticut, employed only a dozen or so by the 1920s. Redcapping attracted a wide range of individuals, from men with no formal education to black college students working during the summer rush to black musicians, lawyers, ministers, and even doctors who were unable to find work in their profession because of discrimination. Despite their subordinate position, many of these men took their jobs seriously and viewed themselves as walking information bureaus capable of advising travelers of arrival and departure times and helping them navigate cities of arrival. Although most redcaps were African American, Japanese workers predominated in Seattle, Washington, while as much as one-third of Chicago's redcap labor force was white throughout the Great Depression.[6]

A lack of uniformity characterized redcaps' wages and working conditions across the country in the early twentieth century. While some received a basic monthly wage, which varied widely from station to station, others relied predominantly on tips; some performed only redcap duties, while others were required to engage in janitorial service as well. Whatever the specifics of their situation, the Great Depression of the 1930s left most redcaps working under harsher conditions for only gratuities. "In the station where I was employed" at the outset of the depression, Willard Townsend later recalled, "the tips had dwindled down to a very, very small amount. There were days when we actually made just about enough to pay our car fare and buy lunch." Not far from the Northwestern Railroad station where Townsend worked, Chicago's Illinois Central Station was purported to be a "bedlam of wrongs, coercion, [and] intimidation" where "special privilege" was "rampant."[7] Like workers in countless industries across the nation, redcaps too turned their attention to union organizing.

The 1930s witnessed not merely an upsurge in trade unionism but also something of a transformation in the relationship between organized labor and African American workers. Until the depression the nation's dominant labor organization—the American Federation of

Labor (AFL)—catered to the interests of its mostly white, skilled craft-worker base, whose unions usually excluded blacks from membership by constitutional provision or ritual or relegated them to second-class auxiliary union locals. For decades, black workers and civil rights organizations had chided the AFL for its hostility toward African Americans, to little avail. The rise of the CIO in the late 1930s changed the relationship of the labor movement and blacks to a considerable extent. Committed to organizing along industrial, as opposed to craft, lines and to enlisting all workers regardless of race, ethnicity, or gender (at least in theory if not always in practice), the CIO in some parts of the country opened its doors to black workers and solicited their support and involvement. By World War II roughly 10 percent of the CIO membership was black. For its efforts the CIO won the unprecedented praise of increasing numbers of black leaders.

The CIO encouraged the growing black working-class protest during the Great Depression but was hardly its sole instigator. From within the ranks of the AFL, socialist A. Philip Randolph led the all-black Brotherhood of Sleeping Car Porters (BSCP) in a ten-year crusade for union recognition from the Pullman Company. Under the Amended Railway Labor Act of 1934, Pullman porters and dining car waiters were able to call upon the National Mediation Board (NMB) to oversee fair union elections, allowing these black workers to make tremendous strides on the collective bargaining front. Inspired by Randolph's BSCP and what observers called the "upsurge of labor," redcaps joined the wave of union organizing sweeping the nation's railroads and other industries and generating significant enthusiasm from both whites and blacks. By the early 1940s as many as 500,000 African American workers were members of trade unions in the United States. Willard Townsend quickly emerged as a dynamic organizer, and the successful unionization of redcaps eventually propelled him into the spotlight as a CIO and civil rights leader.[8]

Townsend was one of the pioneers of redcap unionization in the Midwest. In early 1937 he was one of 200 white and black Chicago railroad and bus station redcaps who founded the Brotherhood of Railroad Depot, Bus Terminal, Airport and Dock Red Caps, Attendants and Porters, affiliating with the AFL as a federal local (that is, one with no formal connection to larger international unions and with little power or influence). The local's first president, Boland L. Hosie, was a white redcap who worked at Chicago's LaSalle Street station, and Townsend became its first vice president. Not content merely to represent Chicago workers, the local's officers hosted a hundred delegates from around the country that May. This interracial endeavor did not last long, however, for white activists came to resent the numerically dominant African Americans in their ranks. When Townsend was elected president of the nascent national body, most white redcaps revolted, quitting to affiliate with the all-white Brotherhood of Railway Clerks. Resentful of blacks' second-class status in a federal AFL local, the new IBRC severed its ties to the AFL. From May until January 1938, Townsend and other black activists traveled across the South and the East, organizing new locals and urging existing redcap unions to join their independent association. At its "unification" conference that January, the IBRC welcomed sixty delegates representing an estimated 4,000 workers. It next turned its attention to the more difficult project of transforming labor relations in the nation's railroad stations.[9]

Redcaps were at a distinct disadvantage in their quest for union recognition and contracts. They possessed no irreplaceable skills, for any man with a strong back could carry luggage, and the economic depression guaranteed a readily available replacement labor force in the event of a strike. Equally important, redcaps had no access to the labor relations machinery established by the New Deal that governed other categories of workers. New Deal labor legislation—particularly the National Labor Relations Act of 1935 and the Amended Railway Labor Act of 1934—conferred a degree of legitimacy on trade unions and established federal agencies to oversee fair union elections and monitor unfair labor practices by employers. In many cases the laws conferred psychological advantages and material benefits on workers seeking to unionize. But redcaps, at least until 1938, fell outside the scope of these laws. Unlike Pullman porters, dining car cooks and waiters, locomotive firemen, brakemen, conductors, and engineers, redcaps had not been legally classified as railroad workers under the terms of the 1934 amendments to the Railway Labor Act. Railroad station managers denied that redcaps were their employees, claiming that they were independent concessionaires. Without official employee status, redcaps could not call upon the NMB to conduct union elections or invoke the National Railroad Adjustment Act to adjudicate disputes between workers and employees. Before they could insist upon any substantive challenge to their working conditions, redcaps first had to fight to be viewed and treated as railroad "employees."[10]

By late September 1938 the IBRC's "March Forward to Job Legality" campaign paid off when the Interstate Commerce Commission concluded, on the basis of numerous surveys and hearings, that redcaps' "independent status" was a fiction and classified them as railroad workers covered by the law. That simple change made all the difference. Drawing upon the services of the NMB over the next two years, the IBRC won election after election in station after station. Although the wage increases won by the IBRC were hardly impressive—they were fiercely resisted by station managers—the union effected significant change in the lives of unskilled black redcaps. In 1941 the U.S. Department of Labor credited the union with winning "seniority rights, decreases in working hours, the elimination of the 7-day week, adjustment procedures, and other changes," including coverage under New Deal-era unemployment compensation and retirement laws.[11] But equally impressive was the struggle Townsend and his union waged against the racist policies of organized white labor.

From the IBRC's start in 1936 and 1937, redcaps had to contend not merely with recalcitrant employers but also with hostile white trade unions, particularly the Brotherhood of Railway and Steamship Clerks (BRSC), which resented the upstart independent union's encroachment on what it perceived to be its "jurisdiction." Until 1934, the Clerks' union largely ignored black workers, officially denying them membership. After 1934 it organized black workers falling under its jurisdiction, such as station porters or freight handlers, into largely powerless AFL federal unions, which were nominally represented by the Clerks in exchange for dues payments. Faced with black protests and competition from the IBRC, the BRSC finally opened its doors, at least partially, to black workers in 1939. Its purpose reflected less an embrace of interracial unionism than a desire to control minority workers more effectively. The new auxiliary locals offered separate and unequal status to blacks, who still possessed no voting rights in the BRSC.

Townsend and the IBRC pleaded with black freight handlers, station porters, and redcaps to fight the BRSC's racially discriminatory policies and instead affiliate with the independent UTSEA. The "best and only way red caps can protect themselves is by their own organization and their own collective strength," the black redcaps insisted. "If they march into the maws of the anti-Negro clique in the AFL, they will find the same protection which the lion furnishes when the walls of his stomach encircle the late lamb."[12] More often than not, black workers heeded the independent union's advice. A "tidal wave of organized protest against the formation of 'jim-crow' auxiliary locals," as the UTSEA put it, involved the defection to the UTSEA of federal AFL locals in Phoenix, Ogden (Utah), the San Francisco Bay Area, Los An-

geles, Santa Barbara, and elsewhere. The UTSEA's often successful challenges to the BRSC in numerous union representation elections heralded a "great day for the step children of American democracy," in the
words of Townsend's co-organizer. "You just simply can't sell this 'white
to the front, colored to the rear' brand of unionism to a group of intelligent, democratic minded working people . . . in this day and age." The
BRSC's defeats were "Jim-Crow's Last Union Stand" among redcaps.[13]

In 1942 the UTSEA voted unanimously to affiliate with the CIO,
bringing to an end the redcap union's five-year experiment as an independent body. Affiliation with the large industrial union federation provided UTSEA leaders with a much firmer and larger organizational
platform from which to attack racism in the railroad industry, the labor
movement, and in American society generally. "We are now a strong
and well established organization," Townsend declared. "We hope that
by our example of seeking organic ties with organized labor, to strengthen
the fight to integrate Negro defense workers and all other workers in
the labor movement and in the industries of our nation." Townsend
soon acknowledged that the CIO had paid a "price for its pan-racial
policy" in the form of losses in labor board elections and "in revolts
among [white] workers." The gains, however, outweighed the losses.
"Hundreds of thousands of Negroes are now working at union scales in
war industries," he argued in early 1944. "When prejudice has broken
down in the shop, the union hall, and the housing project, the results
will have been a gratifying tribute to democracy." Along with formal
affiliation came the appointment of Townsend to the CIO's executive
board, making him the first black appointment to the board and the
highest-ranking African American within the CIO.[14]

Townsend quickly assumed a national role as a critic of American
race relations and as a proponent of civil rights in employment, politics, and housing. "America is sick," he declared following the bloody
race riots in Detroit, Mobile, and other cities in the summer of 1943;
the violent outbreaks were "grave symptoms of a disease that is gnawing
at the vitals of our democracy." Speaking on behalf of the CIO, he
charged that "democracy will survive in America only if its advocates
fight just as hard for the positive values of equality, labor and justice as
its enemies fight for the negative values of racism, terror and exploitation." As a public spokesman for the CIO and for many African Americans, Townsend condemned both restrictive covenants and the Federal
Housing Administration (FHA) for its role in fostering their extension
into new housing developments during and after World War II. The

FHA, he accurately argued in 1946, was "using government power to crystallize current residential segregation patterns," guaranteeing "the extension of such racial patterns of living" and fostering "the spreading and acceptance of the fallacious conception that property values or deterioration is associated with race rather than economic factors."[15]

Townsend's interest in racial equality was not restricted to African Americans alone. Following the U.S. government's internment of Japanese and Japanese Americans in 1942, he defended Japanese redcaps in Seattle's railroad stations as "American sons of Japanese ancestry" who were "giving more and receiving less than many lip-service Americans." When the Illinois Central dismissed some fifty-nine Japanese American track laborers in 1944 after the AFL's Brotherhood of Maintenance of Way Employees threatened to strike, Townsend condemned the union for its "white supremacy" policy and protested, to no avail, the company's action. Before the CIO's annual convention in 1943, the redcaps' leader lashed out at those persons, trade unionists included, who supported "vicious" laws denying equality to Asian Americans.[16]

Notwithstanding his pursuit of racial equality during World War II, Townsend stood aloof from one of the most dramatic challenges of employment and union discrimination. While many African American leaders and activists had invested considerable hope in the newly created Fair Employment Practice Committee (FEPC), Townsend did not. The UTSEA president emerged as one of the foremost black critics of the FEPC, which President Franklin D. Roosevelt had created by Executive Order 8802 in response to the threat by A. Philip Randolph, the militant leader of the black Brotherhood of Sleeping Car Porters, to lead a march on Washington in protest against discrimination in war industries and the armed forces. The FEPC's budget was small, its authority was questioned or undermined by other federal agencies, and its powers were limited by its inability to enforce its orders. Yet many viewed it as a vehicle for exposing racial discrimination and achieving some black economic advancement.

The FEPC's hearings into the extensive racism in the railroad industry in September 1943, held at last after considerable delay and one politically charged cancellation, illustrated the committee's weaknesses. The railroad hearings, Townsend charged, "sounded the death knell" for the FEPC, and its "obituary was written in a blaze of glory, pomp and testimony." Moreover, a "Who's Who in American Professional Negro Leaders" were "cast in the role of pall bearers at the demise and funeral of another projected democratic ideal which never had an even chance." On one level, Townsend was right: the railroad hearings produced dramatic testimony but ultimately no results. Not only did the FEPC lack any power to force discriminatory trade unions or employers to change their policies but the Roosevelt administration, fearful of the industry's power and a conservative backlash in Congress, also effectively postponed any action. In contrast to Randolph and many black activists, Townsend insisted that the FEPC "was created not out of a keen desire to insure the full participation of the Negro in war industry but rather out of a political necessity to placate the growing insistence of the Negro community." The administration's desire to placate conservative whites ensured that the FEPC would be sacrificed to political expediency.[17]

Fiercely committed to racial equality, the New Deal, and the advancement of the labor movement, Townsend also proved to be a sharp critic of the Communist Party (CP). During the 1930s and 1940s, CP activists often proved themselves ardent supporters of black civil rights, and within the CIO they worked as dedicated organizers in numerous unions, including the United Packinghouse Workers of America, the Farm Equipment Workers Union, and the Food, Tobacco, Agricultural and Allied Workers (FTA) union. While never a virulent Red-baiter, Townsend made it clear that he did "not subscribe to the theory that the Communist Party is the answer," nor did he believe "that the Communist Party can serve the best interest of the Negro." Rather, he preferred to continue "in the struggle for human decency within the framework of our so-called democracy."[18]

Within the labor movement, Townsend sparred with members of the CP-influenced AFL Joint Council of Dining Car Employees, whose members he sought to enroll in the UTSEA in the 1940s. At the behest of top CIO leaders, he also used his union to challenge and undermine the vibrant, community-based but Left-led FTA in tobacco factories in North Carolina in the late 1940s and early 1950s. Communists, Townsend charged in 1950, were attempting to "use Negroes in labor to further their ideology."[19] American racial practices, however, provided fuel for the Communists. "We say 'Communism is no good!!' 'Communism is dangerous,' " Townsend argued in 1946. "Yet we do everything in this country to make the Negro Communist-conscious. Bad housing, discrimination, the whole list of grievances that cause him to seek an emotional escape."[20]

What was true of African Americans was true of the world's non-white majority. In his official capacity as a CIO leader and in his weekly column in the *Chicago Defender*, Townsend repeatedly argued that racial inequality undermined the efforts of the United States to compete with the Soviet Union for the loyalty of the world's majority of nonwhite peoples. After the war and through the mid-1950s, Townsend served as a CIO representative to numerous international labor conferences, traveling widely to Cuba, Europe, Japan, China, the Philippines, India, and Korea to promote pro-U.S. and anti-Communist trade unionism.[21]

A shared commitment to anticommunism and racial equality within the labor movement made it logical that Townsend and A. Philip Randolph, the CIO's and the AFL's leading black officials, would enter into a strategic alliance. Indeed, some advocates of black unionization promoted the idea of a unification of redcaps, Pullman porters, and even black dining car workers into a single independent federation or, at a minimum, into a looser alliance. But no such alliance ever came into being. Townsend and Randolph remained at arm's length from one another, each viewing the other as a rival and as an impediment to his own union's ambitious plans. While Randolph offered public support to redcap unionization during the late 1930s, redcaps feared that the BSCP leader sought to subordinate them within the porters' union and preferred autonomy to Randolph's leadership. Compounding these initial tensions were the conflicting ambitions of the two men who led the UTSEA and the BSCP. "Each one of them thought that he was or ought to be the leading black trade unionist," a friend of Townsend's recalled. "There was never really any serious disagreement. . . . Both of them had a great deal of ego and both of them thought they were going to be the savior of the black worker," Ike Golden, the UTSEA's comptroller in the 1940s and early 1950s, concluded.[22]

But more than personality was at stake. Randolph's BSCP was affiliated with the AFL while Townsend's UTSEA was affiliated with the CIO. The very real conflicts between the two labor federations in the late 1930s and 1940s required their members to take active sides. Randolph had committed his BSCP to remaining with the craft-oriented AFL. Acknowledging the deeply entrenched racism of AFL unions, Randolph waged a campaign for racial equality from within, despite the reservations of many porters and even some BSCP officials. Townsend, in contrast, viewed the AFL with disgust, finding top CIO officials far more congenial to his efforts to oppose discrimination. "Today the CIO stands as a national bulwark in the struggle to extend the democratic process into every phase of American life," Townsend wrote in 1944.[23]

By the early 1940s, both Randolph and Townsend attempted to expand beyond their initial membership base and organize black dining car waiters, Pullman laundry workers, shop craft workers, and even locomotive firemen, each man backed by his own federation. Such efforts at expansion put the BSCP and UTSEA on an organizational collision course. Given the entrenched racism in the railroad industry, the resistance of the powerful employers, and the debilitating jurisdictional conflict between the UTSEA and the BSCP, neither black union had much enduring success outside their initial constituencies of redcaps and porters.

Townsend had reached the pinnacle of his career as a labor and civil rights leader by the mid-1940s, but his greatest successes lay behind him, not ahead. The organization he had founded and led had established itself as a bona fide railroad union, but its days as an effective force were numbered. Airplanes, cars, and buses cut sharply into the railroads' business, leading to a significant drop in the number of rail passengers in the decades after World War II. The result was a dramatic cutback in the size of the railroad labor force. Railroad stations carried fewer and fewer redcaps on their payrolls; by the early 1960s, for instance, only several dozen redcaps labored in New York's Grand Central Station, where hundreds had been employed decades before. Broader changes in the larger labor movement also affected the course of Townsend's career. The crusading spirit of the CIO was less in evidence by the late 1940s and early 1950s. When the CIO merged with its archrival, the AFL, in 1955, Townsend joined his former rival, A. Philip Randolph, on the executive board of the new AFL-CIO. But that body proved to be a poor platform from which to launch new civil rights campaigns.

In the years before his death from a kidney ailment at Chicago's black Provident Hospital in February 1957, Townsend's commitment to civil rights and the labor movement did not diminish.[24] During and after World War II he kept up a steady stream of criticism against discriminatory white trade unions and lobbied Congress aggressively against discrimination in employment, unions, and housing markets. He served as a vice president of the National Urban League and the National Association for the Advancement of Colored People as well as a trustee of Hampton Institute in Virginia, whose teachers, he declared in a speech at that school, ought to unionize. Maintaining that racial problems were "workers problems," Townsend insisted that a "racial problem is the problem of all workers of the nation" and that the "labor movement" was the "only vehicle" to achieve "those things we have aspired and hoped for." During World War II he contended that "aggressive unionism becomes the major force for the extension of the rights and progress for the Negro race. It is the only segment of our society where Negroes and whites have been able to work together in common purpose." Until the end of his life, then, Willard Townsend promoted a vision of labor organizing among African Americans, while at the same time he challenged white trade union members to live up to the ideals of interracialism by opposing discrimination in all forms.[25]

Notes

1. *Seattle Northwest Enterprise*, December 23, 1942.

2. *Chicago Tribune*, March 3, 1940; "Willard Saxby Townsend" in Gary Fink, ed., *Biographical Dictionary of American Labor* (Westport, CT: Greenwood Press, 1984), 554–55; *Baltimore Afro-American*, November 28, 1942; *Proceedings of the Fourth Biennial Convention of the United Transport Service Employees of America, CIO, May 17, 18, 19, 1944, Chicago, Illinois* (n.p., n.d.), 69 (copy in Department of Labor Library, Washington, DC); author's interview with Ike Golden (UTSEA's comptroller in the 1940s and early 1950s), April 13, 1995. On the displacement of black dining car waiters on the Canadian National Railway, see *St. Paul Echo*, July 17, 1926, in *Tuskegee Institute News Clippings File* (Tuskegee, Alabama: Division of Behavioral Science Research, Carver Research Foundation, Tuskegee Institute, 1976), reel 26; and James H. Hogans, "Things Seen, Heard and Done among Pullman Employees," *New York Age*, August 14, 1926. The only biographical study of Townsend is Patricia W. Romero, "Willard Townsend and the International Brotherhood of Red Caps" (M.A. thesis, Miami University, Oxford, Ohio, 1965).

3. Remarks of Willard Townsend, *Proceedings of the Fourth Biennial Convention*, 69; author's interview with Ike Golden, April 13, 1995; Hogans, "Things Seen, Heard and Done among Pullman Employees."

4. Lester B. Granger, "Phylon Profile, II: Willard S. Townsend," *Phylon* 5, no. 4 (1944): 331.

5. On employment discrimination in the railroad industry, see Eric Arnesen, " 'Like Banquo's Ghost, It Will Not Down': The Race Question and the American Railroad Brotherhoods, 1880–1920," *American Historical Review* 99, no. 5 (December 1994): 1601–33; and William A. Sundstrom, "Half a Career: Discrimination and Railroad Internal Labor Markets," *Industrial Relations* 29, no. 3 (Fall 1990): 423–40.

6. On the history of redcapping, see Eric Arnesen, *Brotherhoods of Color: Black Railroad Workers and the Struggle for Equality* (Cambridge, MA: Harvard University Press, 2001), 153–60.

7. *William* [sic] *Saxby Townsend et al. vs. The New York Central Railroad Company et al.*, U.S. Circuit Court of Appeals, Seventh Circuit, No. 8177, December 16, 1942, Transcript of Record, 142, 75; Reginald A. Johnson, "Red Caps Seek a Living Wage," *Opportunity* 17 (April 1939): 105; *Bags & Baggage* 1 (August 1937): 1; and *Bags & Baggage* 1 (September 1937): 1. *Bags & Baggage* was a monthly union newspaper that

may be accessed in hard copy at the Department of Labor Library, Washington, DC, as well as on microfilm.

8. *Houston Informer and Texas Freeman*, May 1, 1937. On labor and race in the 1930s, see Arnesen, *Brotherhoods of Color*, 85–87, 93–96, 112, 160–74.

9. Arnesen, *Brotherhoods of Color*, 161–74; (Oklahoma City) *Black Dispatch*, January 28, 1937; *Houston Informer and Texas Freeman*, January 30, 1937; and Ernest Calloway, ed., "The Birth of a Union: What the Press of the Nation Has to Say about the New Red Cap" (Chicago: Educational Department, UTSEA, October 1, 1940), Department of Labor Library, Washington, DC.

10. Ernest Calloway, "The Red Caps' Struggle for a Livelihood" (Part 1), *Opportunity* 18 (June 1940): 175; John L. Yancey, "Our Right to Live," *American Federationist* 46 (March 1939): 259; *Bags & Baggage* 1 (August 1937): 1, 7; 1 (December 1937): 1; 2 (April 1938): 2; and U.S. Department of Labor, Wage and Hour Division, Research and Statistics Branch, "Redcaps in Railway Terminals under the Fair Labor Standards Act, 1938–1941," April 1942, 15, transcript at Department of Labor Library, Washington, DC.

11. Harry Weiss and Philip Arnow, "Recent Transition of Redcaps from Tip to Wage Status," *American Labor Legislation Review* 32 (September 1942): 142; *Bags & Baggage* 5 (May 1942), 2; *Bags & Baggage* 3 (November 1940): 4; and "Red Caps— They Have Come a Longways," *Pulse* 5 (December 1947): 7.

12. *Bags & Baggage* 3 (November 1940): 4.

13. *Bags & Baggage* 4 (March 1941): 1, 3, 4; and Ernest Calloway, "Their World and Ours: Victory over Jim Crow," *Bags & Baggage* 4 (October 1941): 4. On the Clerks' designs on redcaps and other groups of black workers, see Herbert Northrup, *Organized Labor and the Negro* (New York: Harper and Brothers, 1944), 82–92.

14. Willard S. Townsend, "The CIO and the Race Question," *Sunday Chicago Bee*, January 2, 1944; *Chicago Defender*, April 18, May 30, June 6, 1942; and *Bags & Baggage* 5 (May 1942): 1, 2; 5 (June 1942): 1; 5 (July 1942): 2, 4.

15. *Pittsburgh Courier*, July 10, 1943; December 22, 1945; *Chicago Defender*, November 4, 1939; and *Norfolk Journal and Guide*, January 19, 1946.

16. James H. Hogans, "Among Railroad and Pullman Workers: Mr. Townsend and the Japanese," *Baltimore Afro-American*, March 7, 1942; and *Sunday Chicago Bee*, August 6, 1944; November 7, 1943.

17. *Pittsburgh Courier*, October 2, 1943. On the FEPC, see Merl E. Reed, *Seedtime for the Modern Civil Rights Movement: The President's Committee on Fair Employment Practice, 1941–1946* (Baton Rouge: Louisiana State University Press, 1991); and Arnesen, *Brotherhoods of Color*, 181–202.

18. *Chicago Defender*, February 28, 1948.

19. *Pittsburgh Courier*, July 1, 1950.

20. *Pittsburgh Courier*, November 23, 1946; November 12, 1949; and *Chicago Defender*, February 28, 1948.

21. Willard S. Townsend, "Progress of Organized Labor Has Been Swift in Belgium," *Chicago Defender*, July 12, 1952; and Townsend, "Red Parade in Tokyo Snatches Convert from Grip of Democracy," *Chicago Defender*, September 6, 1952.

22. P. L. Prattis, "Labor Everywhere," *Pittsburgh Courier*, September 14, 1946; author's interview with Leon Despres (a white labor attorney who served as counsel for

the Red Caps' Union), December 20, 1994; author's interview with Ike Golden, April 13, 1995; "This Is the Story," in *Convention Journal, The Eighth Biennial Convention of the United Transport Service Employees, June 22–25, 1952, Hotel Manse, Cincinnati, Ohio* (n.p., 1952); *Houston Negro Labor News*, September 13, 1947; Horace R. Cayton, "Railroadmen: Besieged by Two Rival Unions—Randolph, Townsend Should Agree," *Pittsburgh Courier*, July 26, 1941; and Romero, "Willard Townsend," 130, 61.

23. Willard S. Townsend, "One American Problem and a Possible Solution," in *What the Negro Wants*, ed. Rayford Logan (Chapel Hill: University of North Carolina Press, 1944), 183.

24. Harold L. Keith, "Willard S. Townsend, Boss of the Redcaps," *Pittsburgh Courier*, February 16, 1957; and "Willard Townsend Dies," *American Federationist* 64, no. 3 (March 1957): 19.

25. *Proceedings of the Fourth Biennial Convention*, 19–20; and Townsend, "One American Problem and a Possible Solution," 184.

Suggested Readings

The past two decades have witnessed a small explosion in studies of African American workers and working-class and union race relations. Two overviews of recent developments in the field are Rick Halpern, "Organized Labor, Black Workers, and the Twentieth Century South: The Emerging Revision," in *Race and Class in the American South since 1890*, ed. Melvyn Stokes and Rick Halpern, 43–76 (New York: Oxford University Press, 1994), and Eric Arnesen, "Up from Exclusion: Black and White Workers, Race, and the State of Labor History," *Reviews in American History* 26, no. 1 (March 1998): 146–74.

The literature on African Americans in the railroad industry has largely focused on Pullman porters. Key works are Jervis Anderson, *A. Philip Randolph: A Biographical Portrait* (New York: Harcourt, Brace, Jovanovich, 1973); William H. Harris, *Keeping the Faith: A. Philip Randolph, Milton P. Webster, and the Brotherhood of Sleeping Car Porters, 1925–37* (Urbana: University of Illinois Press, 1977); Jack Santino, *Miles of Smiles, Years of Struggle: Stories of Black Pullman Porters* (Urbana: University of Illinois Press, 1991); David D. Perata, *Those Pullman Blues: An Oral History of the African American Railroad Attendant* (New York: Twayne, 1996); and Melinda Chateauvert, *Marching Together: The Women of the Brotherhood of Sleeping Car Porters* (Urbana: University of Illinois Press, 1997). Beth Bates, *Pullman Porters and the Rise of Protest Politics in Black America* (Chapel Hill: University of North Carolina Press, 2001), provides the best study of the BSCP and its broader agenda. Eric Arnesen, *Brotherhoods of Color: Black Railroad Workers and the Struggle for Equality* (Cambridge, MA: Harvard University Press, 2001), explores the worlds of porters, redcaps, locomotive firemen, and brakemen in the nineteenth and twentieth centuries.

Studies of black workers before the CIO era include Daniel Letwin, *The Challenge of Interracial Unionism: Alabama Coal Miners, 1878–1921* (Chapel Hill: University of North Carolina Press, 1997); Tera W. Hunter, *To 'Joy My*

Freedom: Southern Black Women's Lives and Labors after the Civil War (Cambridge, MA: Harvard University Press, 1997); and Eric Arnesen, *Waterfront Workers of New Orleans: Race, Class, and Politics, 1863–1923* (New York: Oxford University Press, 1991).

Among important studies of black workers in the CIO era are Michael Honey, *Southern Labor and Black Civil Rights: Organizing Memphis Workers* (Urbana: University of Illinois Press, 1993); Roger Horowitz, *"Negro and White, Unite and Fight!": A Social History of Industrial Unionism in Meatpacking, 1930–90* (Urbana: University of Illinois Press, 1997); Rick Halpern, *Down on the Killing Floor: Black and White Workers in Chicago's Packinghouses, 1904–54* (Urbana: University of Illinois Press, 1997); Robert Korstad and Nelson Lichtenstein, "Opportunities Found and Lost: Labor, Radicals, and the Early Civil Rights Movement," *Journal of American History* 75 (December 1988): 786–811; Kevin Boyle, " 'There Are No Union Sorrows That the Union Can't Heal': The Struggle for Racial Equality in the United Automobile Workers, 1940–1960," *Labor History* 36 (Winter 1995): 5–23; Rick Halpern, "Interracial Unionism in the Southwest: Fort Worth's Packinghouse Workers, 1937–1954," in *Organized Labor in the Twentieth-Century South,* ed. Robert H. Zieger (Knoxville: University of Tennessee Press, 1991), 158–82; August Meier and Elliot Rudwick, *Black Detroit and the Rise of the UAW* (New York: Oxford University Press, 1979); and Robin D. G. Kelley, *Hammer and Hoe: Alabama Communists during the Great Depression* (Chapel Hill: University of North Carolina Press, 1990).

11

Elmer Henderson
Civil Servant and Civil Rights Activist

Andrew E. Kersten

In the decades following World War II the modern civil rights movement emerged as thousands of ordinary Americans, both black and white, took to the streets and demanded racial equality. The seeds for these mass protests were planted during the Great Depression of the 1930s and World War II. During those years a dedicated group of activists challenged President Franklin D. Roosevelt to support civil rights through legislative initiatives. While Roosevelt, relying on the Democratic Party's traditional white southern voter base, failed to introduce civil rights or antilynching legislation, his New Deal programs benefited many African Americans. A multitude of New Deal agencies offered financial assistance to the unemployed, provided subsidies for poverty-stricken farmers, and created job opportunities for both black and white Americans. In addition, First Lady Eleanor Roosevelt, a staunch supporter of racial justice, was instrumental in recruiting a cadre of highly trained African Americans into high-ranking federal government offices. Known as Roosevelt's Black Cabinet, these civil servants worked in segregated offices, yet they continuously challenged the federal government to assume a leadership role in the struggle for racial equality.

As African Americans found new allies in the White House, black voters shifted their allegiance from the Republican to the Democratic Party. Moreover, the members of the Black Cabinet inspired a generation of black students who enrolled in unprecedented numbers in colleges and universities during the 1930s. Among them was Elmer Henderson, who, as Andrew E. Kersten demonstrates, used his career as a civil servant to pressure the federal government to increase employment opportunities for African Americans, adopt color-blind policies, and promote racial equality.

Early in the afternoon of May 17, 1942, Elmer W. Henderson went to Union Station in Washington, DC, bought a first class ticket, and boarded a Southern Railway train bound for Atlanta, Georgia, en route to Birmingham, Alabama. He was on federal government business. As a newly appointed member of President Franklin D. Roosevelt's Fair Employment Practice Committee (FEPC), he had just received his first big assignment, which was to investigate job discrimination in

Birmingham. The train left the station at two o'clock and at around five made its way into Virginia. About one-half hour later the first call to dinner was announced. Henderson went to the dining car and waited to be seated. As was customary, the two tables at the end of the dining car, those nearest the kitchen and the steward's office, were reserved for blacks. When any black passengers occupied those seats, curtains were drawn between them and the white passengers. There were, however, exceptions to this rule. African Americans were not seated if there was another dining car reserved entirely for blacks or if whites needed the tables. In this case, on May 17, there were more white patrons than dining-car tables. Hence, whites laid claim to those last place settings, and Henderson went without dinner.

Once in Birmingham, Henderson conducted his FEPC work and then filed a complaint with the Interstate Commerce Commission (ICC). Not only did the ICC have jurisdiction over such matters but also the 1887 law that created it explicitly prohibited racial discrimination in interstate travel. It was unlawful, the law read, for a railroad engaged in interstate commerce "to subject any particular person . . . to any undue or unreasonable prejudice or disadvantage in any respect whatsoever."[1] In 1946 the ICC ruled that Henderson had been treated unfairly. In response the Southern Railway Company issued new dining-car rules: ten tables of each dining car were to be reserved exclusively for whites, and one table, near the kitchen, was to be designated for the exclusive use of black patrons. Company officials believed that the new rules would address Henderson's complaint and prevent similar problems in the future. Moreover, they were confident that the new arrangement was perfectly legal and constitutional. After all, since the Supreme Court's 1896 *Plessy v. Ferguson* decision, racial segregation had been the law of the land. Henderson, however, rejected the deal and took his appeal to the Supreme Court, which ruled in 1950. In his famous court brief, Philip Elman, Henderson's lawyer, argued that segregation was a "badge of inferiority" and ought to be struck down. In a near unanimous decision, the Justices agreed with Elman that segregation was a "constitutional anachronism" and forced the Southern Railway to integrate its cars. Thus, the *Henderson v. U.S.* decision overturned the infamous *Plessy* ruling, laying the groundwork for the 1954 *Brown v. Board of Education* case, which mandated desegregation.[2]

Historians and legal scholars have largely overlooked this crucial precedent to the *Brown* decision as well as Henderson's contributions to the struggle for civil rights. Yet Henderson's significant role in the movement for racial justice hinges not merely on his success in fighting discrimination in interstate transportation and employment. Unlike other contemporary civil rights leaders, such as Walter White of the National Association for the Advancement of Colored People (NAACP) or A. Philip Randolph of the Brotherhood of Sleeping Car Porters, Henderson often worked within the government in his pursuit of racial equality. From 1943 to 1982 he maintained that the offices of the federal government as well as other municipal and state agencies should be promoters of civil rights. Using his various governmental positions, he tried to make the United States a place where democracy was adhered to in practice and not just in theory. As Henderson put it in 1943, "working together in a common enterprise without the fetters of a milieu which provoke attitudes of superiority and inferiority, Government workers [have shown] that a democracy which includes all of the people can work, if the will exists to make it work."[3] Henderson's lifelong struggle for racial justice illustrates the efforts of many African Americans who used their government jobs to attack prejudice and bias.

On June 18, 1913, in Baltimore, Maryland, Daisy S. Henderson gave birth to her first son, whom she and her husband named Elmer William. Elmer's mother was the vice principal at Robert Brown Elliot School, No. 104. His father, Elmer Alonzo, worked as the principal of Elementary School No. 101 and later rose to become Baltimore's first black assistant superintendent of schools. Elmer had two younger brothers: Robert, who served in World War II and remained in the army as an administrative officer until 1974; and Douglas, better known as "Jocko," whom *Jet* magazine labeled a "topflight" disc jockey in Philadelphia. Among those who owed some part of their stardom to Jocko were Diana Ross and Stevie Wonder.[4] Although perhaps in less publicly recognized ways, Elmer became as important to the nation as his famous brother.

Elmer Henderson was a precocious child, graduating from Baltimore's Frederick Douglass High School at age fifteen, after having won the Harry S. McCard Medal, a local award for excellence in speech and rhetoric. His debating and oratory skills would later serve him well in his fight for civil rights. In 1937, Elmer graduated with a B.A. in sociology from Morgan State College. Later that year he moved to Chicago and enrolled as a graduate student at the University of Chicago. In 1939 he received his master's degree in sociology.[5] During his graduate student days, Henderson became involved in the local civil rights movement. The personal connections that he made while working for racial justice in the Windy City permanently changed his life. The individual who apparently had the most influence was Earl B. Dickerson, head of the Chicago Urban League, influential member of the Chicago NAACP, and an alderman from one of the city's black wards.[6] The two became lifelong friends. It was Dickerson who helped bring Henderson into the civil rights movement in Chicago and who convinced him of the importance of state activism in the quest to improve the lives of America's minorities.

Elmer Henderson shaking hands with President Jimmy Carter (n.d.). From the private photograph collection of Elmer Henderson, in the Wisconsin Historical Society, Madison. *Courtesy of Earlene Henderson*

Not long after meeting Dickerson in the late 1930s, Henderson joined the Chicago branch of the NAACP and soon became its executive secretary. He used his position to help improve the economic conditions of Chicago's black residents. The Great Depression had hit the Windy City hard. As all laborers made their way down the economic ladder, blacks were pushed continually to a lower rung than whites. New Deal projects did not immediately help many unemployed black workers, while Chicago's white employers hired whites to perform "Negro jobs." As sociologists J. G. St. Clair Drake and Horace R. Cayton documented in their study of black Chicago, African American workers lost out in the intense job competition of the depression years. Moreover, as the Great Depression began to fade when the United States geared up for World War II, African Americans in Chicago remained unemployed. According to a prewar study prepared for the American

Youth Commission, Chicago employment was organized on "a castelike or racial basis." This meant that "such traits as skin color, hair texture, and Negroid features [had] an exaggerated importance in determining social or vocational success." As a result, unlike a majority of Americans, black Chicagoans did not share equally in the economic boom caused by the start of war in Europe.[7]

To investigate the economic condition of the state's black communities, Democratic governor Henry Horner appointed the Illinois Commission on the Condition of the Urban Colored Population in January 1940. The commission was headed by State Senator William A. Wallace, State Representative Ernest A. Greene, A. L. Foster of the Chicago Urban League, and Alderman Earl B. Dickerson. Partly because of Dickerson's recommendation as well as Henderson's reputation as a "young, hard-hitting, serious-minded" activist and intellectual, the commission hired Henderson as its research assistant. Henderson hoped that his work for the state commission would help "to insure equal opportunities for all Illinois' citizens, thus deepening and expanding that democracy which we Americans are now preparing to defend."[8]

Over the next several months, Henderson conducted investigations and public hearings in several cities. His inquiry into the condition of Chicago's black community highlighted problems that were typical throughout the state. On January 3 and 4, 1941, the Horner Commission interviewed city officials and activists. Philip Flum of the Illinois State Employment Service informed the commission that job placements had increased during 1940 as a result of a growth in defense contracts. In August 1940, Flum's office had placed 4,217 workers, 719 of them black. In the following month, 5,071 workers, 795 of them black, got jobs through the state employment service. While black workers constituted 17 percent of all job placements in August 1940 and 16 percent in the following month, African Americans continued to face employment discrimination, and the percentage of those on relief rose steadily. According to a 1941 survey of 358 Chicago defense industries, two-thirds of the companies refused to hire any African American workers. Furthermore, Leo M. Lyons, head of the Chicago Relief Administration, reported that although fewer people were on relief, the percentage of blacks on relief rolls was increasing despite the economic boom. From November 1939 to November 1940 the total relief population decreased 15 percent from 229,305 to 193,721. Yet, Lyons also pointed out that in November 1940, 47 percent of those receiving relief were black, roughly 5 points higher than the rate had been the previous November, while the percentage of whites on relief had dropped 5 points to 53 percent. Perhaps Ishmael P. Flory, a field organizer for the National Negro Congress, a radical civil rights group, described the situation in Chicago and Illinois most clearly. He told the state commission that the barriers to defense employment were merely "an aspect of a whole system of discrimination against Negroes in private industry."9

It may have come as a disappointment to Henderson that his investigative work on the Illinois Commission produced neither immediate social and economic changes nor lasting legislative results. Yet the commission's exposure of racial discrimination in defense industries prompted some African Americans in Chicago to demonstrate against the hypocrisies of the "arsenal of democracy." On February 14, 1941, more than 1,000 people, both white and black, paraded through the streets of Chicago in a march heralded as a "Demonstration for Democracy." Many local civil rights activists, including Henderson, and some Congress of Industrial Organizations (CIO) unionists participated. This combination of government investigation and civil rights activism in 1940 and 1941 must have left an indelible mark on Henderson, who spent most of the rest of his career advancing civil rights through his governmental positions. From those seats of power, he was able to affect not only civil rights but American political culture as well.10

Although important for introducing Henderson to the potential force of government office, his tenure on the Illinois Commission on the Condition of the Urban Colored Population was brief. After the commission, whose mission was only to survey conditions, was dismantled in 1941, Henderson left Chicago for New Orleans and Dillard University where he took a job as an instructor of social anthropology.11 His career in academia was interrupted, however, by another chance to use a state office as an agent for civil rights and social change. In 1943, Henderson joined the most controversial government agency of its time, the FEPC.

In January 1941, A. Philip Randolph, head of the Brotherhood of Sleeping Car Porters, a black labor union, announced that if the Roosevelt administration failed to deal with racial discrimination in defense industries, he would march 100,000 African Americans down Pennsylvania Avenue on July 1, 1941. Roosevelt sought to prevent the protest march for two reasons. First, Washington, DC, culturally a southern city, was still segregated. One hundred thousand black protestors, the president feared, had the potential to spark a race riot. Second, Roosevelt did not want American racism to become grist for the Axis powers' propaganda mills. Throughout that winter and spring, Roosevelt and his advisers negotiated with Randolph in an effort to convince him to cancel the march. Randolph, however, was unwilling to compromise. Finally, five days before the scheduled protest march, Roosevelt gave in to Randolph's demands. On June 25, 1941, the president issued Executive Order 8802, banning employment discrimination on the basis of race, creed, color, or national origin in defense industries, labor unions, and civilian agencies of the federal government. To enforce the executive order, Roosevelt created the FEPC.[12]

Among the first to be selected by President Roosevelt for the FEPC was Dickerson of Chicago. In early 1942, Henderson joined him on the committee's staff. Although the historical records do not indicate why the FEPC hired Henderson, it seems reasonable to assume that Dickerson was instrumental in suggesting him. Henderson served as a roving FEPC investigator until 1943, when he became the head of the committee's Chicago regional office. The city served as his base for fighting job discrimination in Illinois, Indiana, Iowa, Minnesota, and Wisconsin. Because of staff and funding shortages, Henderson mainly concentrated his efforts on combating employment discrimination in Illinois. In a way, this new government job afforded him the means to finish what he had started on the Horner Commission in 1940. Despite setbacks in southern Illinois and in Chicago's plumbers and steamfitters unions, Henderson and his staff had made a significant impact in the state by the end of the war. In Chicago, FEPC officials docketed more than 500 complaints, making the city's FEPC office the third most active in the nation behind New York and Philadelphia.[13] Using his gift for debate and oration, Henderson settled nearly 60 percent of these cases. He strove to eliminate discriminatory job barriers and create job opportunities for individual minority workers. He purposefully avoided setting job quotas, which he and other FEPC officials thought would lead to employment ceilings rather than increased job opportunities. Thus, Henderson shared the views of many depression-era civil rights activists who fought for a society in which individuals could express and realize their desires, dreams, and goals without hindrance. Group solutions to social problems such as separate-but-equal did not ring true to him.[14]

The FEPC, with the cooperation of local labor, civil rights, and government leaders, changed the general employment pattern in Chicago. As had been the case during World War I, the city's black workers had won a place in the area's industries. The percentage of blacks in the labor force rose from 8.6 percent in 1943 to 13.1 percent in 1944, exceeding the national average of 8.3 percent in 1944.[15] Black workers found jobs, both skilled and unskilled, in manufacturing, transportation, construction, and government. As the Chicago Urban League proudly reported toward the end of the war, "industrial democracy has come to be the accepted pattern in the Chicago area. . . . From one end of the city to the other—in hundreds of plants both large and small—in almost every industry of any kind," Urban League officials claimed, "we can cite actual cases" of fair employment.[16] Testifying before the Senate Subcommittee on Education and Labor, in late 1944, the chairman of the Chicago Council against Racial and Religious Discrimination, Arnold Aronson, who would later participate in the postwar push for a permanent federal fair employment law, credited the FEPC for opening job opportunities in the city. "As a result of the activities of the FEPC," Aronson maintained, "employment [has] been secured for thousands of workers in jobs which previously had been closed to them."[17] He publicly thanked the FEPC in general, and Henderson in particular, for their diligent efforts. Henderson had not acted alone. Cooperating with local activists, he had united those fighting for fair employment and illustrated the progress that was possible when government joined hands with proponents of civil rights.[18]

Henderson's other major contribution to civil rights was also the product of his work for the Fair Employment Practice Committee. His legal struggle to ban racial discrimination and segregation in interstate commerce was an eleven-year quest. What sustained him was the fact that he was not alone. Civil rights leaders, sympathetic lawyers, and social activists who immediately recognized the opportunities that his constitutional challenge presented, lined up behind him. Among those who offered encouragement, legal briefs, and advice were Chicago alderman Earl Dickerson, Thurgood Marshall of the NAACP, Will Maslow of the American Jewish Congress, and Arthur J. Goldberg of the CIO. In the end, Henderson needed all their assistance because his fight was not merely with the Southern Railway but also with the ICC. Legally he desired a Supreme Court ruling that would force the ICC, the arm of the federal government responsible for enforcing laws and policies concerning interstate transportation, to end its tacit, de facto approval of racial segregation and discrimination and thus compel integration.[19]

Getting the ICC to do what Henderson wanted was a difficult task. Initially the commission seemed supportive. On March 1, 1946, four years after Henderson filed his complaint, the ICC ruled that he had been subjected to "undue and unreasonable prejudice and disadvantage."[20] Yet the ICC also decided that the Southern Railway's new rules on segregation in dining cars were in compliance with the federal law. Henderson and his lawyers then took both the ICC and the Southern Railway to court. In addition to Marshall, Maslow, and Goldberg, Henderson's legal team included President Harry S. Truman's solicitor general, Philip B. Pearlman.[21] In his government brief, Pearlman argued passionately that "what is separate cannot be equal," an idea that swayed the Justices.[22] On June 5, 1950, Justice Harold H. Burton spoke for the Court, deciding in Henderson's favor, although without explicit reference to the 1896 *Plessy* decision that the ruling overturned. Despite the hoopla and accolades, which included for Henderson a place on the 1950 "Honor Roll of Democracy" of the influential black newspaper the *Chicago Defender*, the fight was not over.[23] Who was going to enforce the decision? In the end it was Henderson who assumed that role, too. For three years after *Henderson v. United States*, he pressured the Southern Railway and the ICC to eliminate racial segregation on dining cars. When in 1952, for instance, the ICC ruled that the Southern Railway's new policy of seating "women with women, men with men, elderly persons with elderly persons, white persons with white persons, and Negroes with Negroes" complied with the law, Henderson again brought suit against the federal agency and the railroad company.[24] In late 1953 the Southern Railway conceded and issued its revised and final diner policy. Patrons were to be seated and served on a first-come basis. Henderson had won.[25]

While engaged in his struggle against discrimination in public transportation, Henderson continued to find ways of using governmental institutions to advance civil rights in other areas. In 1946, when Congress eliminated the wartime FEPC, Henderson joined a municipal agency, the Chicago Human Rights Commission, as its government employment and minority groups expert.[26] The commission's mission was to recommend to the mayor means by which the municipal administration could attack prejudice and discrimination in the city. Perhaps unhappy with the group's advisory role, Henderson left Chicago in 1947 and moved to Washington, DC, where he resumed his academic career at Howard University, teaching sociology and political science. Still committed to social justice, he also joined A. Philip Randolph's civil rights organization, the National Council for a Permanent FEPC.[27]

A professor's life must not have brought much pleasure to Henderson, who by the late 1940s had left his full-time appointment at Howard University to pursue a law career. However, he maintained his ties to Howard University and often taught sociology classes in the evening. In 1948 he enrolled at Georgetown University Law School, becoming one of the first African Americans to do so. Yet he remained active in the civil rights movement and maintained his belief that the federal government should serve as an agent of social change.

In late 1948, Henderson stopped working directly with Randolph's National Council when he was hired as the executive director of the newly formed American Council on Human Rights (ACHR). The ACHR's membership consisted of 75,000 undergraduate students from black fraternities and sororities. The group's mission was to pressure the federal government to enforce existing civil rights legislation "with a special emphasis on interstate travel," to mobilize support for new legislation, and to encourage members to become registered voters. While serving as the ACHR's executive director between 1948 and 1955, Henderson attempted to push the Democratic Party further on civil rights by befriending President Truman and by lambasting Congress. Henderson urged Truman and Congress to act positively on civil rights and sought to convince federal officials to open the doors of opportunity for African Americans.[28]

Henderson had been a fervent Democrat, reflecting the changing political alignment of African Americans during the Roosevelt administration. In fact, this change had been the subject of his master's thesis at the University of Chicago. While Henderson voted for the Democratic Party, he was not blind to the party's problems and mixed record regarding civil rights. During the 1930s and 1940s liberals had led the party, but southern white conservatives often dictated racial policy. Seeking President Truman's support of civil rights, Henderson paid a visit to the White House on March 3, 1951. Accompanied by eleven black civil rights leaders, including A. Philip Randolph, Lester Granger, head of the National Urban League, and Mary McLeod Bethune, an influential member of President Roosevelt's informal Black Cabinet, Henderson presented Truman with a list of demands calling for a new FEPC, more blacks in government employment, and integration of federal agencies. Truman agreed to make their cause his, and in 1952 the president earned the ACHR's annual award for his "great contribution to civil rights in America."[29] Nonetheless, his failure to end discrimination in the federal government as well as his inability to get Congress to pass fair employment-practice legislation prompted Henderson to criticize Truman for not doing everything in his power to advance civil rights.[30]

Henderson recognized that to some extent Truman's hands were tied by a reactionary Congress whose southern leadership bottled up civil rights legislation. Nevertheless, under Henderson, the ACHR joined the NAACP and the American Jewish Congress in voicing extreme disgust at the members of the House and Senate for failing to champion civil rights. In addition to criticizing representatives of both parties, Henderson sought to influence the 1952 national elections. The ACHR wanted both parties to adopt strong civil rights planks in their party platforms. Thus, both presidential candidates as well as congressional office seekers could be held responsible for their actions or inactions. Henderson pulled no punches during the campaign. "If the Democratic Party platform compromises on civil rights and Senator [Richard] Russell of Georgia or one of like mind is placed on the ticket either as the presidential or vice-presidential nominee," Henderson told the black newspaper the *Chicago Defender*, "the Democratic party may consider the Negro vote as lost." Similarly, he warned the Republicans not to count on the black vote, unless the party adopted a civil rights plank. Only the Democrats responded. Both Henderson and the NAACP's Walter White thought that the Democratic Party's 1952 civil rights plank was even stronger than its 1948 one. In 1948 the Democrats merely called on Congress to support the president in "his courageous stand on the issue of civil rights." Four years later the Democrats demanded "Federal legislation effectively to secure [civil] rights to everyone." The Republican Party virtually ignored civil rights in its platform, which was adopted in two minutes by the national convention. In what Henderson labeled a "backward step," the Republican Party retreated from its firm stance in 1948 when it had called for the "enactment and just enforcement of "federal [civil rights] legislation." In 1952 the Republican Party did call for federal fair employment-practice legislation, but it also affirmed the notion that "it is primarily the responsibility of each state to order and control its own domestic institutions."[31]

Soon after the parties' national conventions the ACHR endorsed Democratic contender Adlai Stevenson, and Henderson became one of his closest advisers on racial matters. The failure of Stevenson's campaign might have hardened Henderson's resolve. He continued working for the ACHR for four years even though he had received his law degree and passed the bar in the District of Columbia in March 1952. Shortly afterward he began to practice law, and in 1954 he married Earlene Cobb and started a family.

In 1955, Henderson left his post as the ACHR's executive director when he was once again called into civil service. An old friend from Henderson's Chicago days, William L. Dawson, a black Democratic congressman from Illinois, offered him a job as associate counsel of the House Government Operations Committee, a post he held for nearly thirty years. His work focused on government reorganization, government procurement, and consumer protection. In 1975, Chet Holifield, Democratic congressman from California, elevated Henderson to general counsel, another precedent for African Americans. This promotion provided Henderson with more money and political influence on Congress's main oversight committee.[32]

Although Henderson remained an informal presidential adviser on racial matters, he began to devote most of his professional time to his legal duties on the Government Operations Committee. He also began spending more time with his family. Nonetheless, Henderson kept his belief that the federal government had "an important duty to maintain equality among its citizens and to further the cause of human rights." Although Henderson remained a lifetime member of the NAACP, during the 1960s he did not join any of the protests sponsored by the Southern Christian Leadership Conference, the Student Nonviolent Coordinating Committee, or the Congress for Racial Equality. From time to time, he did lend his voice to the political debates on civil rights.

In 1978, Henderson published an essay that encapsulated his views. Looking back over American history since the Civil War, he saw not only the "tragic results for American blacks of the failure of government to fully meet its responsibilities" but also the enormous progress. Modestly, Henderson glossed over the civil rights contributions of the Supreme Court and his particular landmark case. Similarly he downplayed his work on the FEPC, which to him "represented the use of executive power in the federal government to curb rampant discrimination in employment in the defense industries and government service." Still, this "awakening of federal responsibility," as Henderson put it, culminated in the Great Society reforms of the 1960s "when at long last the federal government agreed to commit itself by statute and policy to equality among its citizens." Finally, he insisted that vigilance was needed to ensure that the transformations in law and society remain. Noting that President Richard M. Nixon had weakened federal involvement in civil rights, Henderson hoped that government officials would maintain the "necessary will and determination" to sustain the "federal arsenal of civil rights protection" to continue to work for justice. Perhaps reflected in these concluding remarks was Henderson's hope that others who shared his passion for justice and agreed with his methods would recognize the great progress that had been made during the age of Roosevelt and carry on the struggle.[33] Elmer Henderson, who had helped make civil rights history, died on July 18, 2001. His widow, Earlene, still lives in Washington, DC.

Notes

1. *Interstate Commerce Act, U.S. Statutes at Large* 24 (1887), 380.

2. Anthony Lewis, "Imposing on Them a Badge of Inferiority," *New York Times*, January 22, 2000; *Henderson v. United States*, 339 US 816 (1950); *Plessy v. Ferguson*, 163 US 537 (1896); and *New York Times*, June 6, 1950, from Elmer Henderson's personal newspaper clipping collection, Wisconsin Historical Society, Madison, Wisconsin.

3. Elmer W. Henderson, "Negroes in Government Employment," *Opportunity* 21 (1943): 143 and 163.

4. Maralyn Lois Polak, "Eee-tiddly-ock . . . Remember the Jock?" *Philadelphia Inquirer*, June 12, 1977, from Elmer Henderson's personal newspaper clipping collection.

5. "E. Henderson Get [*sic*] MA Degree from Chicago U.," unidentified, undated newspaper clipping in Elmer Henderson's personal newspaper clipping collection. Copy in author's possession. His master's thesis was titled "A Study of the Basic Factors Involved in the Change in the Party Alignment of Negroes in Chicago, 1932–1938." Henderson's M.A. was granted in 1939.

6. For more information on Dickerson, see Christopher R. Reed, *The Chicago NAACP and the Rise of Black Professional Leadership* (Bloomington: Indiana University Press, 1997), and Andrew E. Kersten, *Race, Jobs, and the War: The FEPC in the Midwest, 1941–1946* (Urbana: University of Illinois Press, 2000), 19.

7. W. Lloyd Warner, Buford H. Junker, and Walter A. Adams, *Color and Human Nature: Negro Personality Development in a Northern City* (Washington, DC: American Council on Education, 1941), 292; J. St. Clair Drake and Horace R. Cayton, *Black Metropolis: A Study of Negro Life in a Northern City*, 2 vols. (New York: Harper and Row, 1945; reprint ed., 1962), 1:26, 218–32; *Chicago Bee*, August 8, 1940; and Kersten, *Race, Jobs, and the War*, 19.

8. *Chicago Defender*, September 15, 1940, from Elmer Henderson's personal newspaper clipping collection.

9. Verbatim transcripts of the proceedings of the Commission on the Condition of the Urban Colored Population, January 3–4, 1941, *Microfilmed Records of the Fair Employment Practice Committee* (Glen Rock, NJ: Microfilm Corporation of America, 1970), reels 1 and 17.

10. Kersten, *Race, Jobs, and the War*, 26–28.

11. "Elmer Henderson, Jr. Named to Dillard Staff," unidentified, undated newspaper clipping from Elmer Henderson's personal newspaper clipping collection.

12. Kersten, *Race, Jobs, and the War*, 9–20.

13. The FEPC had roughly a dozen of these offices. See Kersten, *Race, Jobs, and the War*, 37–46.

14. Ibid., 35 and 116.

15. Ibid., 58–59, 135; and Robert C. Weaver, *Negro Labor: A National Problem* (New York: Harcourt, Brace, Jovanovich, 1946), 78–81.

16. Chicago Urban League, *Industrial Relations Bulletin: An Informational Service for Management and Labor* (October/November 1944), 1.

17. Senate Committee on Education and Labor, *Fair Employment Practice Act: Hearings on S.R. 2048 before a Subcommittee of the Committee on Education and Labor*, 78th Cong., 2d sess., August 30, 31, September 6, 7, and 9, 1944 (Washington, DC: Government Printing Office, 1944), 65–72.

18. Kersten, *Race, Jobs, and the War*, 47–59.

19. *Henderson v. United States*; American Veterans Committee, *Motion for Leave to File Brief and Brief of American Veterans Committee, Inc., Amicus Curiae* (Washington, DC: AVC, 1949); and Belford V. Lawson Jr., *Before the Interstate Commerce Commission, Docket No. 28895, Elmer W. Henderson v. Southern Railway Company; Brief on Behalf of Complainant* (1949) [brief in Henderson's personal papers, copy in author's possession].

20. *Henderson v. United States*.

21. The Solicitor General's Office handled all federal government business before the United States Supreme Court.

22. *Pittsburgh Courier*, April 7, 1951, from Elmer Henderson's personal newspaper clipping collection.

23. *Chicago Defender*, January 6, 1951, from Elmer Henderson's personal newspaper clipping collection.

24. *New York Herald Tribune*, February 23, 1952, from Elmer Henderson's personal newspaper clipping collection.

25. *Jet* (November 19, 1953): 10.

26. See Chicago Conference on Home Front Unity, *Human Relations in Chicago: Report of the Commission and Charter of Human Relations* (Chicago: The Conference, 1945), 1–5.

27. "Elmer Henderson Becomes FEPC Council Secretary," unidentified, undated newspaper clipping from Elmer Henderson's personal newspaper clipping collection.

28. *Atlanta Daily World*, December 27, 1953, and *St. Louis Democrat*, December 29, 1953, from Elmer Henderson's personal newspaper clipping collection. The student groups comprising the ACHR were: Kappa Alpha Psi, Alpha Kappa Alpha, Phi Beta Sigma, Alpha Phi Alpha, Sigma Gamma Rho, Delta Sigma Theta, and Zeta Phi Beta. See also Elmer W. Henderson, "The Elimination of Segregation through Protest, Propaganda, and Education," *Journal of Negro Education* 20 (Summer 1951): 475–84; *Ebony* (July 1950): 25–28; and *Ebony* (June 1956): 96.

29. *Washington Afro-American*, March 3, 1951, and December 23, 1952, from Elmer Henderson's personal newspaper clipping collection.

30. *Washington Afro-American*, October 30, 1951, from Elmer Henderson's personal newspaper clipping collection.

31. *Washington Afro-American*, May 27, 1952, and September 27, 1952; *Chicago Defender*, April 7, 1951, July 12, 1952 (quote concerning Democratic platform), July 19, 1952 (quote concerning Republican platform), and August 2, 1952; *Chicago Sun-Times*, July 9–11, 1952; and Congressional Quarterly, *National Party Conventions, 1831–1996* (Washington, DC: Congressional Quarterly, Inc., 1997), 93–95, 97–99 (quotes

from party platforms in 1948 and 1952). All newspaper citations are from clippings found in Elmer Henderson's personal newspaper clipping collection.

32. *Washington Afro-American*, September 27, 1952; "Report to the Board of Directors of the American Council on Human Rights," unpublished typescript, October 15, 1952, 2, Henderson's personal files (copy in author's possession); *Chicago Defender*, March 29, 1952; and "Henderson Quits," unidentified, undated newspaper clipping. All newspaper citations are from Elmer Henderson's personal newspaper clipping collection.

33. Elmer W. Henderson, "The Federal Government and the Fight for Basic Human Rights," in *Negotiating the Mainstream: A Survey of the Afro-American Experience*, ed. Harry A. Johnson (Chicago: American Library Association, 1978), 141, 145, 149, and 162.

Suggested Readings

For background on African Americans and the age of Franklin D. Roosevelt consult Patricia Sullivan, *Days of Hope: Race and Democracy in the New Deal Era* (Chapel Hill: University of North Carolina Press, 1996); and Harvard Sitkoff, *A New Deal for Black Americans: The Emergence of Civil Rights as a National Issue* (New York: Oxford University Press, 1978). Allan Winkler, *Home Front U.S.A.: America during World War II*, 2d ed. (Wheeling, IL: Harlan Davidson, 2000), is a fine summary of the wartime era, and Neil A. Wynn, *The Afro-American and the Second World War* (New York: Holmes and Meier, 1975; reprint, 1993), is still the best survey of the black experience during World War II. Other useful studies include Daniel Kryder, *Divided Arsenal: Race and the American State during World War II* (New York: Cambridge University Press, 2000); Desmond King, *Separate and Unequal: Black Americans and the U.S. Federal Government* (New York: Oxford University Press, 1995); and William C. Berman, *The Politics of Civil Rights in the Truman Administration* (Columbus: Ohio State University Press, 1970). Information on Henderson and the FEPC can be found in Andrew E. Kersten's *Race, Jobs, and the War: The FEPC in the Midwest, 1941–1946* (Urbana: University of Illinois Press, 2000). Henderson's personal papers have been donated to the Wisconsin Historical Society, Madison, Wisconsin.

12

Roberta Church
Race and the Republican Party in the 1950s

Beverly Greene Bond

Roberta Church entered Republican Party politics in 1952, at a time when many African Americans had severed their traditional ties to the party. Black allegiance to the Republicans dated back to the Civil War and the Reconstruction period. During the war the Republican president, Abraham Lincoln, had issued the Emancipation Proclamation, and in the years following the war a Republican Congress had passed the Thirteenth, Fourteenth, and Fifteenth Amendments abolishing slavery, acknowledging black citizenship rights, and removing racial restrictions on voting. It is not surprising that African Americans linked emancipation, citizenship, and male suffrage to the party of Lincoln.

By the end of the nineteenth century, however, northern interest in southern politics and the former slaves had waned. Industrialization, urbanization, and imperialism became the watchwords of America's new leaders. Conservative whites regained control of the South, restoring the Democratic Party, introducing segregation, and disfranchising black voters. Some African Americans were disillusioned by the Republican Party's abandonment of southern blacks, yet the majority of them remained loyal to the Republican Party until the 1930s.

During the Great Depression many African Americans bid "Farewell to the Party of Lincoln" and started to support the Democratic Party. This shift in allegiance was largely due to President Franklin D. Roosevelt's New Deal programs, which provided financial assistance to those in need and created jobs for the nation's unemployed. African Americans not only benefited from these programs but were also recruited in large numbers to serve as special racial advisers in various New Deal agencies. Moreover, the president, and particularly First Lady Eleanor Roosevelt, surrounded themselves with an unprecedented number of African Americans. So many black specialists and unofficial advisers were going in and out of the White House that the group came to be known as the Black Cabinet.

African Americans continued to support the Democratic Party after Harry Truman succeeded Roosevelt in 1945. Truman also took the lead in improving the conditions of African Americans. In 1946 he created the first presidential committee to investigate the status of civil rights, and two years later he issued executive orders desegregating the armed forces and requiring fair employment in the federal service. Roosevelt's and Truman's records made it difficult for the Republicans to appeal to black voters in the 1952 election, particularly because their candidate, Dwight D. Eisenhower, was, at best, lukewarm in his support of civil rights.

Still, as Beverly Greene Bond demonstrates, there were African Americans who had never severed their ties to the Republican Party. Although Roberta Church did not become involved in party politics until 1952, her family had been staunch supporters of the Republican Party for several generations.

Roberta Church's thirty-year career in politics and government began in 1952. She was the first African American woman elected to a political office in the state of Tennessee. The daughter of a wealthy southern family, Church was reared in an environment of politics, privilege, and long-standing allegiance to the Republican Party. Although her grandfather and father held unpaid political positions, Roberta was the first in her family to serve in a paid position in a governmental agency. In the 1950s she was the highest-ranking African American female appointee in the Eisenhower administration. Roberta Church was a symbol of the heightened expectations of blacks in the 1950s, as the judicial and executive branches of the national government removed some barriers to black political participation. Yet her work with the Labor Department during both Eisenhower administrations also reflected the limited impact these changes had in altering patterns of systemic racism in American society.

In 1914, Sarah Roberta Church was born into a life of wealth and privilege beyond the reach of most African Americans of her time. Her grandfather, Robert R. Church Sr., was the son of Captain Charles B. Church, owner of two riverboats that cruised the Mississippi River between Memphis, Tennessee, and New Orleans, Louisiana, during the antebellum era. Robert Church's mother, Emmeline, was the slave of a Virginia planter who migrated to Mississippi and Arkansas in the early nineteenth century. Sources do not indicate how Charles B. Church met Emmeline, but neither she nor her son Robert, who was born on June 18, 1839, in Holly Springs, Mississippi, were Church's slaves. Robert was freed at age twelve after his mother's death in 1851. That year, Robert went to live with his father. Robert worked on his father's riverboat as a cabin boy and steward until he moved to Memphis in 1862.

In Memphis, Robert Church Sr. made a fortune in real estate, banking, and business interests and was described by contemporaries as "the wealthiest colored man in the state of Tennessee and probably in the United States."[1] His circle of friends included prominent leaders of the post-Reconstruction black elite such as Virginia congressman John Mercer Langston, Louisiana governor P. B. S. Pinchback, Frederick Douglass and his son Charles, Booker T. Washington, and Blanche K. Bruce, one of two African Americans who represented Mississippi in the U.S. Senate. All of them visited the Church family home or corresponded with the elder Church. Robert Church Sr. also counted many influential whites among his close friends and acquaintances. He was the first Memphian to purchase a taxing-district bond to help pay the city's debt after it lost its charter in 1879. He later donated land and built an auditorium and park for black residents, who were prohibited from using the city's other recreational facilities. President Theodore Roosevelt addressed a large crowd at Church's auditorium when he visited the city in 1902. Although his business interests took precedence over political activities, Robert Church Sr., like many members of the nation's black elite, was a staunch Republican. He never held political office, but his selection as a delegate to the 1900 Republican National Convention began a tradition of political involvement that his son and granddaughter continued throughout the twentieth century.

Robert Church Sr.'s first marriage ended in divorce but produced two children, Mary and Thomas. Thomas became a New York lawyer, but Mary enjoyed a much more prominent career as an educator, writer, clubwoman, and activist during the Progressive Era. After her graduation from Oberlin College, "Mollie" Church rejected her father's demands that she come home to Memphis to live the life of a daughter of wealth and privilege. Instead, she taught school, first at Wilberforce University, an African American college in Ohio, and later at the M Street Colored School in Washington, DC. She married a colleague, Robert Heberton Terrell, who was appointed judge of the District of Columbia Municipal Court by President Theodore Roosevelt. Mary Church Terrell was a leader in the social world of the black elite in Washington as well as a strong advocate for racial and gender equality. She was cofounder and first president of the National Association of Colored Women (NACW), a charter member of the National Association for the Advancement of Colored People (NAACP), an advocate of women's suffrage, and a member of the District of Columbia's Board of Education.

Robert R. Church Jr. and his sister Annette were the children of Robert Sr.'s second wife, Anna Wright, daughter of an antebellum free black woman, Lucy Jane Wright, and Colonel James Coleman, a relative of John C. Breckinridge.[2] Robert and Annette were educated in private boarding schools and, like their half-sister Mary, graduated from

Oberlin Academy and Oberlin College. Robert also attended the Packard School of Business in New York City and followed his father into business. Annette Church, unlike her half sister Mary, returned to Memphis after her college years and spent much of her life within the family fold. She traveled with her parents, vacationed at African American resort communities in Cape May, New Jersey, and Saratoga, New York, and visited the homes of other prominent blacks such as the author Charles W. Chestnutt. She belonged to, but was not a leader in, both the NACW and the NAACP.

The Churches were a close-knit family who corresponded and visited regularly with each other. Although there was a twenty-year age difference between Mary Church Terrell and her younger siblings, Terrell took an active interest in their lives. Her connections gave Robert and Annette entree into the social and political circles of Washington's black elite. In 1911, Robert R. Church Jr. married Sarah "Sallie" Parodi Johnson, a teacher and a member of a well-known Washington family. Sallie Church's death in 1922 left their only child, eight-year-old Roberta, to be reared in a household that included her father, her grandmother Anna Wright Church, her aunt Annette, and Anna's young niece, Violet Wright.

Robert R. Church Jr. traded in his involvement in business and banking for a career in politics in the early twentieth century. In 1916 he created the Lincoln League, a local political organization that grew into the first large-scale effort in the twentieth century to organize African Americans to register and vote.[3] Church was a powerful force in Memphis politics because he and his lieutenants could get out the vote in the city for whichever candidate promised the most rewards to black communities.

Church's command of the African American vote in Memphis brought him up against the city's powerful political boss, Democrat Edward Hull Crump. The two coexisted for decades because of Church's ability to influence black voters and Church's control over Republican patronage in west Tennessee. Church wrested concessions and rewards from the Crump machine, including city jobs, teaching positions, parks, and some paved streets, while remaining essentially independent of Crump's influence. The two men clashed in the late 1930s, and the Crump machine foreclosed on some of Church's tax delinquencies. Church lost much of his Memphis property, left the city in November 1940, and, with his sister Annette, moved to Chicago, where Roberta was working for the Family Service Division of the Chicago Welfare

Administration. Robert, Annette, and Roberta lived together at 6000 Champlain Avenue until the 1950s. In the 1940s, Robert pushed the Republican Party to include a plank in its 1948 platform calling for a permanent Fair Employment Practices Commission. He collided with Senator Robert Taft, a candidate for the party's presidential nomination, over what Church considered Taft's ambivalence on civil rights.

Robert R. Church Jr.'s political activities formed a central focus of his family's life, and the Church women kept up with the events of the times. They shared newspaper descriptions of Robert's actions at meetings and exchanged letters that sometimes included copies of political reports and platforms for them to review. Like many women of their class, the Church women were observers and enablers rather than active participants in the political dramas of their day. Their social contacts drew them into the center of twentieth-century African American political and cultural life. The family's circle of friends, confidantes, and comrades-in-arms included African American poets, writers, and musicians such as Georgia Douglass Johnson, Anna Arnold Hedgeman, W. C. Handy, Charles W. Chestnutt, J. Rosamond, James Weldon Johnson, James Reese Europe, and Bert Williams, as well as political leaders and activists such as Emmett J. Scott, Roy Wilkins, Walter White, A. Philip Randolph, W. E. B. Du Bois, Roscoe Conkling Bruce, and Oscar De Priest. Influential white politicians such as Clare Boothe Luce, Henry Cabot Lodge, Tennessee congressman Howard Baker Sr., Pennsylvania congressman Hugh Scott, and Senators William Langer of North Dakota and Frank Carlson of Kansas considered Bob Church and, by extension, his family their personal friends and political allies.

Robert Church returned to Memphis in 1952. Crump's political machine had suffered an important defeat in the Senate election of 1948, and African Americans pushed for greater influence in the city. Church moved quickly to try to reestablish his political base and actively campaigned for Senator Robert Taft's opponent for the presidential nomination on the Republican ticket, General Dwight D. Eisenhower. Church suffered a fatal heart attack on April 17, 1952, in the midst of a telephone conversation with his old friend Matthew Thornton, the "Mayor of Beale Street," Memphis's historic black business and residential neighborhood. The two men were discussing Eisenhower's presidential candidacy.

After Robert's funeral, local and national party leaders encouraged his daughter to take up the mantle and carry on her father's work against the Taft supporters. Robert Church's national network of social, economic, and political friends and associates facilitated Roberta's entry into politics in 1952. Roberta Church had grown up in a world where affluence, education, social prestige, and political power cushioned, but did not eliminate, racism. She was born in her maternal grandmother's house in Washington, DC, in 1914, grew up in Memphis, and graduated from the city's private LeMoyne High School. She attended Oberlin College for two years and completed her bachelor's and master's degrees in sociology and psychology at Northwestern University. Roberta worked for

Dwight D. Eisenhower and Roberta Church, 1952. From the Roberta Church Collection, Memphis and Shelby County Room, Memphis/Shelby County Public Library and Information Center, Memphis, Tennessee

the Chicago Welfare Administration and the Illinois Children's Home and Aid Society from 1939 to 1953. Roberta Church never married, but she was surrounded by an intimate circle of family and friends, the most influential of whom was her aunt, Annette Church.

Although her father's political activities and her Aunt Mollie's social activism were never far from her consciousness, Roberta Church was a novice when she entered the race for Tennessee's Republican State Executive Committee in 1952. She never had held any office or been actively involved in party politics. She was also an outsider who had lived in Illinois since she left Memphis to attend college in the early 1930s. But she easily qualified for the Tennessee ballot in June because the family had maintained a voting residence in Memphis. She was the only member of the "New Guard" challengers to the Taft regulars from Memphis to win election to the State Committee in the August primary. Her victory made Roberta Church the first African American woman in the South to be elected a state party committeewoman. Beyond these personal triumphs, however, Roberta Church considered her victory a validation of her father's political goals.

Republican Party leaders Hugh Scott, Frank Carlson, and Henry Cabot Lodge congratulated Roberta when she flew to Denver soon afterward to meet with Eisenhower, who had received the party's nomination at the national convention in July. She went on to Washington to confer with party officials on the role she would play in the campaign. In four short months, Roberta Church stepped out of Robert Church's shadow and into the political arena.

Eisenhower's victory in the 1952 election brought the Republican Party back into power for the first time in two decades. But it was a changed nation that the party would lead. President Franklin D. Roosevelt's New Deal had led thousands of African Americans to abandon the Republican Party in favor of the Democratic Party. The migration of African Americans out of the rural South to northern and midwestern cities, which had begun during World War I, had continued unabated in the 1930s and 1940s and contributed to a steady increase in the number of black voters. Moreover, black participation in World War II had heightened the determination of African Americans to challenge segregation, discrimination, and racism. Black protests and lawsuits had forced integrated hiring in defense plants, admission of African Americans to graduate and professional schools, and the integration of the armed forces.

The Roosevelt and Truman administrations also had drawn ever increasing numbers of African Americans to jobs in the nation's capital. Educator Mary McLeod Bethune, who had served as director of the Negro division of the National Youth Administration, was the highest-ranking black woman in the federal government during the New Deal. Bethune, recognizing the need to coordinate the activities of African American administrators and advisers, had organized the Federal Council on Negro Affairs as an unofficial Black Cabinet.[4] Harry Truman had also brought African American advisers into his administration. In 1949,

Anna Arnold Hedgeman was appointed assistant to the Federal Security Administration, later the Department of Health, Education, and Welfare. Beginning in May 1946, Thomasina Johnson-Norford served as chief of the Minority Group section in the Labor Department's Bureau of Employment Security.

Republican leaders had to demonstrate that they were as sympathetic to the needs of African Americans as Democrats had been, and that they were in tune with the nation's changing racial climate. Roberta Church was well aware of the implications of her Tennessee victory for the party's strategy and she moved quickly to position herself for a role in the presidential campaign of 1952. She returned to her job in Chicago to await specific instructions on how her services would be used.

Unlike the other Church women, with the exception of her Aunt Mollie, Roberta had worked since she completed her master's degree in sociology in the late 1930s. She began her career about the time her father and Aunt Annette left Memphis and the family's economic fortunes were waning. Between 1939 and 1942, Roberta worked for the Chicago Welfare Administration in the Family Service Division. In 1942 she began to work for a private welfare agency that was affiliated with the Children's Welfare League of America. In 1952, when Roberta returned to the agency after her victory in the Tennessee elections, its director informed her that she could not continue in her job and participate actively in politics. Roberta assumed that the reason for the director's mandate was the fact that Eisenhower's Democratic opponent, Governor Adlai Stevenson, was on the agency's board of directors, since other women there were also active in political campaigns. Financial difficulties prompted her to approach the Republican national party about a job in the presidential campaign.

But Roberta Church's efforts were blocked by Tennessee Republican leaders. "Congressman Carroll Reece," according to Church, "kept me out of the Tennessee campaign [and] also kept me off the Eisenhower train, which did not even touch Tennessee, solely because my father and I were pre-convention Eisenhower Republicans and I defeated one of his candidates in the committee race and was a threat to his old guard leader George Lee."[5] Reece's decision to limit Church's visibility in Tennessee may have gone beyond this political wrangling. Old Guard Republicans, those who had supported Taft's nomination, controlled the state party and, although they backed Eisenhower's candidacy in the national election, continued to support George Lee. Lee revived the old Lincoln League and tried to convince Memphis black voters, who had shifted to the Democratic Party during the Roosevelt years, to return to the Republican fold. Although she was a Tennessee Republican committeewoman, Roberta Church's political work was limited to unpaid volunteering in Chicago's Citizens for Eisenhower campaign. Nonetheless, the connections she established with national party leaders brought her closer to her goal of a job in the new Eisenhower administration.

Republicans were committed to bringing women and minorities into the administration both to live up to Eisenhower's promises of fairminded inclusiveness and to capitalize on his popularity with voters. Soon after the election, Val J. Washington became the party's top African American adviser and dispenser of patronage. Washington worked with Thavolia Davis Thomas from the Republican Party's Minorities Division to place African Americans in more than 200 government jobs in the nation's capital. In an interview with an African American reporter one year after Eisenhower took office, Washington described how the two had "cracked job barriers in many departments. When we hear of a lily-white agency we send a letter prodding them and ship a copy to the White House. This is in keeping with the President's expressed policy of integration."[6]

African Americans such as Frederick Morrow probably would have questioned Val Washington's political clout. Morrow, who had worked as a field secretary for the NAACP and in the public affairs department of CBS, was a liaison between the Eisenhower campaign and the African American community. Despite the personal humiliations he confronted while traveling with the campaign, Morrow believed that Eisenhower was likable and sincere in his promises. Morrow, however, had a difficult time in making the administration live up to what he assumed were assurances of a postelection job. He resigned from CBS and moved to the capital in early 1953 but was stunned by the city's segregation and overt racism and the administration's waffling. Although he was eventually placed as an adviser in the Commerce Department, it was two years before he was given the job he thought he had been promised during the campaign, as the first African American special assistant to the White House.[7]

Washington and Thomas were successful in placing African Americans throughout the government. Appointees included Vernon Greene at the Post Office Department, Carmel Marr with the United Nations, Paul Williams with the Housing Department, L. B. Toomer as the first black register of the Treasury in forty years, Jane Spaulding as assistant to the secretary of Health, Education and Welfare, Phillip Sadler as a race relations adviser in the Public Housing Administration, Scovel Richardson on the United States Parole Board, J. Ernest Wilkins as acting chairman of the Government Contract Commission, and Joseph Ray and Phillip Sadler at the Labor Department. Washington and Thomas also claimed the appointments of Lois Lippman as a White House secretary and George Robinson as doorkeeper in the House of Representatives among their successes, noting that their only setback was in the appointment of African American congressional pages. Pages were picked by senators and representatives and their positions were tied to admission to segregated private schools.[8]

More African Americans were appointed to high federal posts during the Eisenhower years than by any other administration since that of Theodore Roosevelt. Some Democrats, however, were critical of claims that the administration was breaking new ground with appointments to what many called Eisenhower's Black Cabinet. They charged that instead of opening up new positions, Republicans were simply replacing black Democrats with black Republicans in a game of patronage musical chairs. Critics also questioned the importance of these jobs as minority consultants and assistants to administrators.[9]

Roberta Church's assignment as minority consultant in the Labor Department placed her within this Eisenhower Black Cabinet, but her appointment was credited to the efforts of the Republican Party's Women's Bureau rather than to Val Washington and Thavolia Thomas. Yet in spite of this emphasis on gender rather than race, Church encountered the same reticence on the part of national Republicans as Frederick Morrow had had in getting the party to live up to its preelection promises. After Eisenhower's victory in November 1952, Church sent her résumé to Ivy Baker Priest and Bertha Adkins, who were working on the recruitment of qualified women for patronage positions. Although it seemed to be a foregone conclusion that Church would get a position, party leaders wavered on when and in what agency.

When a job had not materialized six months after Eisenhower's election, Church appealed to U.S. ambassador to the United Nations Henry Cabot Lodge, who had been instrumental in securing the president's nomination. She had been assured, by whom it is not clear, that the position as assistant to the secretary of Health, Education, and Welfare was hers, but that job went to Jane Morrow Spaulding, another prominent black Republican. "To say that I was shocked and amazed is an understatement," Church wrote, "as I have been led to believe since November that this job was selected and set aside for me . . . and no one else was being considered."[10] Church felt that she was entitled to the position because of her father's loyalty to the party and her own educational and occupational qualifications. But she may not have been aware that other equally credentialed and qualified African Americans and women were also competing for what seemed to be a few patronage plums.

Instead, Church blamed Tennessee Republican leaders. "I do not think it is right for me to be pushed around and crucified by people who fought President Eisenhower to the last ditch, while my father was fighting for him. . . . Mr. Reece has the audacity, after fighting Eisenhower, not to want me, the daughter of a man who sacrificed his life for the Eisenhower cause, who ran in his place and was elected to the state Committee on the Eisenhower ticket, to keep me out of the campaign in Tennessee and to try and bar me from an appointment in the Eisenhower Administration."[11] Church called attention to the shifting racial dynamics in American politics when she noted, "It is a rare thing for a young colored woman to be a Republican today, let alone be elected to office by the voters. I belong to a species that is almost extinct and instead of using me as exhibit A it looks as tho the Republican party is trying to bury me."[12]

Her comments were not lost on party leaders. Roberta Church's appointment was already in the works when she drafted her letter to Lodge. "She had enough endorsements," according to one source, "to carry her to Heaven."[13] Many of her endorsements emphasized her father's contributions to the party, but Roberta's personal qualifications were also noteworthy. "She is a lady of excellent character and ability," wrote Tennessee congressman Howard H. Baker, while Clare Boothe Luce had seen her "in action during the Convention in Chicago last year, and I feel certain that her services would be of value in any post." C. Wayland Brooks, a national committeeman from Illinois, noted that Roberta's education and experience fit her for any office she might be assigned to, while the state's national committeewoman, Kitty Dixon, described Roberta as a woman of unusual qualifications. Only R. Douglas Stuart and Bertha Adkins mentioned Roberta's race as a criterion for appointment. Stuart, the treasurer of the Republican National Committee, described her as "a remarkable capable person," who would be an asset because there "is a lot of work to be done with the colored people." Adkins, who had been recruiting qualified women for patronage positions, noted, "I think she could do an excellent job and be a splendid representative of the Republican Party and the Negro."[14] It was clear that the party recognized Church's value and was not going to "bury" her or any other black Republican.

In July 1953, Roberta Church became one of twenty-seven female appointees when she replaced Thomasina Johnson-Norford as the minority consultant in the Labor Department's Bureau of Employment Security. Although, as Democrats had predicted, one African American woman replaced another in this exchange of the torch, Church's appointment was heralded in the black and white media.[15] The story was released to 100 black publications and organizations as well as key national newspapers, major magazines, and 700 labor papers and journals. Family, personal friends, and professional associates also congratulated Church and the administration on the appointment. Roberta's aunt, Mary Church Terrell, wrote, "I have just seen the August 18 *Afro-American* with the headline 'Miss Church gets Labor Dept Post' and I am too proud and happy to be calm and proper!!! From the depths of my heart I congratulate you!" Roberta's friend Dorothy F. Glass noted that the "appointment of Miss Church . . . is not only a personal triumph, but a genuine manifestation of the true American principle of equality of opportunity regardless of race, color or creed." Even black labor leader A. Philip Randolph praised her appointment, claiming that "her service to the Department of Labor will constitute a definite asset to the Department because of her ability and loyalty to the principles of American democracy." Church's appointment did not "crack job barriers" since the position had been held by African Americans in previous administrations, but it added to the image of inclusiveness that the party stressed in the 1950s.[16]

Roberta Church was sworn in at a ceremony attended by her aunt, Annette, Bertha Adkins, and Secretary of Labor Martin Durkin. Church's job was to advise the secretary on the development, review, and improvement of policies, programs, and standards for ensuring equity in employment. In the fall of 1953, Roberta made her first field trip. She traveled to Omaha and Lincoln, Nebraska, and Kansas City and St. Louis, Missouri, to observe employment offices and meet with state employment officials and Urban League representatives. The following spring she visited other cities to gather information on employment trends. Much of Church's work was with new industries moving south for the first time and large chain stores operating in the southern states.[17]

The 1950s witnessed dramatic shifts in American race relations. While African Americans constituted 10 percent of the population, the black unemployment rate was twice that of whites, and the black poverty rate was a staggering 50 percent compared to 20 to 25 percent for whites. Millions of African Americans had migrated from the rural South to urban areas in the Northeast, Midwest, and Far West during the preceding three decades, but millions more still depended on agriculture for their livelihood. They enjoyed greater economic opportunity in areas outside the South, but they still faced discrimination in hiring, promotions, and salary. Key unions in the construction industry, including plumbers, electricians, and Sheetrock workers, barred black laborers. The United Automobile Workers and other unions that accepted African Americans were dominated by whites until the 1960s.

The 1954 Supreme Court decision in *Brown v. Board of Education*, which declared segregation in public schools unconstitutional, climaxed decades of gradual change on segregation. But the Eisenhower administration was in no hurry to spend its political capital by encouraging the enforcement of the *Brown* decision or expanding its scope to include challenges to segregation in other areas of American life. Eisenhower disapproved of the *Brown* decision and did little to endorse it. Indeed, he considered his appointment of Chief Justice Earl Warren, the architect of the decision, "the biggest damn fool mistake I ever made." According to one of his advisers, the president was not "emotionally or intellectually in favor of combating segregation."[18]

Nevertheless, Roberta Church crisscrossed the nation to tout the administration's goals and accomplishments in race relations to black audiences and in the black media. Church praised Eisenhower for bringing about a "more Democratic America" in a speech delivered in Memphis in May 1955. She singled out the president's executive order against discrimination in civilian federal employment, the administration's enforcement of equality of opportunity in the armed forces, and desegregation in the nation's capital as examples of Eisenhower's commitment to civil rights. Moreover, she claimed that the enactment of Fair Employment Practices laws in eleven states, thirty-five cities, and the territory of Alaska was an indication of the impact of the government's commitment to civil rights. Church doubted whether "there is any governmental agency that endeavors to have a more beneficial relationship with individuals" than the Labor Department. Programs for apprentice training, equitable wages, and worker safety as well as child labor laws and cooperation with state governments on job placement and unemployment assistance advanced economic opportunities for all wage earners. Church's own Minority Groups Program promoted and publicized the principles of "hiring workers according to ability, qualifications, and performance on the job, without regard to race, religion, or national origin."[19]

The Eisenhower administration used Church and the other members of its Black Cabinet as evidence of its commitment to racial justice. The visible presence of African Americans in Washington and their active participation in the administration allowed the Republicans to demonstrate their efforts to include them in the political power structure. While Republicans did not push enforcement of the *Brown* decision and, indeed, impeded the progress of desegregation, they offered Church and other appointees as symbols of a commitment to fairness and equity. Whether these appointees were expected to be more than window dressing for conservative Republican politics is debatable.

Roberta Church understood the significance of this "tokenism" for the Eisenhower administration and used it to her own advantage. Her physical attractiveness, her impeccable dress and public demeanor, her family background, her connections to African American social, economic, and political elites, her education, and her stylish Washington apartment all added to her suitability as a 1950s symbol for the Republican Party. Throughout the decade, African American newspapers and magazines published numerous photographs of Church showing her with President Eisenhower soon after her election as a Tennessee Republican committeewoman, with Secretary of Labor Martin Durkin after her appointment and seated next to him during Labor Department meetings, and with representatives from labor unions, the NAACP, and the Urban League. In 1958 a magazine "with a large national circulation among colored citizens" decided to do a story on Church because of, as she put it, "my Republican background [and] the fact that I hold the highest position in the government to which a colored American woman has been appointed by the Eisenhower Administration." Church sent a letter to Secretary of Labor James Mitchell noting that she "thought it would be effective and timely and emphasize your deep interest in the field of human rights, if you could give a few minutes to have a picture taken with me that I could give to the magazine to be included with the article." Mitchell promptly arranged to do so.[20] The article described Church's activities as minority consultant in the Labor Department, the conferences she organized, and the speeches she delivered on behalf of the department.

In 1953, Roberta Church had proffered herself as "Exhibit A" of what she considered a valuable commodity—a young, black, female Republican—and wondered why the party was slow in recognizing an opportunity to placate black voters. By the 1956 election the Republicans could point to Church's appointment and those of other African Americans, the 1954 Supreme Court decision, and the desegregation of federal facilities as examples of their commitment to racial equality. By 1960, however, African American voters, in spite of the elevation of J. Ernest Wilkins to assistant secretary of labor and the use of federal troops to put down resistance to the desegregation of Little Rock's Central High School, could point to the administration's half-hearted efforts at passing civil rights legislation and enforcing the *Brown* decision as indications of the party's lack of sincerity. Some African Americans even questioned whether Republicans had written off black voters in the 1960 election. By a narrow margin of popular votes the Republicans lost that election, and patronage appointees such as Roberta Church were out of a job.

Church had enjoyed her government work. After she resigned from the Department of Labor, she passed a competitive Civil Service examination and accepted a career appointment with the Department of Health, Education, and Welfare as a consultant on disabilities of the elderly for the Office of Vocational Rehabilitation. She was responsible for planning and developing national programs that affected all Americans, not just minorities.[21] In 1970, Republican Richard Nixon appointed her to the President's Council on Adult Education, on which she served two terms, and in 1973 he assigned her to the National Council on Aging.

Roberta Church never married nor did she have a longtime partner. Her closest confidante was her aunt, Annette Church, who had raised Roberta after her mother died, and the two women lived together in Memphis, Chicago, and Washington, DC. Roberta was also close to her cousin, Phyllis Terrell, the daughter of Mary Church Terrell. Roberta retired from government service in late 1981 and returned to Memphis in early 1982. In her later years she was active in the city's social and literary clubs as well as historical societies. She also traveled extensively, often with Alma Roulhac Booth. After her return to Memphis she became a political independent and on one occasion even supported a Democrat who was running for Congress.

Roberta Church was born into a world of racial segregation. Blacks had the constitutional right to vote but were effectively disfranchised by poll taxes, literacy tests, and other legal and extralegal mechanisms. By the time Church died in 1995, grassroots activism, organizational pressure, and congressional, presidential, and judicial actions had brought an end to segregation and disfranchisement. Between 1974 and 1992 the number of African American elected officials skyrocketed from less than 2,500 to more than 8,000 nationwide.[22] African Americans were elected mayors of small and large cities, including Los Angeles, Detroit, Philadelphia, Washington, Atlanta, and New York as well as Church's hometown of Memphis. And in 1989, L. Douglas Wilder was elected Virginia's first black governor. Hundreds of blacks were appointed to positions in local, state, and national government. Unlike the black voters and political power brokers of Church's day, however, those in the second half of the twentieth century were more likely to be Democrats than Republicans. Some rose to positions of influence and power within the Republican Party, but few commanded the influence and patronage that black Republicans had exercised in the first half of the century.

Notes

1. G. P. Hamilton, *The Bright Side of Memphis, A Compendium of Information Concerning the Colored People of Memphis, Tennessee* (Memphis, TN: N.p., 1908), 99.

2. Annette E. Church and Roberta Church, *The Robert R. Churches of Memphis: A Father and Son Who Achieved in Spite of Race* ([Memphis, TN]: A. E. Church, 1974), 37 and 41; Appendix, 236–37. Coleman was a relative of John C. Breckinridge, a Confederate general and statesman who was vice president of the United States from 1857 to 1860. He was nominated for president by Southern Democrats after the party split. Breckinridge and Northern Democratic candidate Stephen Douglas were both defeated by Abraham Lincoln in the election of 1860. James Coleman settled in Memphis after the Civil War and managed a telegraph office where Thomas A. Edison was briefly employed.

3. Church and Church, *The Robert R. Churches of Memphis*, 87–110.

4. Darlene Clark Hine and Kathleen Thompson, *A Shining Thread of Hope: The History of Black Women in America* (New York: Broadway Books, 1998), 252.

5. Roberta Church to Henry Cabot Lodge, April 15, 1953, Roberta Church Papers, Memphis Room, Memphis Public Library, Memphis, Tennessee.

6. "Eisenhower's Black Cabinet," *Our World* 9, no. 2 (February 1954): 24–29.

7. David Halberstam, *The Fifties* (New York: Villard Books, 1993), 424–28.

8. "Eisenhower's Black Cabinet," 24–29.

9. *Pittsburgh Courier*, December 17, 1960.

10. Roberta Church to Henry Cabot Lodge, April 15, 1953, Roberta Church Papers.

11. Ibid.

12. Ibid.

13. *Ebony Magazine* 14, no. 7 (May 1959): 61.

14. General Records of the Department of Labor, Record Group (RG) 174, Box 10, Folder "Roberta Church," National Archives, Washington, DC (hereafter cited as RG 174).

15. Later that year, Adkins wrote Hugh Scott that she also recommended Church as a replacement for Anna Arnold Hedgeman at the Federal Security Administration. Adkins to Scott, December 20, 1953, RG 174.

16. Mary Church Terrell to Roberta Church, September 1, 1953, Church Family Papers, Box 13, Folder 17, Mississippi Valley Collection, McWherter Library, University of Memphis, Memphis, Tennessee; Dorothy Glass to Martin P. Durkin, August 11, 1953, and A. Philip Randolph to Martin P. Durkin, July 24, 1953, RG 174.

17. *Pittsburgh Courier*, July 18 and 25, 1953; *Atlanta Daily World*, May 4, 1954; and *Memphis World*, May 7, 1954.

18. Michael Schaller, Virginia Scharff, and Robert Schulzinger, *Present Tense: The United States since 1945* (Boston: Houghton Mifflin,1996), 128; and William H. Chafe, *The Unfinished Journey: America since World War II* (New York: Oxford University Press, 1991), 154–55.

19. *Tri-State Defender*, May 7, 1955.

20. Roberta Church to James P. Mitchell, October 28, 1958, RG 174, Box 228, Folder "Roberta Church."

21. Annette E. Church to Mr. and Mrs. Patton, July 2, 1961, Roberta Church Papers, Box 1, Memphis Public Library.

22. Darlene Clark Hine, William C. Hine, and Stanley Harrold, *The African-American Odyssey*, combined version (Upper Saddle River, NJ: Prentice Hall, 2003), 565.

Suggested Readings

For material on Church family history, particularly on Robert R. Church Sr. and Robert R. Church Jr., see Annette E. Church and Roberta Church, *The Robert R. Churches of Memphis: A Father and Son Who Achieved in Spite of Race* ([Memphis, TN]: A. E. Church, 1974), and the Robert R. Church Family Papers in the Mississippi Valley Collection of the McWherter Library at the University of Memphis, Memphis, Tennessee. A portion of Roberta Church's papers are also in the Memphis Room at the Memphis Public Library, Memphis, Tennessee. Mary Church Terrell's Papers are located at the Library of Congress, Washington, DC. See also Mary Church Terrell, *A Colored Woman in a White World* (Washington, DC: Ransdell, 1940); Willard B. Gatewood, *Aristocrats of Color: The Black Elite, 1880–1920* (Bloomington: Indiana University Press, 1990); Beverly Washington Jones, *Quest for Equality: The Life and Writings of Mary Eliza Terrell, 1863–1954* (Brooklyn, NY: Carlson Publishing, 1990); and Jacqueline M. Moore, *Leading the Race: The Transformation of the Black Elite in the Nation's Capital, 1880–1920* (Charlottesville: University Press of Virginia, 1999).

13

Edgar Daniel Nixon
A Founding Father of
the Civil Rights Movement

John White

The modern civil rights movement, the concerted effort of African Americans and their white supporters to gain greater social, political, and economic equality through protest, is often dated from the bus boycott that took place in Montgomery, Alabama, between December 5, 1955, and December 21, 1956. On December 1, 1955, a bus driver ordered Rosa Parks to give up her seat to a white passenger. She refused and was arrested. A respected African American resident of Montgomery, Parks worked as a seamstress and was an active member of the local chapter of the National Association for the Advancement of Colored People (NAACP), the nation's leading civil rights organization. Her dignified but determined decision to contest the indignities and daily humiliations of segregated public transportation in the self-proclaimed Heart of Dixie ignited a 381-day grassroots protest by the city's black population. Martin Luther King Jr., a young Baptist minister who had recently arrived in Montgomery, assumed leadership of the boycott's directing agency, the Montgomery Improvement Association (MIA), and took his first steps toward national and international fame.

As John White demonstrates, Edgar Daniel Nixon, who had been a notable figure in Montgomery's African American community for at least twenty years before the bus boycott, played a crucial, yet often forgotten, role in laying the foundations for the protest. During those years, Nixon had worked diligently in an effort to improve the social and economic conditions of Montgomery's black residents. As leader of the local chapters of the NAACP and the Brotherhood of Sleeping Car Porters (BSCP), the nation's first all-black labor union, Nixon headed voter registration and school desegregation drives, challenged discrimination in public transportation, and investigated several incidents of alleged police brutality against black Montgomerians. Moreover, Nixon used his considerable organizational skills as treasurer of the MIA. He raised thousands of dollars to sustain the bus boycott and publicized its aims at meetings and conventions. After Nixon helped launch the bus boycott, he continued to play an active role in mobilizing Montgomery's black community.

In November 1985 part of the fortieth anniversary issue of *Ebony* magazine focused on a celebration of "Four Decades of Black Progress." A photographic essay entitled "40 Who Made a Difference" featured short profiles of "movers and shakers" who had "helped make the world a better place for blacks." Those honored for their civil rights activities included Daisy Bates, who led the desegregation protest at Central High School in Little Rock, Arkansas, in 1957; and Ezell Blair, Joseph McNeil, David Richmond, and Franklin McCain, the North Carolina A & T students who sat down at a Greensboro whites-only lunch counter in 1960. The article also featured James Farmer of the Congress of Racial Equality (CORE), Roy Wilkins of the National Association for the Advancement of Colored People (NAACP), Dorothy Height of the National Council of Negro Women (NCNW), Whitney Young of the National Urban League (NUL), and A. Philip Randolph, organizer of the Brotherhood of Sleeping Car Porters (BSCP) and leader of the 1963 March on Washington. Better known, perhaps, to *Ebony* readers were the Reverend Martin Luther King Jr., "leader of the Montgomery Bus Boycott," and Rosa Parks, whose "refusal to give a White man her seat on a bus in Montgomery, Alabama, became one of the most significant spark plugs in Black history."[1]

Before the month was out, John H. Johnson, publisher of *Jet* and *Ebony*, received an embittered letter from an Alabama subscriber to both magazines, protesting his exclusion from the "listing [of] people that has made some form of contribution to civil rights" in *Ebony*'s feature. Setting the record straight, the author of the letter insisted: "I organized the first Welfare League in 1935; organized the Voters League in 1939; fought for a USO [United Service Organizations] Club for blacks in Montgomery in 1941; in 1944 I led 750 people around the court house to prove to white people that blacks wanted to register just like everybody else. I was the first black to run for public office in Montgomery. I got Mrs. Rosa Parks out of jail and I got her to let me use her case for a test case. It was I who called the people together to organize a Bus Boycott; it was I who selected Dr. M. L. King, Jr., as Chairman and it was I who raised over $100,000 to operate on."[2]

He did not, the writer continued, "want people to build me up just to make me a big man," but simply to tell "children all over the country the truth." Johnson was admonished as "one of the people who ought to tell the truth through your press, because if I had gotten Mrs. Parks out of jail, paid her fine and kept my mouth shut, a lot of people would never have known Rev. King or Mrs. Parks." The civil rights movement, the writer concluded, "grew out of the Bus Boycott, and I started the whole movement." The letter was signed "Respectfully yours, Dr. E. D. Nixon."[3] Despite Nixon's bombastic tone, there was considerable substance in his claims. As an active member of the BSCP and the NAACP, two national organizations that worked to improve the economic and

Edgar Daniel Nixon (right) at ceremony marking the opening of the E. D. Nixon Collection at Alabama State University in 1981. From Special Collections, University Library and Learning Resources, Alabama State University, Montgomery.

political condition of African Americans, Nixon always placed local concerns at the top of his agenda for change.

Nixon's distinguished career also exemplifies the contention that during the Jim Crow era in the South, leaders of African American communities—often divided by intraracial tensions and jealousies—attempted to create "an alternative culture emphasizing collectivist values, mutuality and fellowship" in a hostile environment where "white dominated public space was vigilantly undemocratic and potentially dangerous."[4] These values, in Nixon's case, derived primarily from his identification with the BSCP and its leader, A. Philip Randolph. The testimonies of BSCP members support this view. Mrs. Rosina Tucker, international secretary-treasurer of the Ladies Auxiliary of the BSCP and president of the Washington, DC, chapter, affirmed that membership in the Brotherhood "brought out qualities of strength and courage in the porters and their wives. They became leaders in their communities, bought homes, sent their children to college." The Brotherhood, Mrs. Tucker believed, "laid the foundation for the civil rights movement. It inspired black people by proving that they could get results. The [Pullman] porter changed the image of blacks from strike breakers to strong union men."[5]

Nixon was born in Montgomery on July 12, 1899, the fifth of eight children. His father, Wesley M. Nixon, was a tenant farmer and a Primitive Baptist preacher; his mother, Sue Ann, a cook and maid, died when Nixon was nine. He was brought up in rural Autauga County, which he loathed, by a paternal aunt, Winnie Bates, a laundress and Seventh-Day Adventist. The young Nixon received little more than a third-grade education and left home to become self-supporting at the age of fourteen. After several jobs, including work in a meat-packing plant, on a construction crew, and in a Birmingham store, Nixon became a baggage handler at Montgomery's Union Station. In 1923 he became a Pullman porter, a position he held until his retirement in 1974, and made regular runs from Montgomery to Miami, Chicago, St. Louis, and Los Angeles.

In 1926, Nixon married Alease Curry, the daughter of a Baptist minister. Their son, Edgar Daniel Nixon Jr., was born in 1928. The marriage did not last, and in 1934, Nixon married Arlet, who was from Pensacola, Florida. He had no children with his second wife.

Although Pullman porters were regarded as the elite of the African American working class, Nixon resented the degrading treatment they received from the Pullman Company and white passengers. By 1924,

Pullman porters earned $60.00 per month but were expected to pay for their meals and equipment and were not paid for the time they spent in preparing the coaches for journeys. If a passenger had mislaid his wallet, he might accuse a porter of having stolen it. "A whole lot of porters were searched and humiliated, and [then] they found the man had left it at home."[6] But Nixon's experiences on the railroad also widened his horizons and increased his self-esteem. He liked to recall that "I was over twenty years old before I knew the whole world wasn't like Montgomery. I decided not to be a coward and move up North where things were different, but to keep my home in Montgomery and start fighting for what I thought was right."[7] Moreover, his travels convinced Nixon that southern segregation laws were both unjust and immoral.

Functionally illiterate, Nixon taught himself to read while working as a Pullman porter and remembered: "If you got on a train with a newspaper or book and you left it in your room and went to the dining car, by the time you come back I'd done read it almost. And I made a memorandum of words that I couldn't understand."[8] In 1928, Nixon heard A. Philip Randolph speak at the Young Men's Christian Association in St. Louis, demanding a raise in salary for Pullman porters to $150 per month. Nixon, who was earning only $72.50 per month, put a dollar in the collection box and immediately joined Randolph's fledgling BSCP. He later related that "when I heard Randolph speak, it was like a light. He done more to bring me in the fight for civil rights than anybody."[9]

For Randolph the BSCP was an organization to promote race pride as well as to improve the working conditions of its members. Echoing the motto of Marcus Garvey's Universal Negro Improvement Association, the major black nationalist movement of the 1920s, an early issue of the BSCP's newspaper demanded: "Up with Race Pride and Class Pride, Long Live the Spirit of the New Negro."[10] Aware also of the power of black religion, Randolph, who was a professed atheist, appealed to his members in biblical and evangelical terms and held meetings in black churches. Nixon believed that the BSCP, under Randolph's inspirational leadership, could become a major force in the emerging civil rights struggle.

Nixon founded the Montgomery Division of the BSCP in 1938 and served as its president until 1964, his leadership making it Alabama's most notable black union. But there were problems in recruiting porters for the Brotherhood because the Pullman Company would not allow discussion of union matters during work time. Nixon's solution, derived from Randolph's example, was to find porters wherever he could in Montgomery—in churches, bars, and fraternal lodges—and ask them to join the union. Active involvement in the BSCP increased Nixon's standing in Montgomery's African American community and stimulated his growing political awareness. When the Brotherhood finally secured a contract with the Pullman Company in 1937, Nixon memorized every section of the personnel rules and used them to advantage. On one occasion, a former white railroad employee in Montgomery, who had persistently harassed black porters, obtained a job at a furniture store that they patronized. Borrowing enough money from the bank to pay off the porters' debts, Nixon led his colleagues to the store and informed the manager that unless the individual was sacked, they would close their accounts. The offending employee was promptly fired. Despite Nixon's aggressive and inspiring leadership, the increasing use of the automobile and the decline in rail travel resulted in a nationwide decline in BSCP membership. By 1952 the Montgomery division was desperately short of funds and had only nine paid-up members.

Nixon first became involved in community action in 1925, after two black children drowned while swimming in a city drainage ditch. He organized an unsuccessful petition to build a swimming pool for blacks and later remembered that "after that incident I knew there would not be any recreation or any form of civil rights for black people unless they were ready and willing to fight for it."[11] During the 1930s, Nixon assisted Myles Horton, founder of the interracial Highlander Folk School, a center for labor and civil rights education in Tennessee, in an attempt to organize Alabama's cucumber pickers into a union. Rosa Parks attended a Highlander workshop in May 1955 and later that year, with Nixon's support, instigated the Montgomery bus boycott.

In 1943, Nixon founded the Montgomery Welfare League, which helped indigent African Americans secure relief payments and jobs with the New Deal's Works Progress Administration. He was involved in Randolph's 1941 March on Washington Movement, a threatened mass march on the nation's capital by 100,000 African Americans, which forced President Franklin D. Roosevelt to issue an executive order banning discrimination based on color, creed, or national origin in the federal government and the defense industries. Following a conversation with First Lady Eleanor Roosevelt (with whom he formed a lifelong friendship) when she was a passenger on his train, Nixon secured the provision of a USO club for black military personnel in Montgomery. He also obtained an electric water fountain and toilet facilities for black travelers at Montgomery's Union Station. When he discovered that a separate ticket booth was being constructed at the station for African American passengers—who would then not have any reason to enter the white waiting room—Nixon protested to J. B. Hill, president of the Louisville and Nashville Railroad, and the structure was dismantled.

In 1947, Nixon, on behalf of the NAACP, protested against segregated admission to the Freedom Train—the touring exhibition of such historic documents as the Declaration of Independence, the original manuscript of the "Star Spangled Banner," and the Japanese surrender treaty ending World War II—when it visited Montgomery. Because of Nixon's protests, Montgomerians viewed the Freedom Train exhibits on an integrated basis. The *Montgomery Advertiser* duly reported: "Both white people and Negroes stood side by side to read for themselves the Emancipation Proclamation. Two Negro girls were the first to be admitted when the train opened at 10.00 am for inspection," and until closing time "the one, continuous line which extended for blocks was filled with practically equal numbers of the two races."[12]

Dismayed by the unwillingness of the conservative Montgomery branch of the NAACP to engage in direct action protests, Nixon, in the face of white hostility, organized the Montgomery Voters' League in 1940 to register blacks. Following the Supreme Court's *Smith v. Allwright* decision of April 1944, which invalidated the discriminatory "white primary" in Texas, he led 750 African Americans to the board of registrars, demanding that they be placed on the electoral rolls. Nixon himself had paid the $36.00 poll tax in Montgomery and had tried to register to vote for ten years. Only after filing a lawsuit and threatening another was he registered in 1945. From May to October 1944, Nixon took five months' leave from his porter's job and traveled extensively throughout Alabama in an attempt to organize black voters. Partly as a result of his efforts, the number of African American voters in the state increased from 25,000 in 1940 to 60,000 by 1948. In that year, Nixon described himself as being "very busy in this fight for the right to vote for Negroes," but acknowledged that the "crackers [poor whites] here have done a good job of keeping the Negro afraid and also keeping him unlearned."[13]

As a leading member of the Progressive Democratic Association, a separate organization of black Alabamians excluded from the all-white Democratic Party, Nixon was a cosigner of "An Open Letter" to the *Montgomery Advertiser* in 1953, protesting against a scheduled appearance in Montgomery of Davis Lee, the African American publisher of a

Newark, New Jersey, newspaper. Lee had argued that the desegregation of public schools would result in the loss of many black teachers, a point that Nixon scornfully discounted. When Lee appeared at Montgomery's municipal auditorium, he addressed a meager audience of seventy-five, of whom only twenty-five were African Americans.

In May 1954, Nixon filed as a candidate in the Montgomery Democratic primary for a place on the county Democratic Executive Committee—making him the first African American to seek political office in Alabama since the Reconstruction era—and lost by only ninety-seven votes to the white candidate. He was, however, chosen by the African American readers of the *Alabama Journal* as their "Man of the Year" and characterized as "very unassuming, yet militant, aggressive, yet not a radical."[14]

Nixon made headlines of a different kind the following year when he tried to purchase a ticket to the Democratic Party's Jefferson-Jackson Day Dinner in Birmingham. Refused admission to an all-white gathering, Nixon protested against his exclusion, and in response the principal scheduled speaker, Governor G. Mennen Williams of Michigan, cancelled his appearance.[15] In an editorial on the Jefferson-Jackson Day incident, the African American *Alabama Tribune* noted that despite being a registered Democrat, Nixon had run up against local segregation laws that prohibited integrated political gatherings.[16] Despite this setback, and with the African American vote an increasingly significant factor in Montgomery politics, Nixon successfully pressured county commissioner Dave Birmingham into hiring four black police officers in 1954. The Progressive Democratic Association now began to itemize black grievances, which included the humiliating treatment of African American passengers on Montgomery's buses. Always alert and sensitive to practices of racial exclusion, Nixon went three years during the 1950s without a telephone in Montgomery rather than accept one on a four-party "all-colored" line.

On September 3, 1954, following the Supreme Court's *Brown* decision, Nixon attempted unsuccessfully to enroll twenty-three African American students at the new all-white William R. Harrison High School in Montgomery. Black pupils had previously attended Abraham's Vineyard Elementary School, "an outmoded structure that had been scheduled to be closed and its students bussed elsewhere until black parents petitioned the local school board not to close the neighborhood school."[17] In May the following year the Montgomery chapter of the NAACP planned its celebration of the first anniversary of *Brown*. Nixon was quoted as saying that "we had not done very much about implementing" the Court's landmark decision, and that "the NAACP and other organizations should join in letting it be known in Washington that segregation in public schools must be abolished."[18] Nixon's relations with the Montgomery NAACP were less than harmonious. He was frequently involved in acrimonious disputes with the local chapter and its conservative, middle-class elite, grouped around Alabama State College.

A year after its formation in the summer and fall of 1918, the Montgomery branch of the NAACP had nearly 600 members and was second only to Birmingham among its Alabama chapters. But it quickly became torn by quarrels between its college and noncollege members, and its first secretary, William Porter, lamented the failure of Montgomery's African American working class to appreciate the importance of supporting a pioneering civil rights organization.[19] A founding member of the reorganized Montgomery branch in 1928, Nixon came to believe that it suffered from both corrupt and inadequate leadership. Defeated in his first bid for branch president in 1944, he was elected in 1946 and remained in office until 1950, when Robert L. Matthews, the man he had beaten in 1945, replaced him.

Immediately after his 1944 defeat, Nixon, as president of the Citizens Overall Committee, wrote to Walter White, secretary of the NAACP, complaining that the election had been "one of the most nasty I have ever seen held in a NAACP branch." Matthews, Nixon alleged, had broken "all records in violating the constitution of the Association," and had rigged the election by appointing the nominating committee and recruiting "about 15 people who came to the meeting, paid dues and voted." Nixon also charged Matthews with incompetence, citing as evidence the fact that out of a black population of 50,000, the Montgomery NAACP branch had only about 400 members. Nixon claimed that his bitterness was not over having lost the election but was rather over the manner in which it had been conducted, with Matthews's supporters openly buying votes for their candidate. In a postscript, Nixon restated his 1944 platform, with its call for 3,000 new members "instead of 400," a NAACP office in downtown Montgomery, a program and redress committee, and a voting drive.[20]

Reporting to Ella Baker, the NAACP's director of branches, after a two-day visit to Montgomery in the spring of 1945, Assistant Branch Field Director Donald Jones noted that the branch was in "a bad way due to a lack of competent leadership" and judged Matthews to be "hopeless."

Jones believed that Nixon was "the strongest man in the community in civic affairs, pretty influential among the rank-and-file," and accurately predicted that he would "win the next election and improve the situation." But Jones also added a cautionary postscript: "The big trouble with Nixon is that he fancies himself as an amateur detective. While I was there he was deeply involved in a criminal investigation and his talk was mostly of other cases in which he played the role of sleuth. Were he president, we'd have to watch the branch pretty closely to keep it from turning into a detective bureau and nothing else."[21]

In his 1945 election manifesto, Nixon called attention to the "need of a more aggressive NAACP in Montgomery and vicinity" and pledged to make it a popularly based organization.[22] During his 1945 campaign, Nixon wrote to one of his supporters: "We need a more militant NAACP in Montgomery because we need a program to offer the people, because we need to return the NAACP to the people as their organization."[23]

During his first year in office, Nixon personally signed 2,200 members into the Montgomery chapter but felt that the basic problem was that once most members had paid their annual dues, they felt they had fulfilled their obligation. Those who did engage in branch activities only did so when their jobs and other commitments permitted.

Nixon proved an innovative and aggressive president of the Montgomery branch of the NAACP and also served as president of the Alabama Conference of NAACP Branches. Living up to his characterization by Donald Jones as a "sleuth," Nixon personally investigated many cases involving police brutality, rapes of African American women, lynchings, and murders. In one instance he managed to persuade Alabama Governor Chauncey Sparks to commute the death sentences of three African American men found guilty of raping a white woman, to terms of life imprisonment. On another occasion, Nixon appeared before Sparks to request that a reward be posted for information leading to the arrest of those responsible for the murder of a black schoolgirl, Amanda Baker. A $250 reward was subsequently posted by the governor, the first state reward offered in a crime against a black victim.

In March 1947 the Montgomery branch celebrated the thirty-ninth anniversary of the founding of the NAACP with a rally at Holt Street Baptist Church. The program featured a short profile of the incumbent president as being "well versed in the problems confronting Negroes in Montgomery." Nixon had also "spent long hours working toward the time when the two races will have a better understanding as regards each other," and was "deserving of the full co-operation and support of every Negro citizen in our State and City." Among the contributors to the souvenir program was the Montgomery Division of the BSCP.[24]

By the mid-1950s, Nixon's connections with organized labor and the NAACP, his friendships with prominent white liberals in Montgomery, and his standing with the city's African American working-class community made him a force to be reckoned with. Jo Ann Gibson Robinson, who was to play a pivotal role in the Montgomery bus boycott, recalled that by 1955, Nixon was "acquainted with most of the members of the police and sheriff's departments, with judges and jailers, and with people at city hall. Also, he knew most of the lawyers in the city, black and white." Whenever violations of civil rights occurred, Robinson remembered, "the victims involved would telephone Mr. Nixon, and he would go to their rescue. He was a friend to all who were in trouble and appealed to him for help. He simply seemed to get pleasure out of helping people, especially those who could not help themselves."[25] The Reverend Ralph D. Abernathy, Martin Luther King's successor as leader of the Southern Christian Leadership Conference (SCLC), characterized Nixon as "an aggressive and fearless fighter for the rights of Negro people in Montgomery for many years . . . a Pullman porter [who] does not have a formal education, but a very courageous man. Long before the bus crisis he was meeting threats and turning them back in language as picturesque as a Missouri mule skinner."[26]

In his own account of the Montgomery bus boycott, King called Nixon "a foe of injustice" who had always "worked fearlessly to achieve the rights of his people, to arouse the Negroes from their apathy," and who was "one of the chief voices in the Negro community in the arena of civil rights, a symbol of the hopes and aspirations of the long oppressed people of the State of Alabama."[27] Rosa Parks, who served as Nixon's secretary and general assistant in his work for the BSCP and the NAACP, remembered simply that Nixon "was one of the most active African Americans in Montgomery. He was a proud, dignified man who carried himself straight as an arrow."[28]

Nixon's repeated and sometimes self-serving accounts of his role in the events immediately following Parks's arrest and the formation of the MIA have been variously interpreted. What is certain is that his activities as strategist, treasurer, and fundraiser for the MIA owed much to his differing experiences in the BSCP and the NAACP.

Montgomery's Women's Political Council (WPC), organized in 1949 to urge African American women to vote, had lodged several complaints with the City Commission about the mistreatment of black female passengers on the city's bus line but had achieved little success. Numerous incidents, all involving African American women, had angered the black community, the most notable being the arrest on March 2, 1955, of Claudette Colvin, a teenager who had refused to vacate her seat when ordered to do so by a white bus driver. After Colvin pleaded not guilty to violating Alabama's segregation laws, Nixon discovered that she was unmarried and pregnant and decided that she was not a good choice for a test case against Jim Crow transportation.

The arrest of Parks on December 1, 1955, provided Nixon and Jo Ann Robinson, the most active member of the WPC, with their opportunity. Nixon paid Parks's bail bond and then gained her permission to use her arrest as a test case of the city's segregation laws. Together with the WPC, Nixon decided that the protest should take the form of a one-day black passenger boycott of the Montgomery City Lines. He also called a sympathetic reporter on the *Montgomery Advertiser*, alerting him to the proposed boycott and the pamphlets about to be printed by Robinson advising blacks to stay off the buses on the day of Parks's court appearance. This astute move provided the boycott with valuable and free publicity. Again, it was Nixon who forcefully persuaded the city's African American ministers, who were meeting at Martin Luther King's prestigious Dexter Avenue Baptist Church, to lend their public support to the protest after it was decided to extend the one-day boycott indefinitely. Not least, Nixon supported the election of King as president of the MIA, convinced "that the success of the boycott would depend largely on a black preacher who could communicate with, motivate and inspire the masses."[29]

From the inception of the boycott, Nixon was acutely aware that the MIA needed both publicity and substantial funds to sustain its operations. The warmest responses to his appeals came from southern branches of the BSCP. The Asheville, North Carolina, Division of the BSCP informed him that its members had passed a resolution "commending you and the organizations which you head for the firm, vigorous and courageous stand in behalf of matters of great importance to all concerned."[30]

In March 1956, Nixon was the guest speaker at a BSCP-sponsored meeting of the National Committee for Rural Schools, in New York City. He took the occasion to tell delegates of the origins and progress of the ongoing boycott and of his own role in calling Montgomery's black ministers following the arrest of Parks. He also explained the "many objectives" of the MIA in the third month of the boycott. Although the immediate aim was "to adjust the seating arrangements on the bus[es] within the existing law," Nixon told his audience that the MIA was about to file suit in a federal court, challenging the constitutionality of segregation on Montgomery's public transport system. He also described the organization of the MIA's transportation committee and the operation of the forty-seven pick-up stations and 300 cars that were taking African Americans to work "and providing a better job than the Montgomery bus line has done in 20 years." Nixon stressed that after the MIA achieved its objectives it would stay in existence to fight police brutality and other forms of racial discrimination. He ended by telling a favorite story about a small boy going down the street with a basket, selling puppies. When a lady asked their price, the boy replied "25 cents." She was tempted but decided against a purchase. The next day she met the boy again and asked him if the puppies were still for sale. The boy said that they were and cost 50 cents. Asked why the price had doubled overnight, the boy said: "Their eyes are open." To much laughter, Nixon supplied the moral to this story: "the Negroes' eyes are open in Montgomery and they aren't being sold for 25 cents anymore."[31]

The following day, Nixon's mentor, A. Philip Randolph, informed delegates that it cost $3,500 a week to keep the carpool running and asked for their support. Nixon then stressed the importance of the mass meetings in Montgomery in maintaining the dynamic of the boycott and the need for financial support, which the MIA was receiving from across the country. Montgomery's African Americans, Nixon asserted, were "tired of being Jim Crowed on the Montgomery City Lines or any other form of transportation," and would continue their protest "until the court says they don't have to do it." He ended with an appeal for donations; delegates were urged to "put your hand in your pocket and make a contribution. Whether it's large or small, the MIA will be eternally grateful."[32]

Nixon made a great impression when he appeared in May 1956 at a civil rights rally in Madison Square Garden in New York City, together with Eleanor Roosevelt, Randolph, the Alabama-born film actress Tallulah Bankhead, Congressman Adam Clayton Powell, and Martin Luther King. The last scheduled speaker, Nixon brought the audience of 16,000 people to its feet when he announced: "I'm E. D. Nixon from Montgomery, Alabama, a city that is known as the Cradle of the Confederacy and that has stood still for more than ninety-three years until Rosa Parks was arrested and thrown in jail like a common criminal, and 50,000 Negroes rose up and caught hold of the cradle and began to rock it and the segregated slats began to fall. I am from *that* city."[33] Roy Wilkins, head of the NAACP, was also present and recalled that with Nixon's dramatic statement, "people began to shout and yell and thump one another on the back, and the Garden resonated with enough joy and hope to keep us all going for months afterward."[34]

As the boycott continued, Martin Luther King Jr. was increasingly presented in the media as both its originator and driving force. But Nixon's activities were extensively reported in the *Black Worker*, the official newspaper of the BSCP. The December 1955 issue announced that "Bro. Nixon Steps up the Fight for Civil Rights," and concluded with "our hats are doffed to you once again, Brother Nixon."[35] In April 1956 the Chicago Division of the BSCP hosted "A Salute to A. Philip Randolph" and Nixon was the keynote speaker before 600 guests. The *Black Worker* duly reported that he had given the delegates a graphic account of the events in Montgomery.[36]

Unlike the BSCP, however, the NAACP was to be more critical of the Montgomery bus boycott and the objectives and methods of the MIA. When the newly formed MIA resolved to extend the one-day bus boycott, Nixon hoped that the Montgomery branch of the NAACP would offer its support but was told that the New York office would first have to be consulted. Nixon, who had already decided that a new organization was needed to coordinate the protest, was not prepared to wait. He also knew that the state of Alabama was threatening to outlaw the NAACP, and this action could be fatal to the boycott if the MIA was seen as its auxiliary. His fears were justified. On June 1, 1956, in the sixth month of the boycott, Judge Walter Jones of the Montgomery Circuit Court granted Alabama Attorney General John Patterson an injunction, which banned the NAACP from operating in the state. With a blithe disregard for the truth, Patterson claimed that the NAACP was "organizing, supporting, and financing an illegal boycott by the Negro residents of Montgomery."[37] When the NAACP refused to surrender its membership and contribution lists to Patterson, Jones imposed a fine of $100,000 for contempt and effectively crippled its operations in the state.

In fact, the executive leadership of the NAACP was less than enthusiastic about the initial goals and direct action strategies of the Montgomery bus boycott. Since the MIA's original demands were only for greater courtesy from bus drivers, the hiring of African American drivers for black neighborhoods, and the seating of passengers on a first-come, first-served basis, Roy Wilkins believed that the MIA merely wanted to make segregation "more polite." The NAACP was pledged to "knock it out completely" and was not prepared to go to Montgomery "simply to ask Jim Crow to have better manners."[38]

Only after the mass indictment of boycott leaders and carpool drivers in Montgomery and the MIA's challenge to Alabama's segregation laws in *Browder v. Gayle* (1956) did the NAACP intervene directly in the boycott. Responding to a call from Nixon, Thurgood Marshall, chief counsel for the NAACP, promised that he would assist in the legal defense of those indicted. Wilkins then pledged his total support of the boycott to King. Reflecting twenty years later on the outcome of events in Montgomery, Wilkins claimed it as a victory for "all the years of fighting and organizing done by the BSCP and the NAACP." In particular he praised the efforts and example of Nixon, "the true godfather of the boycott," a man who was "straight as a ramrod, tough as a mule, and braver than a squad of marines," who had "locked Dr. King into history."[39]

A prime strategist of the Montgomery bus boycott, Nixon, in *Roots* author Alex Haley's opinion, "helped to nationalize the Montgomery movement" through his long-standing affiliation with the BSCP and labor unions, which also gave him "the foresight and the organizational skills to impress and mobilize Montgomery's black community."[40] But Nixon was increasingly unhappy with the middle-class leadership of the MIA, irregular accounting methods in its handling of funds, and what he regarded, with some justification, as the patronizing attitude of King. In November 1957, after discussions with King and Abernathy, Nixon submitted his resignation as MIA treasurer. He cited pressure of work as a Pullman porter and dissatisfaction with his treatment by the MIA leadership as prime causes of his departure. Nixon also informed King: "Since I have only been treasurer in name and not reality, it will not be hard to find someone to do what I have been doing, even a school boy." He concluded bitterly: "I resent being treated as a newcomer to the MIA. It is my dream, hope and hard work since 1932."[41]

Never committed to King's philosophy of nonviolent direct action, Nixon was not involved in any of the SCLC's later campaigns in Albany, Georgia; Birmingham and Selma, Alabama; and Chicago. He also criticized the SCLC for moving into local situations that had been initiated by grassroots activists and then stealing the limelight from them. In contrast, after his retirement from the BSCP, Nixon became heavily involved in community work in Montgomery. He raised funds for the care of the sick and organized annual summer camps for the city's black children, including the E. D. Nixon Summer Olympics. He served as community service adviser to Young Forte Village, a housing project in Montgomery with 15,000 residents, most of them teenagers. During the 1970s, Nixon became increasingly concerned with human rights. He worked with the Alabama Coalition against Hunger, the Red Cross, and groups that supported the welfare of the elderly and opposed capital punishment. A lifelong advocate of racial integration, he rejected the rhetoric and separatist program of the Black Power movement during the 1960s. To the consternation of many of his former admirers, Nixon supported the "reformed" George Wallace, an erstwhile diehard segregationist, in his gubernatorial campaigns of 1958 and 1962.

In his last years, Nixon, a founding father of the civil rights movement, complained bitterly that his role in the Montgomery bus boycott had been largely forgotten, and he frequently disparaged King's exaggerated reputation as the instigator and organizer of the protest. Ironically, at the end of his life, the disgruntled Nixon, who died in 1987, was a recipient of many awards and honors, including a Resolution by the Alabama House of Representatives in 1971 commending his outstanding services to the state.

The historic marker, erected on September 6, 1986, in front of Nixon's home on Clinton Street, Montgomery, records that:

> E. D. Nixon, Sr., posted bail for segregation law violator Rosa Parks. In her defense, Nixon gathered the support of Montgomery blacks in implementing the successful 1955–56 Montgomery Bus Boycott. His commitment and active involvement as a grassroots organizer, civic leader and founder of the Montgomery NAACP chapter has paralleled local movements for the advancement of blacks. As chief strategist of the Montgomery Bus Boycott, Nixon spearheaded a local protest, which launched a massive movement of social reform and earned him recognition as "The Father of the Civil Rights Movement."

Curiously absent from this tribute is any mention of Nixon's civil rights activities before 1955 and his lifetime association with the BSCP. Yet, as he fervently believed, the union had not only empowered black workers but also inspired his own determination to destroy the degradations and lunacies of racial discrimination and segregation. Ten years after his retirement from Pullman service, Nixon informed Randolph: "Believe it or not, your guidance have [*sic*] done more to help me in the field of Civil Rights than any person I know of, and for this I am grateful."[42]

Notes

1. *Ebony* 41, no.1 (November 1985): 60–76.

2. E. D. Nixon to John H. Johnson, November 13, 1985, E. D. Nixon Collection, Alabama State University Special Collections, Montgomery. Hereafter cited as EDNC/ASU.

3. Ibid. The signature reflected the honorary doctorate that Nixon had received in 1978 from Alabama State University.

4. Robin D. G. Kelley, " 'We Are Not What We Seem': Rethinking Black Working-Class Opposition in the Jim Crow South," *Journal of American History* 80 (June 1993): 79, 102.

5. Jack Santino, *Miles of Smiles, Years of Struggle: Stories of Black Pullman Porters* (Urbana: University of Illinois Press, 1989), 52.

6. Studs Terkel, *Hard Times: An Oral History of the Great Depression* (New York: Pantheon Books, 1970), 144.

7. Eliot Wigginton, *Refuse to Stand Silently By: An Oral History of Grass Roots Social Activism in America, 1921–1964* (New York: Doubleday, 1991), 23–24.

8. Ibid., 23.

9. Terkel, *Hard Times,* 119.

10. *Black Worker*, November 15, 1929, in the New York Public Library, New York City.

11. Interview with Norman Lumpkin, Statewide Oral History Project: Alabama Center for Higher Education, Tuskegee Institute, Tuskegee, Alabama, 1963, 3:1.

12. "Priceless Documents Draw 10,000 to Freedom Train," *Montgomery Advertizer*, December 28, 1947.

13. Paula F. Pfeffer, *A. Philip Randolph: Pioneer of the Civil Rights Movement* (Baton Rouge: Louisiana State University Press, 1990), 173.

14. *Alabama Journal*, November 22, 1954.

15. *Montgomery Advertizer/Alabama Journal*, October 2, 1955.

16. "According to Their Rules," *Alabama Tribune* 15, no. 23, October 14, 1955.

17. Edward R. Crowther, "Alabama's Fight to Maintain Segregated Schools," *The Alabama Review* 42 (July 1990): 215.

18. NAACP Minutes: Montgomery Branch, 1954–56, Schomburg Center for Research in Black Culture, New York Public Library, New York City.

19. Dorothy A. Autrey, "The National Association for the Advancement of Colored People in Alabama, 1913–1952" (Ph.D. diss., University of Notre Dame, 1985), 96, 102.

20. Nixon to Walter White, December 14, 1944, NAACP Papers, Library of Congress, Washington, DC.

21. Donald Jones to Ella Baker, September 14, 1945, NAACP Papers.

22. EDNC/ASU.

23. Nixon to W. G. Porter, November 13, 1945, NAACP Papers.

24. "Let the Record Show," undated pamphlet, EDNC/ASU.

25. David J. Garrow, ed., *The Montgomery Bus Boycott and the Women Who Started It: The Memoir of Jo Ann Gibson Robinson* (Knoxville: The University of Tennessee Press, 1987), 28.

26. Ralph D. Abernathy, "The Natural History of a Social Movement: The Montgomery Improvement Association," in *The Walking City: The Montgomery Bus Boycott, 1955–56*, ed. David G. Garrow (Brooklyn: Carlson Publishing, 1989), 111, 143.

27. Martin Luther King Jr., *Stride toward Freedom: The Montgomery Story* (New York: Harper and Row, 1958), 39.

28. Rosa Parks with Jim Haskins, *Rosa Parks: My Story* (New York: Dial Books, 1992), 72–73.

29. Lewis V. Baldwin and Aprille V. Woodson, *Freedom Is Never Free: A Biographical Portrait of E. D. Nixon* (Atlanta: United Parcel Service, 1992), 51.

30. Western Union Telegram (no date), EDNC/ASU.

31. Joseph F. Wilson, *Tearing Down the Color Bar: A Documentary History of the Brotherhood of Sleeping Car Porters* (New York: Columbia University Press, 1989), 246.

32. Ibid., 258.

33. Howell Raines, *My Soul Is Rested: Movement Days in the Deep South Remembered* (New York: G. P. Putnam's Sons, 1977), 37.

34. Roy Wilkins with Tom Mathews, *Standing Fast: The Autobiography of Roy Wilkins* (New York: The Viking Press, 1982), 236–37.

35. *Black Worker*, December 1955.

36. Ibid., April 1956.

37. Taylor Branch, *Parting the Waters: America in the King Years, 1954–63* (New York: Simon and Schuster, 1988), 186.

38. Wilkins, *Standing Fast*, 228.

39. Ibid., 225–28.

40. Baldwin and Woodson, *Freedom Is Never Free*, xi.

41. Nixon to Martin Luther King Jr., June 3, 1957, Martin Luther King Papers, Special Collections, Mugar University Library, Boston University.

42. E. D. Nixon to A. P. Randolph, January 2, 1974, EDNC/ASU.

Suggested Readings

E. D. Nixon never published an autobiography, but there are numerous transcripts of his conversations with sympathetic interviewers that shed light on his civil rights activities. See especially: Earl and Miriam Selby, *Odyssey: Journey through Black America* (New York: G. P. Putnam's Sons, 1974), 48–54; Howell Raines, *My Soul Is Rested: Movement Days in the Deep South Remembered* (New York: G. P. Putnam's Sons, 1977), 37–39, 43–51; Milton Viorst, *Fire in the Streets: America in the 1960s* (New York: Simon and Schuster, 1981), 19–51; and Eliot Wigginton, *Refuse to Stand Silently By: An Oral History of Grass Roots Social Activism in America, 1921–1964* (New York: Doubleday, 1991), 23–28, 219–28.

Lewis V. Baldwin and Aprille V. Woodson, *Freedom Is Never Free: A Biographical Portrait of E. D. Nixon* (Atlanta: United Parcel Service, 1992), offers a brief summary of his life and achievements. On Nixon's acknowledged mentor see Jervis Anderson, *A. Philip Randolph: A Biographical Portrait* (New York: Harcourt Brace Jovanovich, 1973); and Paula F. Pfeffer, *A. Philip Randolph:*

Pioneer of the Civil Rights Movement (Baton Rouge: Louisiana State University Press, 1990).

Nixon's role in the Montgomery bus boycott is discussed in Taylor Branch, *Parting the Waters: America in the King Years, 1954–63* (New York: Simon and Schuster, 1988); and David J. Garrow, *Bearing the Cross: Martin Luther King, Jr., and the Southern Christian Leadership Conference* (New York: William Morrow and Company, 1986). See also John White, "Nixon *Was* the One: Edgar Daniel Nixon, the MIA and the Montgomery Bus Boycott," in *The Making of Martin Luther King and the Civil Rights Movement*, ed. Brian Ward and Tony Badger (London: Macmillan Press, 1996), 45–63.

14

Sgt. Allen Thomas Jr.
A Black Soldier in Vietnam

James E. Westheider

Black soldiers had fought in all of America's wars before Vietnam, but they had done so largely in segregated units. Vietnam was the first war since the American Revolution in which the armed forces were fully integrated from the beginning. Moreover, unlike the typical black experience during previous wars, the U.S. military in Vietnam did not relegate African Americans to noncombat duties and menial tasks. The official sanction of military segregation and racial quotas, limiting both the number of black soldiers and their advancement in the armed forces, ended with Executive Order 9981. Issued on July 26, 1948, by President Harry S. Truman, the order called for "equality of treatment and opportunity for all persons in the Armed Services." The Selective Service Act of the same year initiated a peacetime draft that placed no limits on black enlistments. Thus, in the years following World War II, a growing number of African Americans viewed a career in the armed forces as a chance to advance economically without having to face the racial barriers that existed in civilian employment.

However, the military's reputation as the most integrated institution in America began to fade as the nation's commitment to the war in Vietnam expanded. In 1965, the year following the Tonkin Gulf Resolution, the first American ground troops arrived in Vietnam. By 1968 nearly 500,000 Americans served in Southeast Asia, and the military needed ever increasing numbers of new recruits and draftees. While African Americans had in the past fought for the right to serve their country in arms, they were now beginning to wonder if black men were being asked to carry a disproportionate load of the fighting and dying.

Black criticism focused particularly on college deferments, charging that they provided white men with safe havens from the draft while most black families could not afford college tuition. Claims that the draft was racially biased rang true for many African Americans when heavyweight boxing champion Muhammad Ali's application for a religious deferment was rejected on April 28, 1967. Stripped of his title by the World Boxing Association, Ali was convicted on charges of draft evasion and sentenced to five years in prison. Black disillusionment hit rock bottom when Dr. Martin Luther King Jr. was assassinated on April 4, 1968.

During these critical years, Allen Thomas Jr. was among the more than 300,000 African Americans who served in Vietnam. Thomas, who had chosen a career in the military, was not a reluctant draftee like most of the black recruits. Serving three tours of duty, he spent more time "in country" than most American servicemen. While in Vietnam, Thomas observed the soldiers' growing disillusionment with America's involvement in the war and a corresponding decline in troop morale. He also witnessed an increase in racial tensions, particularly following King's assassination. Large numbers of young black recruits, who had come of age during the civil rights era, became increasingly impatient with their status as second-class citizens. In defiance of whites and military authority, they embraced a militant rhetoric and style. They wore symbols of racial pride and black power, called each other "brother," and greeted each other with a ritualized handshake, the "dap." Tracing the life and military career of Thomas, James E. Westheider takes the reader on a journey into the jungles of Southeast Asia and explores what it was like to be black in Vietnam.

Allen Thomas Jr. was born on September 25, 1939, in Covington, Kentucky, located opposite Cincinnati on the Ohio River. His father, Allen Thomas Sr., was originally from Covington, Louisiana. In 1917, at age fourteen, he had joined hundreds of thousands of African Americans who were leaving the South during the Great Migration and heading North in search of work. Thomas's mother, Fredericka, was a native Kentuckian. Like so many other black families, the Thomases struggled to overcome poverty, racism, discrimination, and segregation. Child mortality rates were particularly high among African Americans, who had limited access to medical care. Thus, Allen Jr. was the only one of seven children to reach adulthood. But family, church, and community ties were strong, and Thomas grew up in a supportive and protective environment. "We were supposed to be poor, but we didn't know it," he recalled. This strong sense of community also helped him cope with living in a Jim Crow society. He learned early in life how to deal with hatred and racism by watching his parents, uncles, and minister as well as the Pullman porter who lived down the street. "I was never angry, just confident . . . that if you did the best you could, you could get ahead. It was opportunity, not revenge, so we were trying to get along . . . but the whites were not."[1]

Thomas and other African Americans of his generation had good reason for feeling somewhat confident. They were growing up in a victorious and prosperous post-World War II America. More important, the legalized segregation and discrimination that still prevailed throughout much of the country and kept many blacks from sharing in that prosperity was beginning to crumble. In July 1948, when Thomas was eight years old, President Harry S. Truman issued Executive Order 9981, ending segregation in the armed forces, a policy that had been initiated during the Civil War. Years later, Truman's decision would have a tremendous impact on Thomas's life and career, but it was another battle against Jim Crow that the future army sergeant would remember fondly as "a highlight of my life." On May 17, 1954, Thomas was sitting in his math class at the all-black Lincoln Grant High School when the school's public address system announced that the U.S. Supreme Court unanimously had just struck down segregation in public education in the *Brown v. Board of Education* decision.

Sgt. Allen Thomas Jr., at left, is awarded the Army Commendation Medal for Meritorious Service in Vietnam in 1968. *Courtesy of Allen Thomas Jr.*

In 1957, Thomas graduated from Lincoln Grant and later that year, on the morning of his eighteenth birthday, entered the army. Like other young black men, particularly those of modest economic means, he viewed military service as an opportunity. Thomas had gotten married in 1956 and was unable to find a job that could support him together with his wife and child. Thomas recalled that the army was "fine by me. . . . The upper strata had a chance for college, but all the poor kids like me joined the service."[2]

Military service, however, was popular among African American men not only because it offered economic advantages. By the late 1950s the U.S. Army had won a well-deserved reputation in the black community for racial fairness and equal opportunity. After initially resisting President

Truman's 1948 desegregation order, white military leaders began to see the advantages of an "equal opportunity" armed forces. It had tremendous cold war propaganda value, especially in the emerging nations of Africa and Asia. More important, it was cost effective. In 1951 the army's "Project Clear" study found that racially integrated units were more efficient than segregated units and performed quite capably. Another study, conducted by Johns Hopkins University, reported that contrary to the fears of many white officers, black and white soldiers not only accepted integration but worked well together with little friction. A change in leadership at the military's top echelons also helped. Segregationists such as Gen. Douglas MacArthur were retiring and being replaced by a new generation of racially enlightened officers.

By the fall of 1957, when Thomas entered boot camp at Fort Knox, Kentucky, the military was probably the most integrated institution in America. During basic training at Fort Knox, Thomas remembers being treated well, especially by his platoon sergeant, despite the new recruit's "attitude." He appreciated the opportunities the military offered him, such as sending him to Fort Gordon, Georgia, for advanced training in the Signal Corps in 1958. But at Fort Gordon, Thomas also got a harsh reminder of the differences between military and civilian race relations in the late 1950s. Kentucky and Georgia, like all southern states of that era, had state and municipal segregation statutes. Black soldiers were aware of local rules and practices that limited their freedom off base and generally observed them, knowing that any protest could lead to charges of misconduct and result in a dishonorable discharge. Thus, in the communities surrounding Fort Knox, black military personnel avoided confronting racism and stayed out of segregated areas.

At Fort Gordon, however, manifestations of racism were blatant and the racial climate was worse. Racist signs warned African Americans not to patronize "white only" establishments or enter restaurants through the front door. Thomas and his wife and baby were thrown off a local bus for attempting to ride in the front. White post commanders, even those who enforced the army's equal opportunity standards on their base or in their units, were seldom willing to challenge local practices. Instead, white officers distributed maps among African American troops, listing establishments that refused to serve blacks as "off limits" to enlisted personnel. "We were told to put up with it and stay safe," Thomas recalled. The white officers "thought they were doing a good thing, being careful of our personal safety."[3] Whether it was concern about the safety of black troops or fear of embroiling the army in the civil rights movement, the distribution of the maps demonstrates the limits of the military's commitment to racial integration and equal opportunity.

Thomas left the army and returned briefly to civilian life in 1960. The Signal Corps had trained him to do sophisticated electronics work and he hoped to find employment either in that field or in his original career choice as a baker. But after being a civilian for only thirty-three days and being offered only menial jobs in restaurants or as a security guard, Thomas reenlisted and made the army a career. It was a path many young black men chose in the 1960s. In 1966, 66 percent of all African Americans eligible to reenlist in the armed forces did so, compared to only about 12 percent of eligible whites.[4] Alfonza Wright Jr., for example, left the navy for a job in a steel mill near Baltimore, but when he became frustrated with the overt racism there he reenlisted, this time in the army. Likewise, black army private James Williams claimed that he knew "a lot of brothers that will stay in the Army because they're afraid to get out and face what's out there."[5] Thus, a career in the military not only provided African Americans with job training and economic opportunities but also shielded them, at least to some degree, from racism and discrimination.

A career in the army, however, also entailed many personal sacrifices as soldiers were reassigned to different posts, forcing them and their families to relocate frequently, often with little advance notice. Moreover, as America's military involvement in Vietnam escalated in the aftermath of the 1964 Tonkin Gulf Resolution, it meant an almost certain tour of duty in Vietnam. Thomas, who had advanced to the rank of sergeant, was assigned to Southeast Asia in 1965. "First time I went I didn't even know where the hell I was going," he recalled. "I got an APO for San Francisco, not my eventual destination." Like all those assigned to an overseas tour, Thomas had only sixteen days to relocate his wife and six children from Fort Huachuca, Arizona, where he was stationed, back home to Covington, Kentucky. At the time he was more concerned for their safety and comfort than he was about America's reasons for fighting the war. "I was brainwashed . . . anti-Communist, pretty much supported the war," he stated. "You have to remember this was in the early sixties, before all hell broke loose. We were still patriotic, and I thought I was up to the job . . . what did I know!"[6]

Thomas's views were fairly representative of the majority of black soldiers who served in Southeast Asia during the early stages of America's military involvement. In 1967, journalist Wallace Terry found that the vast majority of black troops in Vietnam supported the war effort, while many criticized civil rights leader Dr. Martin Luther King Jr. and heavy-weight boxing champion Muhammad Ali for speaking out against it. Like the nation in general and the black community in particular, Thomas's views of America's role in Vietnam changed in the aftermath of the 1968 Tet Offensive, when the North Vietnamese and Vietcong launched a massive coordinated assault on South Vietnam. Thomas, who was on his second tour of duty in 1967–68, concluded that American involvement was a mistake and a "big lie." Likewise, Wallace Terry found that in 1970 "a majority of black GI's . . . feel they have no business fighting in Southeast Asia."[7]

Thomas, like most African Americans, saw Vietnam as yet another opportunity to convince white Americans that black soldiers were just as capable and as patriotic as white troops. "The brother does all right here," a black officer told *Ebony* magazine in 1968; "you see it's just about the first time in his life that he finds he can compete with whites on an equal—or very close to equal—basis. He tries hard in this kind of situation and does well."[8] Patriotism was also a major motivating factor, but, as in previous wars, many blacks had to "fight for the right to fight." Sgt. Pinkie Hauser, for example, turned down several choice assignments and had to reenlist for six years in order to volunteer for Vietnam. "I felt like I wasn't serving my country enough," she recalled.[9] Maj. Gen. Frederic E. Davison had to fight the Pentagon before he was allowed to command troops in Vietnam. "I wanted to go very badly," he recalled. "There was no plans to take me. And I god damn nearly lost my family—lost my family because they couldn't see why the hell I had to volunteer to go to Vietnam."[10]

The hard work, courage, and sacrifice of black soldiers did not go unnoticed. In previous wars, African Americans had been castigated as inferior and cowardly, but in Vietnam a new positive stereotype was emerging, that of "the good soldier." Gen. William C. Westmoreland, commander in chief of Military Assistance Command, Vietnam (MACV), summed up this new appraisal of black military skills when he remarked that "the performance of the Negro servicemen has been particularly inspirational to me. They have served with distinction."[11] Thomas and his comrades were finally getting the recognition they deserved, often in the form of medals and official commendations. Thomas won three Bronze Stars, several army commendations, a Meritorious Service medal, and a Civil Action Award for work with Vietnamese villagers. Colin Powell, future chairman of the Joint Chiefs of Staff, was awarded eleven medals in Vietnam, including a Bronze Star and a Purple Heart. Twenty of the 237 Medals of Honor awarded during the conflict went to African Americans, including one to Pvt. James Anderson, who became the first black marine to win the nation's highest military award.

The military recognitions and awards came with a steep price. Although African Americans were not assigned disproportionately to Vietnam, they tended to be concentrated in combat rather than support or administrative units. They made up approximately 10 percent of U.S. personnel in Vietnam but constituted more than 20 percent of the combat strength. In some infantry units more than half of the soldiers were black. Henry Parker, a white company commander, claimed that 60 percent of his men and 95 percent of his noncommissioned officers were black. Thomas's unit reflected a similar racial composition; eighteen of the twenty-five noncommissioned officers were black.

The concentration of African Americans in combat units resulted in an alarmingly high black casualty rate, especially early in the war. In three tours of duty, Thomas defied the odds; he lost not a single man under his command. However, several soldiers, including himself, were wounded. "Got blowed up twice," he recalled, but it was nothing serious. Survival depended on skill and experience as well as sheer luck. Thomas remembered putting on his helmet, "and I never wore my helmet," seconds before the 2.5-ton truck in which he was riding struck a mine. "Blew the whole front of the truck off," but Thomas escaped with only minor injuries.[12]

Others were not as lucky. In 1965, which marked the arrival of American ground combat troops as well as Thomas's first year in Vietnam, one out of every four Americans killed in action was black. In all, 7,241 African Americans died in Southeast Asia, constituting about 12.6 percent of American losses between 1957 and 1973. To put this percentage figure into perspective, consider that blacks constituted 9.1 percent of the U.S. population in 1950, 10.5 percent in 1960, and 11.1 percent in 1970.[13] Some African American soldiers viewed these numbers with a sense of gruesome pride and vindication. "I feel good about it," commented Lt. Col. George Shoffer, one of the highest-ranking black officers in the army. "Not that I like the bloodshed, but the performance of the Negro in Vietnam tends to offset the fact that the Negro wasn't considered worthy of being a front line soldier in other wars."[14]

Many African Americans, however, were not as sanguine as Shoffer. They did not view the high black casualty rates as proof of valor but as evidence of racism and discrimination in the armed forces. Race relations and black expectations were rapidly changing in America in the mid-1960s. After years of crusading for racial equality, civil rights leaders had made some progress, including the 1965 Voting Rights Act. Emboldened by their success, African Americans were more determined than ever to fight racism and less willing to tolerate it. A growing sense of urgency and frustration pervaded much of the black community. The Pentagon, preoccupied with Vietnam, had paid little attention to these changes in civilian society. Moreover, military leaders were content that they had implemented Truman's desegregation order and failed to address legitimate concerns and complaints of black service personnel. As a consequence, the military's reputation for fairness and equal opportunity suffered among African Americans. Black leaders who had once praised the services now questioned whether African Americans were being asked to do more than their fair share for a nation and its armed forces that still treated them as second-class citizens.

Many African Americans singled out the Selective Service system as a prime example of institutional racism. Black criticism grew particularly following the expansion of U.S. military forces in Vietnam in the aftermath of the 1964 Tonkin Gulf Resolution. On December 31, 1964, the United States had 23,300 military personnel in Vietnam, most of them serving as advisers or in support and logistical capacities. In the following year, when Thomas served his first tour of duty, the United States initiated a massive troop buildup that topped out at 540,000 Americans "in country" by mid-1968. The U.S. government had initially relied on voluntary enlistment, but in response to the growing need for troops in Vietnam, the Johnson administration decided to raise the number of draftees.

The Vietnam-era draft was governed by the Selective Service Act of 1948, which provided for a deferment system that exempted college students as well as individuals with certain skills. In the years prior to America's military involvement in Vietnam, draft calls were low, and deferments generated little controversy. Even in early 1966, with both the war effort and black casualties rising, a Gallup poll for *Newsweek* found that 75 percent of African Americans thought the draft was racially fair. But as the war escalated and draft calls increased, it became more and more obvious that the deferments provided a way out of military service for those who could afford college tuition. The burden of the draft fell on the unlucky ones who could not afford it, largely African Americans and poor whites. By June 1969 nearly half of all African Americans believed that the draft was racially biased. They had good reason for their suspicions. Although blacks made up nearly 11 percent of the draft-eligible population during the Vietnam War, they accounted for roughly 16 percent of all draftees.

Many of these new recruits were also more militant than their predecessors and more reluctant to serve in an organization they viewed as racist. They entered military service expecting to find discrimination and bigotry, and often their concerns were justified. Racism and race-based double standards existed and affected black service personnel in virtually every aspect of their military careers from training through promotion, especially in the application of justice.

In the armed forces, justice is administered at two levels. Major transgressions are handled through courts-martial, similar to civilian trials. During the Vietnam War era, blacks were far more likely to be brought up on charges than whites. A 1971–72 Department of Defense investigation found that African Americans were defendants in more than 34 percent of the courts-martial. On the other hand, relatively minor infractions are generally dealt with through a procedure known as "Non-Judicial Punishment," referred to in the army and air force as "Article 15" and in the navy and marine corps as a "Captain's Mast." Non-Judicial Punishment provides the accused with a hearing, but guilt and any penalty are determined by the defendant's commanding officer, with little room for appeal. Since the presiding officer has such wide discretion, the system is ripe for abuse and of racially based double standards. In a 1972 investigation of the application of military justice, the Congressional Black Caucus found that "no military procedure has brought forth a greater number of complaints and evidences of racial discrimination than the administration of nonjudicial punishment." The National Association for the Advancement of Colored People, the nation's oldest civil rights organization, concurred, calling Article 15 "a major source of grievance among black servicemen," adding that "there seem to be two sets of rules: one for whites and the other for blacks."[15]

Thomas witnessed examples of this double standard in military justice everywhere he was stationed. Blacks received Article 15 for wearing Black Power symbols such as slave bracelets woven out of bootlaces, while whites in the same units were not disciplined for wearing peace symbols or fraternity rings, which were also violations of the uniform code. There were exceptions, particularly for troops "out in the woods" on combat duty, but racism was still a powerful factor even on the front lines. During his second tour of duty in 1967–68, Thomas once missed out on a promotion because he deliberately was not notified until 11:00 P.M.

the night before about a promotion board meeting the next day. An all-night truck ride from Dak To to Pleiku failed to get him to the hearing on time.

Thomas and other black soldiers did what they could to fight inequities and racism through official channels. Black sailors at the navy's submarine base at Groton, Connecticut, for instance, successfully petitioned their commanding officer to increase the number of black-oriented products sold at the base post exchange as well as the ratio of black music played at the enlisted men's and noncommissioned officers' clubs. But they were also aware of the risks involved in challenging the system. "Being the military they don't take kindly to suggestions anyway," Thomas observed. "They view suggestions as criticism, and automatically assume you are rebelling." Especially if "you were black and spoke up, you were a trouble maker, an instigator, whatever. If you were white, you were considered an innovator." In 1969 black marines at Camp Lejeune, worried that even a conservative plea for mild reforms could result in retaliation, petitioned their commanding officer anonymously and signed their letter "Semper Fidelis"—the Marine Corps's motto—to emphasize their loyalty.[16]

Thomas eventually got his promotion because he knew his job and did it well. As a ten-year veteran he also now knew "the system, the right people, and how things really got done." Since trying to work through official channels was often difficult and dangerous, seasoned noncommissioned officers such as Thomas usually found it "easier to just change things in your little part of the world. Hopefully it will catch on and become regulation."[17] Instead of petitioning the military for more black-oriented products in post commissaries, Thomas and others learned to contact various manufacturers directly or to call or write church and civic groups back home. Motown Records, for example, sent the black troops in Vietnam the latest Soul music coming out of Detroit. Mainstream corporations were often just as responsive. In 1968, for example, Kraft Foods sent free Kool-Aid to Thomas and his men at their base at Kontum after he wrote the company that they missed the soft drink.

In addition to the institutionalized racism, African Americans also had to endure the bigotry, taunts, and violence of whites. Racist graffiti, such as "Niggers eat shit" or "I'd prefer a gook [Asian] to a nigger," defaced the walls of latrines and barracks from Camp Lejeune to Cam Ranh Bay. Using a common black nickname for whites, one black trooper in Vietnam stated that "Chuck's all right until he gets a beer under his belt, and then its Nigger this and Nigger that . . . Chuck ain't too much fun, you dig?"[18] Often "Chuck" seemed oblivious to the callous nature of his remarks. One white soldier from Mississippi bluntly informed Thomas that "for a nigger you're a pretty good guy. If you were white we could be friends." Language like that often precipitated a fight, but Thomas was mature enough to put things in perspective. "I didn't say much back. Any fool saying that to you when you've got all these weapons and grenades, has just got to be a fool." On another occasion, a white man from Louisiana told Thomas that he was not "going to take orders from a nigger." Eventually the man "turned out to be a pretty good kid," though only after spending thirty days in the stockade for disobeying a direct order.[19]

Most of the incoming black recruits, however, lacked Thomas's skills and experience. Moreover, unlike many of the older black veterans, they felt alienated, isolated, and often afraid of service in a white-controlled and -dominated institution. Many of the black men were reluctant draftees and more than a few embraced the militancy of Malcolm X or Stokely Carmichael. They were more interested in "Black Power" than "Freedom Now," the mantra of earlier civil rights crusaders. They called each other "brother" and in response to what they viewed as a hostile and uncaring military, in the middle of a war in the jungles, mountains, and rice paddies of Vietnam, began to seek comfort and support in racial solidarity. They separated themselves from whites and started to wear the symbols of racial pride. The stereotype of the good soldier gave way to that of the black militant.

Thomas and other African Americans, particularly older men who had chosen the military as a career, were often torn between the demands of the young black militant draftees and their professional obligations. Thomas had been active in the civil rights movement since he was fourteen years. His heroes were men such as Dr. Martin Luther King Jr. and Asa Philip Randolph, leader of the Brotherhood of Sleeping Car Porters, America's first all-black labor union. "You've got to understand where I came from," Thomas explained. "Malcolm X scared the hell out of me; just like he scared a lot of white folks, he scared the hell out of a lot of black people too." There was also his career in the armed forces to take into consideration. "Anything out of the mainstream was out if you were going to be a professional in the army."[20]

The trend toward black solidarity, and in some cases militancy, was apparent by the time Thomas arrived at Cam Ranh Bay for his second tour of duty in 1967–68. "Nobody was trying to hide it," recalled Thomas, "the tone was changing." Many of the black men were wearing slave bracelets, chalking "Black Is Beautiful" or "Black Power" on their helmets, and giving the "dap" handshake. Visible signs of racial pride often became a source of friction and trouble. "Whites were not used to blacks taking a stand, voicing an opinion," Thomas remembered. "Dapping was big, scared the majority of whites, two or three black guys get together . . . what are they up to?"[21] Many white soldiers were convinced that African Americans were dapping to antagonize them and viewed it as a deliberate annoyance. "Well, the favorite time for blacks to do that was in line in the mess hall," commented one white officer. "Sometimes they would go into a five- or ten-minute dapping period, and the whites would not be real thrilled about waiting in line while a couple of bros went through their dapping procedures." Even Thomas conceded that "it did get annoying sometimes."[22]

Whites also engaged in behavior that in turn annoyed and antagonized African Americans, such as creating a "White Power" salute to mock dapping or, even more galling, flying Confederate flags in Vietnam. The use of the Stars and Bars probably infuriated blacks more than any other symbol of white supremacy, but the older noncommissioned officers such as Thomas were usually able to keep things in perspective. "There were lots of those around, didn't really make me mad as long as they (the whites flying the flags) left me alone," Thomas remembered years later. "But I felt then the same way I do now, the American flag means more to me."[23]

Thomas knew he could not allow anger to guide his actions. As part of the chain of command it was his duty to prevent racial friction from escalating to racial violence. There were some all- or predominantly white or black hootches (GI slang for living quarters, derived from the Vietnamese term for a thatched-roof hut) at Dak To, but Thomas and some of the other noncommissioned officers tried to set a positive example by living in integrated quarters. There were minor "day to day" problems, but generally, "everybody got along . . . intermingled together." In fact, Thomas claims that in both his second and third tours in Vietnam the men of his company did not separate along racial lines. Rather, separation in his company was based on the recreational drug of choice. The heavy users of alcohol, or "juicers," tended to congregate, as did the "heads," who preferred marijuana, opium, or psychedelics.

The fragile racial harmony in Thomas's unit, as in others, was sorely tested following Martin Luther King Jr.'s assassination in Memphis on April 4, 1968. Thomas recalled that "some of the younger guys were angry, and just wanted to hurt someone," but mostly everyone was in shock. "When the word got to us in the field, we just sat down, talked, cried. We put ourselves in stand-down for the next three days." There were words exchanged and a few fistfights, but serious violence was avoided because Thomas and the other black sergeants convinced the company commander to "back off" and let the men work through their grief and anger.[24]

The company commander, like many whites, was sympathetic, but some were hostile and reveled in King's assassination. Upon hearing the news of King's death, some whites at Cam Ranh Bay donned makeshift Ku Klux Klan outfits and paraded a Confederate flag around the base. Most whites, though, were simply apathetic. But for African Americans, King's death changed everything. Pvt. Morocco Coleman observed that "everywhere here you can see the unity which exists among the Negro soldiers. After the assassination of Dr. M. L. King you could also feel the malcontent." Another black soldier concurred, claiming that King's death "made a lot of people angry—angry people with guns."[25] King's assassination touched off a widespread wave of racial violence among American soldiers, ranging from confrontations between small groups of whites and blacks to large-scale rumbles involving dozens and sometimes hundreds of participants. Thomas, however, could not recall a single serious racial incident in either his second or his third tour in Vietnam. Both times he served in combat units that spent considerable time in the field. As a rule, front-line companies had fewer problems because the officers and noncommissioned officers tended to be more experienced than those commanding many of the support or administrative units. Moreover, combat kept the troops busy and served as a constant reminder that they had to rely on each other, regardless of race.

Racial warfare was only one of many problems plaguing the U.S. military late in the war. In 1970, when Thomas returned to Vietnam to begin his third and final tour, he found a chaotic and deteriorating situation. Morale had all but collapsed in many areas. There had been mostly volunteers and career military personnel in Vietnam during Thomas's first tour and a mix of professionals and draftees during his second. Thomas liked working with the majority of the draftees because they tended to be older, better educated, and more capable than many of the volunteers. During his last stint "in country," however, most of the men were reluctant and angry draftees and "substandard" volunteers, who were often poorly led by inexperienced or inept officers. Drug and alcohol use was rampant and discipline hardly apparent. No one wanted to fight because after the 1968 Tet Offensive the United States had essentially abandoned any hope of winning the war. By 1970 the goal had become "Vietnamization," President Richard Nixon's plan to withdraw American forces after achieving "Peace with Honor" and turn responsibility for the war over to the South Vietnamese. Thomas no longer believed the war could be won either, but he was a professional and "wanted to do a good job." Yet he became increasingly frustrated: "We saw what was happening. They called it Vietnamization, but everybody was just running for the door. It was just survival. Nobody wanted to be the last person to die."[26]

Throughout the war, Americans often vented their frustrations on the South Vietnamese peasants. In a war that pitted white and black Americans against Asians, race and racism were always factors. Some of the American soldiers looked down on the Vietnamese, calling them "gooks," "slopes," or other racial epithets. Thomas, as do many black veterans, contends that African Americans generally displayed more kindness and understanding toward the Vietnamese than did their white counterparts. "I had a hootch, but I was seldom there," he recalls; "eight guys in the hootch, four black, four white. We had Vietnamese to clean it, take care of things. The whites were racist, condescending. The blacks did not call them (the Vietnamese) names and they paid them well. We respected them, they've been through four thousand years of crap. We've also been oppressed, so we understood. Besides, hear some white guy call them a gook and you know what's coming next."[27]

The abuse went beyond racial slurs. The conflict in Vietnam was ultimately a civil war, and it was often difficult to determine which side a person really supported. The friendly rice farmer by day could be a Vietcong guerrilla at night. Some Americans did not bother to distinguish between friend and foe and treated everyone as a potential enemy. The worst known atrocity occurred on March 16, 1968, when a company under the command of Lt. William Calley massacred at least 122 unarmed civilians in the hamlet of My Lai, but there were others. There were some blacks under Calley's command who participated in the slaughter, but, reflecting a strongly held belief among black veterans, Thomas argues that it was mostly whites who were responsible for the atrocities, or for at least giving the orders that led to incidents such as My Lai.

Sometimes frustrated and angry American soldiers turned on each other. One of the most telling signs of the breakdown in morale and discipline late in the war was the rise of a phenomenon known as "fragging," the killing of an officer or sergeant in your unit. The term is derived from the most popular weapon of choice for the task, a fragmentation grenade. Everyone carried them; they could easily be rigged into a booby trap, and they left little in the way of incriminating evidence. Unlike for guns and bullets there is no ballistics test for hand grenades. Racial hostility, drug abuse, poor morale, and bad leadership all contributed to an epidemic of fraggings as America attempted to disengage itself from Vietnam. The Department of Defense admits to 788 fraggings or attempted fraggings between 1969, the first year it began to track them, and 1972. The actual number is probably much higher because many went unreported. A congressional inquiry documented 1,016 cases by the end of the war.

It was poor leadership that led to an attempted fragging during Thomas's final tour in Vietnam. The intended victim was a young lieutenant who was new to Vietnam and eager to prove his mettle in combat. His eagerness and inexperience posed a danger to the men. As Thomas observed, "this new guy, a first lieutenant, a platoon leader, didn't know what he was doing." What made it worse, Thomas explained, "was that he would not listen to the veterans, he wouldn't follow advice and he was going to get someone killed." Thomas prevented the fragging when he caught a group of eight black and white men attempting to wire a mine to the front entrance of the lieutenant's sleeping quarters. The young officer owed his life to the fact that Thomas had to use the latrine. Otherwise, "I would never have found out about it," he mused. Thomas eventually solved the problem, first talking to the lieutenant and then arranging a meeting between him and his would-be assassins. It was a sign of just how surreal things had become in Vietnam that the attempted murder of an officer was never reported and none of the soldiers was ever brought up on charges. Even Thomas admitted, "I didn't think much of it at the time, nor do I now."[28]

In 1971, Thomas returned home from his final tour in Vietnam, but in more ways than one the conflict followed him to the United States. The plane that brought Thomas and other noncommissioned officers back from the war touched down at the Seattle-Tacoma airport during huge antiwar demonstrations. Protesters and police barricades filled the streets around the airport. Authorities were reluctant to allow a bus with Thomas and other veterans on board to drive through the crowd, fearing for their safety. To Thomas and the others returning from the war the situation was both ludicrous and funny. After fighting in

Vietnam, the last thing they feared was a group of antiwar protesters. Contrary to police orders, the veterans left the bus and marched through the crowd, only to discover, to their amusement, that the crowd was there not to harass or abuse them but to prevent them from being *sent* to Vietnam in the first place.

Generally, though, the returning veterans found that American society shunned or ignored them. Thomas discovered that most of the veterans' organizations did not want him or other Vietnam servicemen. Often veterans of previous wars branded Vietnam returnees as "losers." Part of the ostracism was also due to racism. Many of the Veterans of Foreign Wars chapters and American Legion posts were either all-white or nearly all-white and did not want large numbers of black members. An all-white American Legion post near Thomas's home in northern Kentucky rejected his application for membership, and its commandant advised him to seek out an all-black post.

Like most returning veterans, Thomas had problems in his postwar adjustment and could never quite shake his connection to Vietnam. "I'm still there, I haven't really returned yet," he remarked almost thirty years later. His second tour of duty cost him his first marriage, and all three tours have left him with post-traumatic stress disorder. For years he battled nightmares, flashbacks, and severe headaches. For five years he periodically lost the vision in one of his eyes. Three decades have helped to ease the pain, but Thomas is still bothered by nightmares, though they are less frequent and less intense. Thunderstorms or the aroma of Asian food can trigger intense anxiety or melancholy, and Thomas is still dealing with a variety of physical ailments related to the war. But in his own words, "we were the lucky ones, the survivors."[29]

Thomas believes that it was a bit easier for him to overcome his problems because he stayed in the military after the war. Not that the military itself provided much help. "They didn't know what to do with us," he confided. It was other veterans, especially a group of old friends, who helped Thomas readjust. They talked about their experiences together and eventually "things did become better after the war." The military learned from its mistakes and began to take complaints about racism seriously. The Pentagon initiated a series of reforms and made race-relations training mandatory. "By 1974 you couldn't get promoted without it." Thomas added ruefully, "Of course they brought in college experts to tell them what the sergeants already knew, and were doing."[30]

Like the vast majority of Vietnam veterans, Thomas has dealt with his problems and forged a happy and productive life since his return to the United States. He remarried and credits Patricia, his wife of more than thirty-two years, for the success of their marriage, despite "some hard days of about eight years" in the beginning. Thomas is now the proud father of eight children and grandfather to sixteen. In 1979, after a successful twenty-one-year career in the army, he became sergeant of security at Northern Kentucky University, retiring from that post in January 2000. Today, Thomas lives in Erlanger, Kentucky, and remains active in church, civic, and veterans' organizations. He is a member of the Vietnam Veterans of America and post commander of his chapter of the Veterans of Foreign Wars. He has started a third career of sorts, talking and lecturing to various groups and organizations about the war and the African American experience in Vietnam. After helping to forge American history in Southeast Asia, he wants to ensure that future generations never forget the sacrifices and the lessons of Vietnam.

Notes

1. Allen Thomas Jr., interview with the author, Erlanger, Kentucky, July 25, 2000 (hereafter cited as Thomas, 2000 interview); and Allen Thomas Jr., interview with the author, Highland Heights, Kentucky, March 22, 1995 (hereafter cited as Thomas, 1995 interview).

2. Thomas, 2000 interview.

3. Ibid.

4. Jack D. Foner, *Blacks and the Military in American History* (New York: Praeger Publishers, 1974), 208.

5. Sol Stern, "When the Black GI Comes Back from Vietnam," *New York Times Magazine*, March 24, 1968.

6. Thomas, 2000 interview.

7. Wallace Terry, "Bringing the War Home," *Black Scholar* (November 1970): 7.

8. Thomas Johnson, "Negroes in the Nam," *Ebony* (August 1968): 31.

9. Kathryn Marshall, *In the Combat Zone: An Oral History of American Women in Vietnam* (Boston: Little, Brown and Co., 1987), 37.

10. Major General Frederic E. Davison Interview, Senior Officer, Oral History Project, Blacks in the Armed Forces Series, U.S. Military History Institute, Carlisle Barracks, Pennsylvania, 1977, 26.

11. Thomas Johnson, "The U.S. Negro in Vietnam," *New York Times*, April 29, 1968.

12. Thomas, 2000 interview.

13. Lawrence M. Baksir and William Strauss, *Chance and Circumstance: The Draft, the War, and the Vietnam Generation* (New York: Random House, 1978), 8; and L. Deckel McLean, "The Black Man and the Draft," *Ebony* (August 1968): 62.

14. Stern, "When the Black GI Comes Back," 37.

15. James E. Westheider, *Fighting on Two Fronts: African Americans and the Vietnam War* (New York: New York University Press, 1997), 39.

16. Thomas, 2000 interview; and Thomas, 1995 interview.

17. Thomas, 2000 interview.

18. Johnson, "Negroes in the Nam," 38.

19. Thomas, 2000 interview; and Thomas, 1995 interview.

20. Thomas, 1995 interview.

21. Thomas, 2000 interview.

22. Westheider, *Fighting on Two Fronts*, 89.

23. Thomas, 2000 interview.

24. Thomas, 1995 interview.

25. Westheider, *Fighting on Two Fronts*, 98.

26. Thomas, 2000 interview.

27. Ibid.

28. Ibid.

29. Ibid.

30. Ibid.

Suggested Readings

Several excellent firsthand accounts can be found in Wallace Terry, *Bloods: An Oral History of the Vietnam War by Black Veterans* (New York: Random House, 1984); Stanley Goff and Robert Sanders, *Brothers: Black Soldiers in the Nam* (Novato, CA: Presidio Press, 1982); and James Daley and Lee Bergman, *A Hero's Welcome* (Lawrence: The University Press of Kansas, 2000). For accounts of black women in Vietnam, see Kathryn Marshall, *In the Combat Zone: An Oral History of American Women in Vietnam* (Boston: Little, Brown and Co., 1987). For a comprehensive study of African Americans and the Vietnam War, see James E. Westheider, *Fighting on Two Fronts: African Americans and the Vietnam War* (New York: New York University Press, 1997). Robert Mullen, *Blacks in America's Wars: The Shift in Attitudes from the Revolutionary War to Vietnam* (New York: Pathfinder Press, 1973), does a fine job of detailing the range of arguments and opinions about the war in the black community. For biographies of black generals during the war, see J. Alfred Phelps, *Chappie: The Life and Times of Daniel James Jr.* (Novato, CA: Presidio Press, 1991), and Benjamin O. Davis Jr., *Benjamin O. Davis Jr., An Autobiography* (Washington, DC: Smithsonian Institution Press, 1991). Probably the best general account of African Americans in the armed forces, and one of the first to examine the black experience in Vietnam, is Jack D. Foner's *Blacks and the Military in American History* (New York: Praeger Publishers, 1974). Some good primary accounts include Thomas Johnson, "The U.S. Negro in Vietnam," *New York Times*, April 29, 1968, and the entire August 1968 edition of *Ebony*.

About the Contributors

ERIC ARNESEN is professor of history and African American studies at the University of Illinois at Chicago. He received his Ph.D. in history from Yale University in 1986. His *Waterfront Workers of New Orleans: Race, Class, and Politics, 1863–1923* (1991) won the American Historical Association's John H. Dunning Prize, and his *Brotherhoods of Color: Black Railroad Workers and the Struggle for Equality* (2001) won the American Historical Association's Wesley-Logan Prize. He is also the coeditor, with Julie Greene and Bruce Laurie, of *Labor Histories: Class, Politics, and the Working-Class Experience* (1998) and the author of *Black Protest and the Great Migration: A Brief History with Documents* (2002).

BEVERLY GREENE BOND is assistant professor of history at the University of Memphis. She received her Ph.D. in history from the University of Memphis in 1996. She is the author of " 'The Extent of the Law': Free Women of Color in Antebellum Memphis, Tennessee," in *Negotiating Boundaries of Southern Womanhood: Dealing with the Powers That Be*, ed. Janet Coryell et al. (2000), and "Every Duty Incumbent upon Them: African American Women in Nineteenth-Century Memphis," in *Trial and Triumph: Essays in Tennessee's African American History*, ed. Caroll Van West (2002). She is currently completing *"Troublesome Times": African American Women in Memphis, Tennessee, 1820–1905* for the University of Illinois Press.

RONALD E. BUTCHART is professor and department head in the Department of Social Foundations at the University of Georgia. He received his Ph.D. in history from the State University of New York at Binghamton in 1976. A former president of the History of Education Society and the American Education Studies Association, he is the author of *Northern Schools, Southern Blacks, and Reconstruction: Freedmen's Education, 1862–1875* (1980) and *Local Schools: Exploring Their History* (1986). His *Classroom Discipline in American Schools: Problems and Possibilities for Democratic Education* (1998) won the 1998 American Educational Studies Association Critics' Choice Award and the 1998 *Choice* Magazine's Outstanding Academic Book Award. He is currently completing a book on the freedmen's teachers.

SUSAN CURTIS is professor of history and chair of the American studies program at Purdue University, Indiana, where she has taught since 1989. She received her Ph.D. in history from the University of Missouri-Columbia in 1986 and is the author of *A Consuming Faith: The Social Gospel and Modern American Culture* (1991; reprint, 2001), *Dancing to a Black Man's Tune: A Life of Scott Joplin* (1994), and *The First Black Actors on the Great White Way* (1998). She is now working on a biography of Lester A. Walton tentatively entitled *Lester A. Walton and the American Century*.

S. SPENCER DAVIS is professor of history at Peru State College in Peru, Nebraska, and past president of the Nebraska State College Education Association. He received his Ph.D. from the University of Toronto in 1982. Davis specializes in African American intellectual and cultural history. He has presented numerous papers and has published articles and encyclopedia entries on American and European history.

GARY R. ENTZ is an assistant professor of history at McPherson College, Kansas. He earned his Ph.D. from the University of Utah, Salt Lake City, in 1999. He is the author of "Image and Reality on the Kansas Prairie: 'Pap' Singleton's Cherokee County Colony," *Kansas History* (Summer 1996). His "Zion Valley: The Mormon Origins of St. John, Kansas," *Kansas History* (Summer 2001), won the Western History Association's 2002 Arrington-Prucha Prize for best article in Western Religious History.

DAVID M. FAHEY is professor of history at Miami University, Oxford, Ohio. He received his Ph.D. from the University of Notre Dame in 1964 and is the author of *Temperance and Racism: John Bull, Johnny Reb, and the Good Templars* (1996), editor of *The Black Lodge in White America: "True Reformer" Browne and His Economic Strategy* (1994), and co-editor of *Alcohol and Temperance in Modern History: An International Encyclopedia* (forthcoming).

PAUL HARVEY received his Ph.D. from the University of California at Berkeley in 1992. He was a postdoctoral fellow at Valparaiso University in Valparaiso, Indiana, and since 1996 has taught American history at the University of Colorado at Colorado Springs. He is the author of *Redeeming the South: Religious Cultures and Racial Identities among Southern Baptists, 1865–1925* (1997), and *Freedom's Coming: Religion, Race, and Culture in the South, 1860–2000* (forthcoming).

ANDREW E. KERSTEN received his Ph.D. in history from the University of Cincinnati in 1997 and is now an associate professor of history at the University of Wisconsin at Green Bay. He is the author of *Race,*

Jobs, and the War: The FEPC in the Midwest, 1941–1946 (2000) and co-editor of *Politics and Progress: American Society and the State since the Civil War* (2001). He is now working on a history of the American Federation of Labor during World War II.

CHRISTINE LUTZ received her Ph.D. in history in 2001 from Georgia State University, Atlanta, where she is a visiting lecturer. She is the author of *They Don't All Wear Sheets: A Chronology of Racist and Far Right Violence, 1980–1986* (1987). She is currently working on a monograph about the Hunton family.

JACQUELINE M. MOORE received her Ph.D. in history from the University of Maryland-College Park in 1994 and is currently associate professor of history, director of Asian Studies, and chair of the Department of History at Austin College in Sherman, Texas. She is the author of *Leading the Race: The Transformation of the Black Elite in the Nation's Capital, 1880–1920* (1999), and *Booker T. Washington, W. E. B. Du Bois, and the Struggle for Racial Uplift* (2003). Her next monograph focuses on cowboy masculinity. She is also co-editor of Scholarly Resources' African American History Series.

A. J. SCOPINO JR. has been a member of the Department of History at Central Connecticut State University in New Britain since 1985. He received his Ph.D. in American history from the University of Connecticut, Storrs, in 1993. He is the author of *The Progressive Era, 1900–1917* (1996), *World War I: The Great War* (1997), and *The Struggle for Religious Freedom in America* (1998) as well as several articles, encyclopedia entries, and book reviews.

JAMES E. WESTHEIDER received his Ph.D. in history from the University of Cincinnati in 1994 and is now assistant professor of American history at the University of Cincinnati–Clermont College. He is the author of *Fighting on Two Fronts: African Americans and the Vietnam War* (1997). He is working on a monograph on Camp Des Moines, the first black officers' training camp.

JOHN WHITE received his Ph.D. in American Studies from the University of Hull, England, in 1975. His publications include *Black Leadership in America: From Booker T. Washington to Jesse Jackson* (1985; rev. ed. 1990), *Billie Holiday: Her Life and Times* (1987), and *Artie Shaw: Non-Stop Flight* (1998). His "Kansas City, Pendergast, and All That Jazz," in Brian Holden Reid and John White, eds., *American Studies: Essays in Honour of Marcus Cunliffe* (1991), received the 1992 Arthur Miller American Studies Prize for the best journal-length article on an American Studies topic published in the United Kingdom. His most recent publication is "John Hope Franklin: Southern History in Black and White," in Glen Feldman, ed., *Reading Southern History: Essays on Interpreters and Interpretations* (2001), and he is currently working on a book on the Montgomery bus boycott.

Index